Reading for the Citizen of the World
世界公民读本（文库）

FOUNDATIONS of DEMOCRACY

R G Reading for the Citizen of the World
世界公民读本（文库）

Foundations of Democracy
民主的基础丛书

主编　赵文彤

Justice
正义

〔美〕Center for Civic Education (公民教育中心)　著

刘小小　译

隐私
PRIVACY

责任
RESPONSIBILITY

正义
JUSTICE

权威
AUTHORITY

金城出版社
GOLD WALL PRESS

FOUNDATIONS of DEMOCRACY

AUTHORITY PRIVACY RESPONSIBILITY JUSTICE

English Edition Copyright ©2009. Center for Civic Education. Calabasas, CA, USA.

著作权合同登记图字：B11002794-01-2011-3501

图书在版编目(CIP)数据

正义 ／（美国）公民教育中心著；刘小小译. —北京
：金城出版社，2011.6
　　（世界公民读本文库/赵文彤主编）
　　书名原文：Justice
　　ISBN 978-7-80251-927-5

　　Ⅰ．①正… Ⅱ．①美… ②刘… Ⅲ．①正义-青年读
物②正义-少年读物 Ⅳ．①B82-49

中国版本图书馆CIP数据核字（2011）第075251号

正义

作　　者	CENTER FOR CIVIC EDUCATION(美国)公民教育中心
责任编辑	袁东旭
开　　本	710毫米×1000毫米 1/16
印　　张	20.75
字　　数	318千字
版　　次	2011年8月第1版 2011年8月第1次印刷
印　　刷	北京联兴华印刷厂
书　　号	ISBN 978-7-80251-927-5
定　　价	45.00元

出版发行	金城出版社 北京市朝阳区和平街11区37号楼　邮编：100013
发 行 部	(010)84254364
编 辑 部	(010)64210080
总 编 室	(010)64228516
网　　址	http://www.jccb.com.cn
电子邮箱	jinchengchuban@163.com
法律顾问	陈鹰律师事务所　(010)64970501

本书承蒙郭昌明基金资助印行

该基金以一位年近百岁的母亲的名字命名，她和中国近百年来一代又一代的普通母亲一样，将自己对人生和世界最美好的希望全部寄托给了成长中的中国式的世界公民。

CENTER FOR CIVIC EDUCATION

5145 Douglas Fir Road
Calabasas, CA 91302 - USA
818.591.9321 - Fax 818.591.9330
cce@civiced.org
www.civiced.org

人类命运与责任共同体时代呼唤世界公民

——世界公民读本（文库）出版说明

刘建华

引子

　　早在大约 250 年前，中国与世界公民 (The Citizen of the World) 这个英文词组，就有过一次美丽的的邂逅。18 世纪 60 年代，中国在西方的许多思想家那里，被理想化为一个美好而神秘的国度，哥德斯密 (Oliver Goldsmith，1728—1774) 就是在这样的时代背景下，以"中国人的信札" (Chinese Letters) 为名，发表连载文章，借此讥讽英国的社会弊病，两年后（1763）结集出版，题名为：The Citizen of the World or Letters of a Chinese Philosopher living in London to his Friends in the East. 翻译成中文，是《世界公民——　一位旅居伦敦的中国哲学家写给他的东方朋友的信札》。

　　此后过了约 150 年，大约距今 100 年前的 1914 年，一个在美国的中国人应验了歌德斯密的这个噱头式的玩笑。根据邵建先生发表在《大学人文》（广西师范大学出版社 2008 年 5 月版）的文章，这一年，在美国康奈尔大学的学生宿舍里，胡适在自己的一篇日记中，以《大同主义之先哲名言》为题，抄录了以下数则关于"世界公民"的先哲名言，这些名言以无言的方式，影响了无数个"胡适"们，并通过他们在后来的一个世纪里影响了无数中国人——

　　亚里斯提卜说过，智者的祖国就是世界。
　　——第欧根尼·拉尔修：《亚里斯提卜》第十三章

当有人问及他是何国之人时，第欧根尼回答道：
"我是世界之公民。"
——第欧根尼·拉尔修：《亚里斯提卜》第十三章

苏格拉底说，他既不是一个雅典人，也不是一个希腊人，
只不过是一个世界公民。
——普卢塔：《流放论》

我的祖国是世界，我的宗教是行善。
——T.潘恩：《人类的权利》第五章

世界是我的祖国，人类是我的同胞。
——W.L.加里森：《解放者简介》

一

进入 21 世纪以来，全球气候变暖的危机日益明显，与此相关的多种全球性危机日益增多，人类仿佛在一夜之间变得比以往任何时代都更加亲如兄弟、情同手足，地球比以往任何时候都更像是一个风雨飘摇中的小小的村落。这不只是全球经济一体化和信息技术与交通高度发达的结果，也不只是人类追求世界大同理想社会的结果，而是任何一个国家和民族都无法单独应对的全球共同的危机，让我们人类不得不彼此靠近，不能不唇齿相依，除了学会成为彼此一家的世界公民，学会互相之间兄弟姐妹般的友善和宽容，我们已经别无选择。

二

我们因此正在走向"人类命运共同体和全球责任共同体"的特殊时代，世界各国人民因此必须走出宗教文化壁垒，跨越意识形态障碍，超越政治制度边界，以世界公民的身份，与其他国家和民族的人民一道，共同承担起人类社会的可持续发展责任。我们每一个人不仅需要具有自觉的世界公民责任意识，更需要具有能承担起世界公民责任的基本素质和技能——在这样一个事关我们每一个人现在的生存质量、决定我们每一个家庭明天的

生活希望的全球性危机时代，我们每一个人都不能不从头开始，学会以世界公民的方式生存。

三

我们因此需要一个全球普遍适用的世界公民教育体系，但我们又身处多元格局的差异化社会之中，我们因此永远不可能有一部放之四海而皆准的世界公民统编教材，但是我们却可以而且必须互相参考和借鉴。我们因此倡导"互相阅读"和"比较阅读"式的世界公民教育，这本身就是一种承担共同责任的世界公民行为，是人类面对全球性危机时，首先需要的一种协商、协调、协同的智慧和行为。我们相信，尽管一方面，世界各国发展不平衡，世界各民族和地区的文化各不相同，应对全球性危机和承担世界公民责任的方式、方法和路径各不相同，但是，另一方面，世界各国无论贫富，世界各地无论远近，世界各民族文化无论有多么地不同，都毫无例外地、没有差别地、不可逃避地承受着同样的全球性危机的影响和压力，都必须协调一致，在人类的共同拯救行动中才能最终拯救自己。

四

综观世界各国的公民教育，无论是发达国家还是发展中国家，基本素质和基本技能都是公民教育的核心内容，唯其如此，世界各国的公民教育经验才具有互相参考和借鉴的可能性，不同语言的公民教育读本才具有互相阅读的必要性。

在众多国家出版的众多公民教育读本中，美国公民教育中心的一整套教材，在这方面最具有代表性。这套公民教育读本，可以说是"最高地位的社会名流邀请最高学问的专家一道，弯下腰来，以最低的姿态，奉献给他们认为是最高大的幼儿、少年、青年们的《公民圣经》"。这套由美国以及世界上多个国家多方面领域的专家经过多年精心编修的读本，没有高深的理论，没有刻板的道理，没有号称伟大的思想体系，没有不可置疑的绝对真理，而是结合人生成长的不同阶段，针对不同年龄青少年的学习、生活和成长实际，引导学生，通过自己的独立判断、反思鉴别、团队合作、谈判妥协、陈述坚持、提案答辩等理性的方法和智慧的工具，在观察、发现、认知、处理身边各种与公民权利和责任有关的问题的过程中，成长为一个具有公民美德基本素质和履行社会责任的基本技能的合格公民。

五

我们深知，无论多么好的公民素质和技能，离开了养成这种素质和技能的国度，就不一定有效，我们因此只是将这套美国公民教育读本作为中国公民的参考读物，原原本本地译介过来，用作借鉴，而非直接用作教材；我们深知，无论多么好的公民教育读本，离开了产生这种读本的文字语言环境，就很难领略其中丰富的意蕴，我们因此采用中英文对照的方式出版，即便是当作学习美国英语的泛读教材，也不失为一种明智的选择，因为这套读本用最基本的词汇和最浅显的文体，最准确地阐释了美国最基本的社会实质和美国公民最基本的生活真实。

六

《世界公民读本》（文库），是一项长期性的、庞大的公益出版计划，其宗旨在于倡导全社会的"公民阅读"。公民阅读和私人兴趣阅读不一样的地方在于，私人阅读更关注个体自身的心灵世界、个人的知识需求和个性化的审美愉悦，而公民阅读更关心的是公共生活的领域、人类共同的价值和世界更好的未来。从这个意义上来说，公民阅读是一种更加需要精神品德和高尚情怀的开放式阅读、互动式阅读和参与式阅读，也正是在这个意义上，可以说，我们翻译出版给国人阅读的这套《世界公民读本》，其实也是真正意义上的《好人读本》、《成功读本》、《领袖读本》，是每一个人，要想成长、成熟、成功的基本教科书，是任何人一生中的"第一启蒙读本"。

七

我们的民族是一个崇尚"好人"的民族，深受"穷则独善其身，达则兼济天下"的自我完善文化影响，更有所谓"不在其位、不谋其政"的古老训条，这些都很容易被借用来为我们远离社会理想、逃避公民责任构建自我安慰的巢穴。人们因此更愿意以"独善"的"好人"自居，而怯于以"兼济"的"好公民"自励。

　　尽管我们的传统是一个没有公民的好人社会传统，但我们的时代却是一个需要好公民的大社会时代，在这样的文化纠结中，就让我们用世界公民的阅读方式延续中国的好人传统，用好人的传统善意理解当今的公民世界。这可以说是我们编辑出版《世界公民读本》（文库）的初衷。

八

　　我们期待着有一天，公民这个称呼，能够像"贤人"一样，成为令每一个中国人都值得骄傲的赞许；世界公民这个身份，能够像"圣人"一样，成为中华传统至高无上的美德的代名词。

　　我们相信有一天，一个普通的中国人面对世界的时候，也能够像美国的奥巴马一样，以世界公民的身份向世界的公民们说：

　　"Tonight, I speak to you not as a candidate for President, but as a citizen—a proud citizen of the United States, and a fellow citizen of the world."（今晚，我并不是以一个总统候选人的身份在这里向大家演讲，而是以一位公民—— 一位以美国为荣的公民和一位世界公民的身份跟大家讲话。）

　　"I am a citizen of the world."我是一个世界公民。你准备好了吗？

编者语

　　这是一些将民主与法治当作信仰，相信它能够成为社会的秩序原则与社会运行方式，并坚信理性力量的知识精英，历经数年共同精心编纂的一部书。他们满怀激情、充满智慧，以建筑一座理想中恢宏大厦的决心，做着构建最扎实地基的工作——公民教育。

　　被命名为《民主的基础》的这一辑的读者对象，是甫将开始独立社会生活的青年。这些青年，正是保证前人着力思考过、倾心建设过的民主与法治机制——同时也是具有普世价值的文化传统和社会生活信念，能够得以延续的基石。

　　作为美国高中的课程读本，《民主的基础》由《权威》、《隐私》、《责任》、《正义》四个部分构成。所涉问题常常会触碰到个体的自我面对群体的他者时的一些核心价值冲突，令我们本能、直觉的感受纠结与困扰。但是，我们都知道，这世界是由一个个独立的个体组成的一个共同体，社会共有的秩序与幸福是达成个体幸福的基础。在纷繁复杂的人际社会中、在相互冲突的利益与价值面前，必须权衡利弊，做出理性的思考与选择。因此，只有当一个社会有更多能够独立思考的人、以社会的共同利益为目标捍卫个人权利的人，我们才能够期待这个社会更加和谐美好。

　　该丛书的要旨不仅是带领研习者广泛而深入的思考权威、隐私、责任、正义这些至关重要的问题，更是通过思想智慧、知识经验给出了一个叫做"知识工具"的东西。"它是一种思想工具，是研究问题和制定决策的一系列思路与方法的集合。"运用这些工具，不仅能帮助我们更好地解析这些核心理念，更通过由理念到操作层面的分析与权衡，令研读者通过熟练运用具体的指标体系，形成对研究对象的判断与决策，在面对多重利益交叠的复杂的社会政治生活、决定我们的态度和行动方式的时候，超越情感，不是凭主观感受，而是理性、平和、有序的使用知识工具做出衡量与选择。

　　可以说，这套书是一部精粹的法治文化及公民教育领域的思想方法读本，是了解美国核心民主法治建构理念与公平公正处世方略的钥匙，是把握理性权衡与处置个体与社会共同体之间利益与冲突的工具，同时也是学习最简洁、规范、实用的文化英语和法律英语的范本。相信该丛书会从多个方面给予我们启迪。

Foundations of Democracy introduces you to four ideas which are basic to our constitutional form of government: authority, privacy, responsibility, and justice. These are not only ideas that need to be grasped in order to understand the foundations of our government, but they are crucial to evaluating the important differences between a constitutional democracy and a society that is not free.

《民主的基础》将向你们介绍美国政府的宪政模式中的四种基本观念：权威、隐私、责任和正义。理解和掌握这四种观念，不仅有助于理解美国政府的立国之本，更是评估和区分"宪政民主"与"不自由的社会"的关键。

Preface

Foundations of Democracy introduces you to four ideas which are basic to our constitutional form of government: authority, privacy, responsibility, and justice. These are not only ideas that need to be grasped in order to understand the foundations of our government, but they are crucial to evaluating the important differences between a constitutional democracy and a society that is not free.

There are costs or burdens that we must bear in order to preserve our freedom and the values on which our nation was founded. There are many situations in which hard choices need to be made between competing values and interests. In this course of study, you will be challenged to discuss and debate situations involving the use of authority and the protection of privacy. You will be asked to decide how responsibilities should be fulfilled and how justice could be achieved in a number of situations.

You will learn different approaches and ideas, which we call "intellectual tools," to evaluate these situations. Intellectual tools help you think clearly about issues of authority, privacy, responsibility, and justice. They help you develop your own positions, and support your positions which reasons.

The knowledge and skills you gain in this course of study will assist you not only in addressing issues of public policy, but also in everyday situations you face in your private life. By thinking for yourself, reaching your own conclusions, and defending your positions, you can be a more effective and active citizen in a free society.

前　言

　　《民主的基础》将向你们介绍美国政府的宪政模式中的四种基本观念：权威、隐私、责任和正义。理解和掌握这四种观念，不仅有助于理解美国政府的立国之本，更是评估和区分"宪政民主"与"不自由的社会"的关键。

　　为了维护我们的国家得以建立的自由和价值，我们必须付出代价或承担责任，我们也必须在许多相互冲突的价值和利益中做出选择。在本课程的学习中，你们将会针对运用权威和保护隐私的案例进行讨论和辩论，你们将要回答在一系列情况下应当如何承担责任、怎样才能实现正义的问题。

　　在本课程中，你们将学到各种不同的方法和观念（在这里我们统称为"知识工具"），并运用这些工具来评估不同的案例和情况。知识工具不仅将帮助你们对有关权威、隐私、责任和正义的问题进行更清晰的思考，也将有助于你们形成自己的观点，并通过推理来论证自己的观点。

　　在本课程学习过程中所获得的知识与技能，不仅将有助于你们应对未来的公共政策问题，也能帮助你们面对个人生活中的日常情况。通过独立思考，形成自己的观点并对此进行论证。作为一个公民的你，将更有效、更主动地投身于自由的社会中。

JUSTICE
Table of Contents

目录

 What issues of justice were raised by Martin Luther King, Jr.'s "I Have a Dream" speech during the 1963 civil rights march on Washington?

1963年华盛顿民权运动游行上马丁·路德·金的"我有一个梦想"的演讲提出了什么有关正义的问题?

Introduction

> I have a dream that my four little children will one day live in a nation where they will not be judged by the color of their skin, but by the content of their character.

Martin Luther King, Jr.'s speech from the steps of the Lincoln Memorial on August 28, 1963 quoted above, was a call for justice that continues to inspire us. It is almost impossible for a day to go by in which we do not think of something that is just or unjust; for issues of justice arise in our daily lives, in the news media, on entertainment programs, and in the actions of our government and others. The Preamble to the U.S. Constitution states that one of the main purposes of our government is to establish justice in our nation; and the Pledge of Allegiance ends with the phrase with liberty and justice for all.

The central idea of justice is fairness, but despite our belief in justice, it is not always easy to decide what is fair in many situations. This course of study will provide opportunities for you to examine and make decisions about justice in a number of specific situations. In this way, you will learn to apply several sets of intellectual tools to different types of problems of justice.

Intellectual tools are ideas and sets of questions useful in examining issues and making decisions. They are tools of the mind that, if used thoughtfully and with skill, will build understanding. Your use of these tools should help you gain a better understanding of the subject of justice and a greater ability to deal effectively with issues of justice when they arise in your daily life.

导言

> "我梦想有一天，我的四个孩子将在一个不是以他们的肤色，而是以他们的品格优劣来评价他们的国度里生活。"

以上摘自1963年8月28日小马丁·路德·金在林肯纪念堂台阶上发表的演讲，演讲中对正义的呼声一直激励着我们。几乎在过去的每一天里，我们都会考虑某件事是否公正。正义问题出现在我们的日常生活中，在新闻媒体、娱乐节目、我们的政府和其他人的行动中。联邦宪法的前言当中写道："美国政府的主要目标之一就是建立一个公平正义的国家"。"效忠誓词"的最后一句也正是以"自由"和"正义"这两个词汇结束的。

正义的主要观念是公平。但是，尽管我们相信正义，在很多情况下仍然很难判断什么是公平。在本课程的学习中，你们将有机会对一系列具体情况中的正义问题进行研究并做出判断。通过这种方式，你们将学会几组知识工具，并将它们运用于不同种类的正义问题。

知识工具是有助于研究问题和制定决策的一系列观念与问题的集合，这也是一种思想工具，如果使用时经过深思熟虑并且熟练地运用，就能形成对研究对象的理解。运用这些工具，应当能够帮助你们更好地理解与正义相关的问题，并使你们在日常生活中遇到正义问题时具备有效处理这些问题的能力。

Unit One: What Is Justice?

> ### Purpose of Unit
>
> What is justice? How can you decide whether or not something is just? This unit will sharpen your ability to deal with such questions. As you will see, the essence of justice is fairness, and situations can be fair or unfair in different ways. For example, someone may not get his or her fair share of something that is being distributed; someone may not get a fair chance to explain his or her side of the story; or someone may suffer a punishment that is unfair in relation to his or her wrongful conduct.

Issues of justice can be divided into three categories: distributive justice, corrective justice, and procedural justice. This unit introduces you to these three categories of justice. When you have completed this unit, you should be able to identify issues of justice and explain why it is useful to do so. You also should be able to identify examples of issues of distributive, corrective, and procedural justice in your daily life.

第一单元：什么是正义？

单元目标

什么是正义？如何判断某件事是否公正？

本单元将提高你们处理类似问题的能力。正如你们将学到的，正义的本质是公平，某些特定情况在不同方面可能是公平的，也可能是不公平的。例如，在分配某些物品时，有人可能没有得到他或她应得的那一份；有人可能都没有一个公平的机会为自己辩解；有人会受到相对于他或她的错误行为来说不公正的惩罚。

正义问题可以分为三类：分配正义、矫正正义和程序正义。本单元将向你们介绍这三类正义。学完本单元后，你们应该能够识别和区分正义问题，并说明这样做为什么是有用的。你们也应该能够在日常生活中找到分配正义、矫正正义和程序正义问题的例子。

 How do these photographs illustrate the difference between distributive justice, corrective justice, and procedural justice?

这些照片如何反映出分配正义、矫正正义和程序正义之间的区别？

LESSON 1

What Are the Different Kinds of Issues of Justice?

> ### Purpose of Lesson
>
> This lesson introduces you to three types of issues or problems of justice that you will examine and discuss. When you have completed the lesson, you should be able to classify issues of justice and explain the usefulness of doing so.

Terms to Know

distributive justic   benefits

corrective justice   burdens

procedural justice

The law, in its majestic equality, forbids the rich as well as the poor to sleep under bridges, to beg in the streets and to steal bread.

Anatole France, La Lys Rouge, 1894

 Can justice always be achieved by treating people equally? ☞

第一课：正义问题有哪些不同种类？

本课目标

本课介绍了你们将研究和讨论的三类正义问题。学完本课后，你们应当能够识别不同的正义问题并解释这么做的用处。

掌握词汇

分配正义	利益	矫正正义
负担	程序正义	

"法律，在它崇高的平等之下，禁止富人也不允许穷人睡在桥下、在街上乞讨和偷一块面包。"

——阿纳托尔·法朗士《红百合》，1894 年

是否总能通过公平对待他人来实现正义？

Critical Thinking Exercise

EXAMINING ISSUES OF JUSTICE

We think of the essence of justice as fairness, and the essence of fairness as treating people equally. But as the Anatole France quotation shows, issues of justice can arise even if everyone is subjected to the same rules, and even if everyone who breaks the rules receives the same punishment. Issues of justice are often complex and multifaceted, and they require careful analysis. At the outset, it is important to recognize and to be able to distinguish different types of issues of justice. As you read the following situations, ask yourself what is fair or unfair about them. Then answer the "What do you think?" questions. Be prepared to share your answers with the class.

• At the end of the week, Jane received her paycheck. It was for $275. She was upset and angry when she learned that Paul had received $410 for doing the same type and amount of work.

• During the riot, the secret police arrested Hans, dragged him off the street, and threw him into a small cell. That night he was taken to a room and three angry men questioned him for about ten minutes. Just as he began to realize that they were trying him, the man in the center banged a gavel on the table and declared, "Guilty of rebellion against the government. Sentenced to death by firing squad at once!" They took Hans outside, stood him against a wall, and shot him.

• Jean Valjean, the principal character in Victor Hugo's novel Les Miserables, was sentenced to prison for stealing a loaf of bread to feed his sister and her children who were starving.

What do you think?

1. What is fair or unfair about each of the situations above?

2. What similar experiences have you had or observed?

3. How are each of the situations similar to things that happen in your community?

重点思考练习

我们认为，正义的本质即公平，公平的本质即平等待人。但正如上文引述阿纳托尔・法朗士的话所说，即使在每个人都遵守同样的规则、甚至犯规的人也会受到同样的惩罚时，有关正义的问题也会出现。正义的问题往往是复杂且多方面的，需要进行仔细分析。首先，重要的是要承认并能区分不同类型的正义问题。阅读下面的材料，问问自己，对材料中描述的当事人来说，什么是公平的？什么是不公平的？然后回答"你怎么看？"这一部分的问题。准备好与全班分享你的答案。

・周末，简领到了她的薪水，一共是275美元。当她得知跟她做同样工作且工作量相同的保罗拿到了410美元工资时，她感到非常沮丧和愤怒。

・在骚乱期间，秘密警察逮捕了汉斯，把他从大街上拖走，扔到了一间小牢房里。当晚汉斯被带到一个房间里，三个男人粗暴地讯问了他大约10分钟。正当他开始意识到他正在接受审讯的时候，其中一个男人在桌子上敲槌宣布："反政府叛乱罪名成立！判处死刑，立即执行枪决！"随后有几个人把汉斯带走，命令他靠墙站着，并开枪杀死了他。

・维克多・雨果的小说《悲惨世界》里的主人公冉・阿让因为偷了一块面包给他的姐姐和她正在挨饿的孩子而被判入狱。

你怎么看？

1. 上述各种情况哪些是公平的？哪些是不公平的？
2. 你有没有经历过或者看到过类似的事情？
3. 上述各种情况与发生在你们社区的事情有什么相似之处？

4. What customs, rules, or laws do you know that are designed to promote justice or fairness in the kinds of situations described?

5. In the situations, are the issues of justice similar in any way? Are they different in any way? Explain.

Why do we divide issues of justice into different categories?

As you read each of the situations on page 153, you may have had a common reaction: "That's not fair!" or 'That's not just!" Each example illustrates a type of issue of justice. The intensity of our feelings about justice and our desire to achieve it have helped to shape history and have led to numerous controversies in both private and public life in our communities, our nation, and the world.

For more than 2,000 years, scholars dealing with the subject of justice have divided issues of justice into three categories. These categories are the following:

DISTRIBUTIVE JUSTICE. Issues of distributive justice concern the fairness of the distribution of something among several people or groups. Whatever is distributed or divided can be a benefit, such as pay for work or the right to speak or vote, or it can be a burden, such as taxes, household chores, or homework.

CORRECTIVE JUSTICE. Issues of corrective justice concern the fairness of the response to a wrong or injury to a person or group. Common responses include making a person who has wronged or injured another suffer some form of punishment, give back something that was stolen, or pay for damages.

PROCEDURAL JUSTICE. Issues of procedural justice concern the fairness of how information is gathered and/or how a decision is made. For example, a person suspected of a crime might give information through careful, unbiased investigation or by torture. People making a decision might hear from all people interested in an issue or might make the decision without such a procedure. It is important to emphasize that procedural justice deals with the fairness of how we gather information or make decisions, not with what information we gathered or decision we make.

4. 有没有什么传统、规则或法律是用来促进上述材料中描述的正义或公平问题的？

5. 上述各种情况中描述的正义问题在哪些方面是相似的？在哪些方面是不同的？请说明。

为什么我们将正义问题分成不同种类？

阅读上页描述的每一种情况时，你们可能有一个共同的反应："这不公平！"或者"这不公道！"上述每一件事例分别代表了一类正义问题。我们对正义的热忱和对实现正义的愿望有助于改变历史，同时也在我们生活的社区、国家乃至全世界，在私人生活和公共生活中引发了许多争议。

两千多年来，研究正义问题的学者们将正义分成了以下三类：

分配正义：分配正义问题关注的是，在某些个人或某些团体中分配某些事物的公平性。被分配的可能是某种福利，例如工作的报酬、言论或投票的权利；也可能是某种负担，例如缴税、家务活，或者做功课。

矫正正义：矫正正义问题关注的是，对某些个人或团体造成的某种错误或伤害做出的回应的公平性。常见的回应包括要求那些犯了错或伤害他人的人承受某些形式的惩罚，例如，偿还偷窃的某些物品或赔偿损失等。

程序正义：程序正义问题关注的是，获取信息的方式和（或）做出决策的方式的公平性。例如，涉嫌犯罪的某个人可能会在认真、公正的调查中提供案件信息，也可能是在酷刑之下招供。要对某事做决策的人可能会听取所有对这个问题感兴趣的人的意见，也可能完全忽略这个步骤而自行决定。在这里，需要强调的是，程序正义针对的是我们获取信息或做出决策的方式的公平性，而不是我们获得的信息或我们所做的决定的公平性。

This division of issues of justice into different categories is helpful because each category requires the use of a different set of ideas or intellectual tools. In other words, to determine whether a situation is fair from the standpoint of distributive justice, you need to ask a different set of questions than the questions you would ask to determine whether the situation is fair from the standpoint of corrective justice. This explanation might be illustrated best by an analogy. Suppose you wanted to repair an automobile engine, paint a picture, or mend some clothing. Obviously, you would not use a paintbrush to mend the clothing or a sewing machine to repair the automobile engine. Each task would require the use of different tools.

It is the same with issues of justice. Dealing with issues in each of the three categories requires the use of a different set of ideas or intellectual tools. Fortunately, you do not have to reinvent all the tools because they have been developed during the past several thousand years by such people as philosophers, judges, political scientists, and statesmen.

Before trying to use the intellectual tools to analyze issues of justice, however, it is important to identify those issues as being distributive, corrective, or procedural so you will not try to use a sewing machine to repair an automobile engme.

Critical Thinking Exercise

IDENTIFYING ISSUES OF DISTRIBUTIVE, CORRECTIVE, AND PROCEDURAL JUSTICE

Work with a study partner or in small groups to complete this exercise. As you read each of the following examples, identify whether it raises an issue of distributive, corrective, or procedural justice. Then answer the "What do you think?" questions.

1. In a recent court case, a man sued the driver who ran into his car for $5,000 in damages to his automobile, $4,300 in medical bills, and $1,000 for inconveniences caused by the accident.

2. Police departments usually hire only those people who are physically able and who have had adequate education and experience for the police force.

　　将正义问题划分为不同种类是有必要的，因为每一类正义问题都需要用到不同的观念或知识工具。换句话说，从分配正义的角度判断某一种情况是否公平时，你需要提出一组问题，这些问题不同于从矫正正义的角度提出的问题。比如说：假设你打算修理汽车发动机，或者你想画一幅画，缝补一下衣服。很显然，你不会用画笔来修补衣服，也不会用一台缝纫机来修理汽车发动机。因此，为完成每项不同的任务，都需要使用不同的工具。

　　解决正义问题也一样。在解决以上三类正义问题中任何一类时，都需要使用不同的观念或知识工具。幸运的是，你们不必进行新的发明创造，在过去的几千年里，哲学家、法官、政治学家和政治人物们已经创造了许多解决这些问题的工具。

　　在我们尝试用知识工具来分析正义问题之前，重要的是要识别并区分这些正义问题是分配正义、矫正正义或程序正义，这样你就不会打算用缝纫机去修理汽车发动机了。

重点思考练习

识别分配正义、矫正正义和程序正义问题

　　与一位同学一起或分成小组来完成本次练习。当你们阅读以下案例时，判断当中提到的是分配正义、矫正正义，还是程序正义问题，然后回答"你怎么看？"这一部分的问题。

1. 在最近的一宗法庭案件中，一名男子控告那位撞到他的车的司机并要求赔偿 5000 美元汽车修理费、4300 美元的医疗费用，以及 1000 美元用于弥补此次事故对他造成的诸多不便。

2. 警察部门通常只聘用那些身体健康、受过一定程度的教育以及有过警察部队经验的人。

3. Five boys were accused of vandalizing a school on a weekend. On the following Monday, they were brought to the principal's office and asked if they were guilty. Two boys said they were not and had been at the homes of friends at the time of the incident. The principal questioned their friends to check on the boys' stories. He then called the parents of the boys to his office to further verify their stories.

4. Before hiring a person to fill a vacancy in a governmental agency, the agency must advertise the availability of the position and provide all applicants the opportunity to take a written examination and to have an interview.

5. Each year the federal government gives fellowships to outstanding students under the Fulbright Act. These fellowships pay for American students to study, conduct research, or teach in foreign countries.

6. In the 1880s, thousands of Irish immigrants came to the United States. Often they were denied employment opportunities because of their Irish ancestry.

 What might be some ways to fairly distribute employment opportunities among citizens and recent immigrants to the United States? ☞

3. 某个周末，5 名男孩被指控破坏了学校的公物，之后的那个星期一，他们被带到了校长办公室并接受询问，当中有两名男孩说，他们没有做这件事，事情发生的时候他们在朋友家里。校长询问了他们的朋友，以此来判断这两名男孩说的是否属实。随后他请两位男孩的父母到学校来，以便进一步验证他们的说法。

4. 在聘用某个人担任某政府机构的职位之前，该机构必须公示这个职位的招聘启示，并为所有申请人提供参加笔试和面试的机会。

5. 根据《富布赖特法案》，美国联邦政府每年都会为优秀的学生提供奖学金以支付美国学生到国外学习深造、进行研究或担任教职的费用。

6. 在 19 世纪 80 年代，成千上万的爱尔兰人移民来到美国，但他们常常因为其爱尔兰血统而被剥夺就业机会。

在美国，有哪些方法可以保障公民和新移民之间就业机会的公平分配？

7. During the Middle Ages, people were sometimes forced to confess to crimes by the use of torture.

8. Tom borrowed his friend's car and dented a fender. He agreed to pay for the repair.

9. If you are accused of a crime, the government has the obligation to provide a lawyer to assist you at public expense if you cannot afford one.

10. Before making a decision on which textbooks to adopt, a state curriculum commission must hold public hearings to enable interested persons or groups to present their views on the textbooks being considered.

11. In some cities, unauthorized parking in a handicap zone is punishable by a fine of $330.

12. To qualify for a driver's license you must have an adequate knowledge of traffic laws, adequate driving skills, and be at least a certain age.

What do you think?

1. Which examples raise issues of the following:

distributive justice?

corrective justice?

procedural justice?

2. What do you think is fair or unfair about each of the above situations? Explain your reasoning.

3. Think about your reasoning in the twelve examples involving issues of justice. How did you evaluate whether the situation was fair or just?

- What questions did you ask or what things did you consider in the situations involving issues of distributive justice?

- What questions did you ask or what things did you consider in the situations involving issues of corrective justice?

- What questions did you ask or what things did you consider in the situations involving issues of procedural justice?

7. 在中世纪，有时在残酷的刑罚折磨之下，人们不得不认罪。

8. 汤姆借了朋友的车，但他在用车的时候把车子的挡泥板刮花了，他同意为此支付修理费。

9. 如果你被控犯有某项罪行，政府有责任提供一名律师协助你。如果你无法负担律师费用，则由政府使用公费来支付。

10. 在决定是否批准使用某版教科书之前，国家课程委员会必须举行公开听证会，让有兴趣的人士或团体提出他们对于此版教科书的意见。

11. 在一些城市的残疾人专用区域违例停车要被处以330美元的罚款。

12. 为了获得驾驶执照，你必须拥有足够的交通法规知识、充足的驾驶技术，并至少符合一定的年龄条件。

你怎么看？

1. 上述哪一个案例中提到了以下正义问题：
   • 分配正义？
   • 矫正正义？
   • 程序正义？

2. 以上案例中你认为哪些是公平的？哪些是不公平的？请说明你的推理。

3. 想想上述12个有关正义问题的案例中你的推理。你是如何评价某个案例是否公平或公正的？
   • 在有关分配正义的案例中，你提出了哪些问题？或你考虑了什么因素？
   • 在有关矫正正义的案例中，你提出了哪些问题？或你考虑了什么因素？
   • 在有关程序正义的案例中，你提出了哪些问题？或你考虑了什么因素？

4. What situations have you experienced or observed that raised issues of justice similar to those in the examples?

Using the Lesson

1. Write a brief description of a situation you have observed or experienced that raised an issue of distributive, corrective, or procedural justice.

2. Watch a television news program and identify reports on issues that involve distributive, corrective, and procedural justice. Describe those issues to your class.

3. Review newspapers and newsmagazines for articles that deal with situations involving distributive, corrective, and procedural justice. Bring these clippings to class and be prepared to explain them.

4. 你曾经历过或看见过哪些与上述案例中描述的正义问题相似的情形？

知识运用

1. 简单描述某个你看见过或经历过的有关分配正义、矫正正义或程序正义问题的情况。

2. 观看一档电视新闻节目，找出某个有关分配正义、矫正正义和程序正义的新闻报道，并向全班描述这些问题。

3. 浏览报纸和杂志上有关分配正义、矫正正义和程序正义的文章，将新闻剪报带到班上，并准备向全班描述这一新闻报道。

LESSON 2

How Do Our Nation's Founding Documents Promote Justice?

Purpose of Lesson

The Founders of our nation were dedicated to the ideal of justice. In this lesson, you have a chance to look at excerpts from the two most important founding documents of the United States-the Declaration of Independence and the Constitution and evaluate which types of issues of justice the excerpts address.

When you have completed this lesson, you should be able to explain how the Declaration of Independence and the Constitution promote issues of distributive, corrective, and procedural justice.

Terms to Know

Naturalized	indictment Jurisdiction	grand jury
bill of attainder	compulsory process	
ex post facto law	poll tax	
common law	probable cause	
habeas corpus corruption of blood	oath or affirmation	

Critical Thinking Exercise

EXAMINING JUSTICE-A NATIONAL IDEAL

Each of the following excerpts from the Declaration of Independence and the Constitution of the United States is designed to protect and promote one or more of the kinds of justice you have been studying. Your teacher will divide your class into groups to complete this exercise. Each group should examine the excerpts they have been assigned and do the following:

第二课：美国的立国文献如何促进了正义？

本课目标

我们国家的立国者致力于实践正义的理想。在本课中，你们将有机会阅读美国最重要的两份立国文献——《独立宣言》和《美国联邦宪法》的选段，并判断每一段材料中提出的不同种类的正义问题。

学完本课后，你们应该能够解释《独立宣言》和《美国联邦宪法》如何促进了分配正义、矫正正义和程序正义问题。

掌握词汇

归化	管辖	公民权利剥夺法案
追溯既往的法律	习惯法	人身保护权

血统玷污（译者注：禁止重罪犯享有继承财产、称号等的法律规定，此法律在英国已于 1870 年废除）

起诉	大陪审团	强制程序
人头税	合理根据	宣誓或代誓宣言

重点思考练习

研究一种国家理想——正义

以下阅读材料均摘自《独立宣言》和《美国联邦宪法》，这两份文献都旨在保护和促进我们正在学习的一种或几类正义。老师将会把全班分成小组来完成本次练习，每个小组应当阅读各自被分配的段落，并完成以下任务：

- Decide whether the excerpts are designed to deal with issues of distributive, corrective, or procedural justice. Some may deal with more than one type of Issue.

- Develop answers to the "What do you think?" questions that follow the list of excerpts and be prepared to report your group's answers to the class.

Group 1

An Excerpt from the Declaration of Independence

We hold these truths to be self-evident, that all men are created equal; that they are endowed by their Creator with certain inalienable rights; that among these are life, liberty, and the pursuit of happiness.

Excerpts from the Constitution of the United States

AMENDMENT I (Bill of Rights, 1791)

Congress shall make no law respecting an establishment of religion, or prohibiting the free exercise thereof; or abridging the freedom of speech, or of the press; or the right of the people peaceably to assemble, and to petition the Government for a redress of grievances.

AMENDMENT VIII (Bill of Rights, 1791)

Excessive bail shall not be required, nor excessive fines imposed, nor cruel and unusual punishments inflicted.

Do the First Amendment rights of assembly and petition promote distributive, corrective, or procedural justice? ☞

- 判断该段材料的目的是解决分配正义、矫正正义还是程序正义问题。某些材料中可能会包含一种以上的正义问题。
- 回答材料后"你怎么看？"部分的问题，准备向全班报告你们组的答案。

第一组

摘自《独立宣言》：

我们认为下面这些真理是不言而喻的：人人生而平等，造物者赋予他们若干不可剥夺的权利，其中包括生命权、自由权和追求幸福的权利。

摘自《美国联邦宪法》：

第一修正案（1791年权利法案）：国会不得制定关于下列事项的法律：确立国教或禁止宗教活动自由；限制言论自由或出版自由；或剥夺人民和平集会向政府请愿申冤的权利。

第八修正案（1791年权利法案）：不得要求过多的保释金，不得处以过重的罚金，不得施加残酷和非常的惩罚。

保障了集会和请愿权利的第一修正案是否促进了分配、矫正或程序正义？

Group 2

Excerpts from the Constitution of the United States

AMENDMENT XIV, Section 1 (1868)

All persons born or naturalized in the United States, and subject to the jurisdiction thereof, are citizens of the United States and of the State wherein they reside. No State shall make or enforce any law which shall abridge the privileges or immunities of citizens of the United States; nor shall any State deprive any person of life, liberty, or property, without due process of law, nor deny to any person within its jurisdiction the equal protection of the laws.

ARTICLE I, Section 9, Clause 3

No bill of attainder or ex post facto law shall be passed.

AMENDMENT VII (Bill of Rights, 1791)

In suits at common law, where the value in controversy shall exceed twenty dollars, the right of trial by jury shall be preserved, and no fact tried by a jury, shall be otherwise re-examined in any Court of the United States, than according to the rules of the common law.

 Does the Fourteenth Amendment guarantee of equal protection of the laws promote distributive, corrective, or procedural justice?

第二组

摘自《美国联邦宪法》:

第十四修正案,第一款(1868年):凡在合众国出生或归化合众国并受其管辖的人,均为合众国和他们居住州的公民。任何一州,都不得制定或实施限制合众国公民的特权或豁免权的任何法律;不经正当法律程序,不得剥夺任何人的生命、自由或财产;对于在其管辖下的任何人,亦不得拒绝给予平等法律保护。

第一条第九款(三):不得通过公民权利剥夺法案或追溯既往的法律。

第七修正案(1791年权利法案):在习惯法的诉讼中,其争执价值超过20美元,由陪审团审判的权利应受到保护。由陪审团裁决的事实,合众国的任何法院除非按照普通法规则,不得重新审查。

保障平等法律保护的第十四修正案是否促进了分配、矫正或程序正义?

Group 3

Excerpts from the Constitution of the United States

ARTICLE I, Section 9, Clause 2

The privilege of the writ of habeas corpus shall not be suspended, unless when in cases of rebellion or invasion the public safety may require it.

ARTICLE II, Section 2

The President... shall have power to grant reprieves and pardons for offenses against the United States, except in cases of impeachment.

AMENDMENT V (Bill of Rights, 1791)

No person shall be held to answer for a capital, or otherwise infamous crime, unless on a presentment or indictment of a grand jury, except in cases arising in the land or naval forces, or in the militia, when in actual service in time of war or public danger; nor shall any person be subject for the same offense to be twice put in jeopardy of life or limb; nor shall be compelled in any criminal case to be a witness against himself, nor be deprived of life, liberty, or property, without due process of law; nor shall private property be taken for public use, without just compensation.

AMENDMENT XXVI, Section I (1971)

The right of citizens of the United States, who are eighteen years of age or older, to vote shall not be denied or abridged by the United States or by any State on account of age.

 Does the Twenty–sixth Amendment guarantee of voting rights for eighteen–year–olds promote distributive, corrective, or procedural justice? ☞

第三组

摘自《美国联邦宪法》：

第一条第九款（二）：不得中止人身保护状之特权，除非发生内乱或外患时公共安全要求中止这项特权。

第二条第二款（一）：总统……有权对危害合众国的犯罪行为颁赐缓刑和赦免，但弹劾案除外。

第五修正案（1791年权利法案）：无论任何人，除非根据大陪审团提出的报告或起诉，不得受判处死罪或其它不重罪之审判，惟发生在陆、海军中或发生在战时或出现公共危险时服现役的民兵中的案件，不在此限。任何人不得因同一犯罪行为而两次遭受生命或身体的危害；不得在任何刑事案件中被迫自证其罪；不经正当法律程序，不得被剥夺生命、自由或财产；不给予公平赔偿，私有财产不得充作公用。

第二十六修正案第一款（1971年）：年满18周岁或18周岁以上的合众国公民的选举权，不得因为年龄而被合众国或任何一州加以剥夺或限制。

保障18岁以上公民投票权的第二十六修正案是否促进了分配、矫正或程序正义？

Group 4

Excerpts from the Constitution of the United States

ARTICLE III, Section 3, clause 2

The Congress shall have power to declare the punishment of treason, but no attainder of treason shall work corruption of blood, or forfeiture except during the life of the person attainted.

AMENDMENT VI (Bill of Rights, 1791)

In all criminal prosecutions, the accused shall enjoy the right to a speedy and public trial, by an impartial jury of the State and district wherein the crime shall have been committed, which district shall have been previously ascertained by law, and to be informed of the nature and cause of the accusation; to be confronted with the witnesses against him; to have compulsory process for obtaining witnesses in his favor, and to have the assistance of counsel for his defense.

AMENDMENT XIII, Section 1 (1865)

Neither slavery nor involuntary servitude, except as a punishment for crime where of the party shall have been duly convicted, shall exist within the United States, or any place subject to their jurisdiction.

AMENDMENT XXIV, Section 1 (1964)

The right of citizens of the United States to vote in any primary or other election for president or vice president, for electors for president or vice president, or for senator or representative in Congress, shall not be denied or abridged by the United States or any. state by reason of failure to pay any poll tax or other tax.

 Does the Sixth Amendment protection of the right to counsel promote distributive, corrective, or procedural justice? ☞

第四组

摘自《美国联邦宪法》：

第三条第三款（二）：国会有权宣告对叛国罪的惩罚，但对因叛国罪而被褫夺公民权的人，其后人继承财产的权利不受影响，叛国者的财产只能在本人生存期间才能被没收。

第六修正案（1791年权利法案）：在一切刑事诉讼中，被告享有以下权利：由犯罪行为发生地的州和地区的公正陪审团予以迅速而公开的审判，该地区应事先已由法律确定；得知被控告的性质和理由；同原告证人对质；以强制程序取得对其有利的证人；取得律师帮助为其辩护。

第十三修正案第一款（1865年）：在合众国境内或受合众国管辖的任何地方，奴隶制和强迫劳役都不得存在，惟作为对依法判罪者犯罪之惩罚，不在此限。

第二十四修正案第一款（1964年）：在总统或副总统、总统或副总统选举人、或国会参议员或众议员的任何预选或其他选举中，合众国公民的选举权不得因未交纳人头税或其他税而被合众国或任何一州加以剥夺或限制。

保护律师帮助权的第六修正案是否促进了分配、矫正或程序正义？

Group 5

Excerpts from the Constitution of the United States

ARTICLE III, Section 2, Clause 3

The trial of all crimes, except in cases of impeachment, shall be by jury; and such trial shall be held in the state where the said crimes shall have been committed; but when not committed within any state, the trial shall be at such place or places as the Congress may by law have directed.

ARTICLE IV, Section 2

A person charged in any State with treason, felony, or other crime, who shall flee from justice, and be found in another State, shall on demand of the executive authority of the State from which he fled, be delivered up, to be removed to the State having jurisdiction of the crime.

AMENDMENT IV (Bill of Rights, 1791)

The right of the people to be secure in their persons, houses, papers, and effects, against unreasonable searches and seizures, shall not be violated, and no Warrants shall issue, but upon probable cause, supported by oath or affirmation, and particularly describing the place to be searched, and the persons or things to be seized.

AMENDMENT XIX, Section I (1920) The right of citizens of the United States to vote shall not be denied or abridged by the United States or by any State on account of sex.

 Does the Nineteenth Amendment guarantee of voting rights for women promote distributive, corrective, or procedural justice? ☞

第五组

摘自《美国联邦宪法》：

第三条第二款（三）：除弹劾案外，一切犯罪皆由陪审团审判；此种审判应在犯罪发生的州内举行；但如犯罪不发生在任何一州之内，审判应在国会以法律规定的一个或几个地点举行。

第四条第二款（二）：在任何一州被控告犯有叛国罪、重罪或其他罪行的人，如逃脱该州法网而在他州被寻获时，应根据他所逃出之州行政当局的要求将他交出，以便解送到对犯罪行为有管辖权的州。

第四修正案（1791 年权利法案）：人民的人身、住宅、文件和财产不受无理搜查和扣押的权利，不得侵犯。除依照合理根据，以宣誓或代誓宣言保证，并具体说明搜查地点和扣押的人或物，不得发出搜查和扣押状。

第十九修正案第一款（1920 年）：合众国公民的选举权，不得因性别而被合众国或任何一州加以剥夺或限制。

保障妇女投票权的第十九修正案是否促进了分配、矫正或程序正义？

What do you think?

1. Which of the excerpts deal with the following:

Distributive Justice-For the excerpts focusing on distributive justice, what benefits or burdens do they deal with? What values or interests does each excerpt seem to protect or promote?

Corrective Justice-For the excerpts focusing on corrective justice, what responses do they deal with? What values or interests does each excerpt seem to protect or promote?

Procedural Justice-For the excerpts focusing on procedural justice, what procedures do they deal with? What values or interests does each excerpt seem to protect or promote?

2. Which excerpts deal with more than one type of issue of justice?

Using the Lesson

1. Ask a lawyer or judge to help you find a court opinion or excerpts from an opinion that deals with an issue of justice. Read and analyze the opinion to determine the principles, values, and interests that underlie the position reflected. Some landmark cases of the Supreme Court which might be analyzed include the following:

• Brown v. Board of Education (347 U.S. 483; 1954)

• In re Gault (387 U.S. 1; 1967)

• Stanford v. Kentucky (492 U.S. 361; 1989)

2. Each of the following novels contains situations that raise issues of justice. Read one and then describe to the class the situations in the novel that involve issues or questions of distributive, corrective, or procedural justice.

• To Kill a Mockingbird, by Harper Lee

• Animal Farm, by George Orwell

• The Adventures of Huckleberry Finn, by Mark Twain

你怎么看?

1. 以上材料涉及了以下哪类正义问题:

分配正义:在有关分配正义的材料中,涉及了哪些利益或负担?每段材料试图保护或促进的价值或利益是什么?

矫正正义:在有关矫正正义的材料中,涉及了哪些回应?每段材料试图保护或促进的价值或利益是什么?

程序正义:在有关程序正义的材料中,涉及了哪些程序?每段材料试图保护或促进的价值或利益是什么?

2. 哪段材料涉及到一种以上的正义问题?

知识运用

1. 请一位律师或法官帮助你们找一个有关正义问题的法庭判例,或摘录一段法庭判决书。阅读并分析这些判例的观点中所包含的原则、价值和利益。可以从以下高等法院的里程碑式案件中选择一个来进行分析:
   - 布朗诉教育委员会案(347 U. S. 483;1954)
   - 高尔特案(387 U. S. 1;1967)
   - 斯坦福诉肯塔基州案(492 U. S. 361;1989)

2. 以下每篇小说都有涉及正义问题的内容。阅读其中一篇小说,并向全班描述其中有关分配正义、矫正正义或程序正义问题的具体情节:
   - 哈珀·李:《杀死一只知更鸟》
   - 乔治·奥威尔:《动物庄园》
   - 马克·吐温:《哈克贝利·费恩历险记》

Unit Two: What Is Distributive Justice?

> ### Purpose of Unit
>
> In Unit One you learned that we divide issues of justice into three categories: distributive justice, corrective justice, and procedural justice. This unit deals with the issues (or problems) of distributive justice, that is, how fairly we distribute benefits or burdens among persons or groups in society.

In some situations it can be relatively easy to decide what is fair when a benefit or a burden is distributed among several people. For example, it is usually considered fair for all students in a class to have the right to take part in a discussion, provided they respect the right of others to speak. In other situations, however, fair decisions can be more difficult to make. For example, how good should a student's work be to earn an A? How much money, if any, should people who earn moderate incomes contribute to help support people who need help?

Some of the most difficult problems we face in our daily lives have to do with distributive justice. This unit will help you develop the knowledge and skills that will be useful to you in dealing with such issues. It provides you with a set of intellectual tools you can use to examine issues of distributive justice and take reasoned positions on those issues.

第二单元：什么是分配正义？

单元目标

在第一单元中你们已经学会将正义问题区分为三类：分配正义、矫正正义和程序正义。在这一单元中，你们将学习分配正义问题，即如何在社会中的个人和团体之间公平地分配利益或负担的问题。

在某些情况下，要决定如何在几个人之间公平地分配某个利益或负担，相对是比较容易的，例如，如果一个班上所有学生都有权参与班级讨论，通常人们认为这对所有同学来说都是公平的，只要他们尊重别人的发言权。然而，在其他情况下，要做出公平的决定却比较困难。例如，学生的作业应该写多好才能得到Ａ？一个中等收入的个人应该拿出多少钱来帮助那些需要救助的人？

我们在日常生活中面临的某些最困难的问题，都与分配正义有关。本单元将增进你们处理类似问题的相关知识和技能，将向你们介绍一组知识工具，用来研究分配正义问题，并对这些问题形成合理的观点。

 How do these photographs illustrate issues of distributive justice?

这些照片如何反映了分配正义问题？

LESSON 3

What Intellectual Tools Are Useful in Examining Issues of Distributive Justice?

Purpose of Lesson

This lesson introduces you to a set of intellectual tools helpful in dealing with issues of distributive justice. When you have completed this lesson, you should be able to use these tools and explain how they are useful.

Terms to Know

principle of similarity	relevant
need	values
capacity	interests
desert	

What are some issues of distributive justice?

As you have learned, distributive justice deals with the fairness of the distribution of benefits and/or burdens among two or more people or groups in society.

Benefits may be such things as pay for work or the right to speak or to vote, They may include almost anything that can be distributed among a group of people that would be considered useful or desirable, such as praise, awards, opportunities for education, jobs, membership in organizations, or money.

第三课：研究分配正义问题时应当使用什么知识工具？

本课目标

本课将向你们介绍一组用于解决分配正义问题的知识工具。学完本课后，你们应当能够运用这些工具，并说明其用途。

掌握词汇

相似原理	相关的
需求	价值
能力	利益
值得与否	

什么是分配正义问题？

正如之前你们所学到的，分配正义涉及到两个或多个人之间、社会中的团体之间在利益和（或）负担分配上的公平性。

利益可以是工资、言论自由或选举自由，也可能包括在一群人中分配的、所有被认为是有用的、值得拥有的事，例如：赞扬、奖励、受教育的机会、工作、组织机构的会员资格或者金钱。

Burdens may include obligations, such as homework or chores, working to earn money, paying taxes, or caring for another person. They may include almost anything that can be distributed among a group of people that would be considered undesirable, such as blame or punishment for wrong doing.

Making decisions about what is fair may be relatively easy in some situations, for example, when a decision has to be made about what members of a team can play in a game or what students can vote in school elections. In other situations, however, deciding what is fair is not easy and requires careful thought. In some instances, a solution that is distributively just may not be proper when considering other values and interests.

Difficult problems of distributive justice may arise over such questions as the following:

- Should all people have to pay the same amount of taxes or should the government require some to pay more than others? If so, how much more and why?

- Should all people receive the same educational opportunities at public expense, or should some people receive greater assistance and opportunities than others?

- Should part of the income of people who work go to those who are not working for one reason or another? If so, why? How? To whom? How much?

- Should the wealth of developed nations be used to assist developing nations?

These questions raise a few of the difficult issues of distributive justice that face all of us as individuals and as a society, within our nation and in other nations.

负担可能包括义务和责任，例如家庭作业或家务活、工作赚钱、纳税或照顾其他人，也可能包括在一群人中分配的、所有被认为是不受欢迎的、不需要的事，例如：因为做错事而受到责骂或惩罚。

在某些情况下，判断什么事情是公平的，可能相对来说很容易，例如：当需要决定一个团队中谁可以参加比赛，或者在学校竞选中哪些学生可以投票时。但在其他情况下，要进行这样的判断就不太容易了，需要经过仔细的思考。在有些情况下，考虑到其他价值和利益时，某种公平分配的解决方法也许就不那么合理了。

有关分配正义的疑难问题可能出现在以下方面：

是不是所有人都要缴纳同样额度的税收？或者政府是否要求某些人支付比其他人更多的税收？如果是这样，要高出多少？为什么？

是不是所有人都应当有接受同样的公费教育的机会？或者某些人是否应当有比其他人接受更多的帮助和机会？

出于某些原因，有工作的人的部分收入是否应当给那些没有工作的人？如果是，为什么？怎么给？该给谁？应当给多少？

发达国家的财富是否应当被用来帮助发展中国家？

这些问题提出了一些有关分配正义的疑难之处，也是我们作为个人和社会的一份子都要面对的问题，无论是在美国还是其他国家。

How can you decide issues of distributive justice?

Once you have identified an issue of distributive justice (as different from issues of corrective or procedural justice), there are several useful intellectual tools to aid you in examining and in making decisions about such issues. The first of these tools is the principle of similarity. Stated briefly, the principle means that in a particular situation, people who are the same or similar in certain important ways should be treated the same, or equally. In that situation, people who are different in certain important ways should be treated differently, or unequally. For example, suppose that out of ten people stranded on an island, three are sick and there is a limited amount of medicine. The three sick people are similar in an important way: need. They all have equal needs for the medicineandit would be fair to give each of the three persons the same amount. The seven other people are different from the sick people in an important way: need. They do not need the medicine, so it would be fair to treat them differently from the sick people and not give them the medicine.

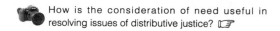

How is the consideration of need useful in resolving issues of distributive justice? ☞

如何判定分配正义问题？

在确认某个分配正义的问题（区别于矫正正义或程序正义问题）之后，以下将介绍几种有助于对这类问题进行研究和决策的知识工具：第一种工具是相似原理。简单地说，这一原理意味着在某种特殊情况下，某些重要条件一样或相似的人们应当得到同等或平等的对待，某些重要条件不同的人们应当得到不同或差别对待。例如：假设有 10 个人困在一个岛上，其中有 3 个人生病了，但药物有限，因此，在某种重要条件——需求上，3 个病人是相似的，他们都有相同的对药品的需求，公平就是给这三个人每人配发均等的药。剩下的 7 个人与这 3 个病人在某种重要条件——需求上是不同的，他们都不需要药，因此公平就是将这 7 个人和病人区别对待，不给他们配发药品。

考虑需求因素将如何有助于解决分配正义问题？

What considerations are useful in applying the principle of similarity?

In the previous section, we looked at similarities and differences among people in terms of their needs. In other situations, we may look at similarities and differences in terms of people's capacities (or abilities), and also in tenms of desert-in other words, how deserving they may be. One or more of these three considerations need, capacity, and desert-are necessary when we use the principle of similarity.

Following are brief definitions of these terms and some simple problems that show the use of each consideration. In reality, many common problems of distributive justice are not as simple as the examples, and more than one of the following considerations should be used to develop a reasonable position on an issue of distributive justice.

NEED. To what degree are the persons or groups being considered similar or different in terms of their need for whatever is being distributed? Types of needs that might be considered include: physiological needs, such as hunger; psychological needs, such as affection or security; economic needs, such as money; or political needs such as influence.

Example: Suppose you have food to distribute among fifty people. Seventeen have not eaten for three days and the rest have eaten regularly.

1. All other things being equal, how should you distribute the food? Why?

2. How is the consideration of need useful in applying the principle of similarity in making such a decision?

CAPACITY. To what degree are the persons or groups being considered similar or different in terms of their capacity to deal with whatever is being distributed? Types of capacities that might be considered include physical, psychological, intellectual, economic, and spiritual.

Example: Suppose ten men and six women apply for jobs with the fire department. Eight men and three women pass the department's rigorous physical strength and conditioning test that establishes their ability to satisfy the physical demands of the job.

运用相似原理时需要考虑哪些因素？

在上文中，我们研究了人们在自身需求方面的相似和不同之处；在其他情况下，我们会考察人们之间在能力方面的相似和不同之处；还要依据值得与否（即他们是否值得）来考察彼此之间的异同。这三种考虑因素（需求、能力和值得与否）当中的一种或一种以上都是我们运用相似原理时所必需的。

以下是对这三种考虑因素及其概念的简要定义，以及运用每一种考虑因素的某些简单案例。在现实生活中，有关分配正义的许多问题通常并不像案例中的问题这么简单。要为分配正义问题寻找一种合理的解决方案，需要以下一种或更多考虑因素：

需求：无论要分配的事物是什么，个人或团体对分配事物的需求在多大程度上是相似的或不同的？需求的种类可能包括：生理需求，例如饥饿；心理需求，例如安全感；经济需求，例如金钱；政治需求，例如影响力。

例：假设你要给50个人分配食物，当中有17个人3天没有吃东西了，而其他人则有规律的饮食。

1. 在其他条件都相同的情况下，你应当怎么分配食物？
2. 运用相似原理做决定时，考虑需求因素有何作用？

能力：无论要分配的事物是什么，要参与分配的个人或团体在能力方面多大程度上是相似的或不同的？能力可能包括以下几种：生理上的、心理上的、智力上的、经济上的和精神上的。

例：假设有 10 名男性、6 名女性同时申请消防局的工作，当中有 8 名男性和 3 名女性通过了严格的身体强度和体能测试，这足以证明他们的能力可以满足这份工作的生理需求。

1. All other things being equal, if there are three jobs available, who should be hired? Why?

2. How is the consideration of capacity useful in applying the principle of similarity in making such a decision?

DESERT. Consider the degree to which the persons or groups described are similar or different in terms of deserving whatever is being distributed, either because of their conduct or because of their status (position). Do similarities in the conduct or status of the persons or groups justify similar treatment? Or do differences in their conduct or status justify different treatment?

Example: Suppose that in the America's Cup boat race sailboats from Australia and the United States qualified for the finals, a series of seven races. At various stages of the competition each day, different boats were ahead, but at the finish the boat from the United States was first over the line four times, and the boat from Australia was first over the line three times.

1. Which team should receive the America's Cup trophy? Why?

2. How is consideration of desert useful in applying the principle of similarity to make the decision?

Example: The Twenty-Sixth Amendment to the Constitution of the United States includes the following statement: The right of citizens of the United States, who are eighteen years of age or older, to vote shall not be denied or abridged by the United States or any State on account of age.

1. What reasoning might underlie giving all who have the status of being eighteen years or older the right to vote? Does the Amendment prohibit exceptions being made on the basis, for example, of capacity? Might it be fair in some situations to deny the right to vote to those eighteen years or older in consideration of capacity or desert?

2. How is the consideration of desert useful in applying the principle of similarity in deciding who should have the right to vote?

What difficulties may arise in applying the principle of similarity?

Two of the most common areas in which disagreements arise about issues of distributive justice are

- deciding what kinds of similarities or differences (need, capacity, or desert) should be used or considered relevant in a particular situation

1. 在其他条件都相同的情况下，如果只有 3 个职位空缺，你应当选择谁？为什么？

2. 运用相似原理做决定时，考虑能力因素有何作用？

值得与否：无论要分配的事物是什么，无论是出于他们的行为或是身份（地位），个人或团体是否值得获得分配对象？这在多大程度上是相似的或不同的？这些个人或团体在行为或地位方面的相似性是否值得获得相似的对待？或者他们在行为或地位方面的不同是否值得获得不同的对待？

例1：假设在美洲杯帆船赛上，决赛将在澳大利亚队和美国队之间进行，这将是一系列共7场比赛。在每天比赛的过程中，两队都互有先后，但在终点线上美国队率先冲线4次，澳大利亚队率先冲线3次。

1. 哪一只帆船队将最终获得美洲杯帆船赛的冠军？为什么？

2. 运用相似原理做决定时，考虑"值得与否"因素有何作用？

例2：美国联邦宪法第26条修正案中有以下声明：联邦或任何一州都不得因年龄而否认或剥夺已满18岁或18岁以上的美国公民的选举权。

1. 赋予所有已满18岁或18岁以上公民以选举投票权有什么内在原因？宪法修正案是否禁止例外的存在，例如以能力为基础来给予选举权？如果考虑"能力"或"值得与否"等因素，在某些情况下否定已满18岁或18岁以上公民的选举权，这样会公平吗？

2. 运用相似原理来决定谁应当获得投票权时，考虑"值得与否"因素有何作用？

在运用相似原理的过程中会出现什么疑难问题？

有关分配正义问题最常出现分歧的其中两个领域是：

· 在某种特定情况下，决定应当运用或考虑哪些异同因素（需求、能力或值得与否）

• determining to what degree members of a group are similar or different in terms of their needs, capacities, or desert

The following exercise illustrates these difficulties.

Critical Thinking Exercise

IDENTIFYING RELEVANT CONSIDERATIONS

Work with a study partner to complete both parts of this exercise. Be prepared to share your answers with the class.

1. Discuss and identify which considerations (need, capacity, or desert) are most relevant in the distribution of the following:

• welfare benefits • fines

• driver's licenses • political rights

• college scholarships

2. Suppose 100 people were to apply for twenty-five openings in the freshman class of a college. What considerations (need, capacity, or desert) should you use in determining whom to admit? How could you determine to what degree applicants were similar or different in terms of the considerations you decided were relevant?

What values and interests should be considered?

Deciding what would be just or fair using the principle of similarity and the consideration of need, capacity, or desert is essential in many situations. Before taking action on a decision regarding what would be just, however, it is important to take into account values and interests other than distributive justice. A value is something that you think is worthwhile and important, something that is right or good, that you ought to try to achieve, such as kindness, honesty, loyalty, privacy, and freedom. An interest is something that you want or that you are concerned about, such as free time, good health, or rewards of one kind or another.

·根据团体成员的需求、能力或值得与否因素，来判定他们在什么程度上是相似的或不同的

以下练习中将说明这些疑难问题。

重点思考练习

识别相关考虑因素

与一位同学一起完成本次练习的两个部分。准备与全班分享你们的答案。

1. 讨论并找出哪些考虑因素（需求、能力或值得与否）在分配以下事物时是最相关的：

· 罚款

· 政治权利

· 大学奖学金

· 驾驶执照

· 福利

2. 假设有 100 个人要申请某大学大一新生班里的 25 个空缺名额，应该用哪些考虑因素（需求、能力或值得与否）来决定人选？根据你所选择的这些相关考虑因素，应该如何判断申请者在什么程度上是相似的或不同的？

应当考虑什么价值和利益?

在很多情况下，运用相似原理和需求、能力或值得与否的考虑因素来判断什么是公平或正义是非常重要的。然而在判定什么是正义之前，我们有必要考虑除了分配正义之外的其他价值和利益。价值是某些你认为是值得的和重要的、正确或良好的、你应当努力实现的事物，例如:仁慈、诚实、忠贞、隐私和自由。利益是指某些你想要的或你关注的事物，例如：自由的时间、健康的身体或各种各样的奖励等。

Example: Suppose a state created a program to help local communities finance the construction of flood-control systems. Under the program, the state would pay half the cost of needed improvements, provided the local community paid the other half with property taxes. Suppose that voters in a particular town repeatedly had rejected proposals to raise taxes to construct a flood-control system that would protect the town from a nearby river. After a series of heavy rains one spring, the river overflowed its banks and flooded the town. It destroyed thousands of homes and businesses, and the people of the town appealed to the state government for help in dealing with the disaster.

A narrow, or limited, idea of distributive justice might call for the state government to reject the request for help. However, the consequences of such a decision would include vast suffering by many people. Thus, considering such other values as kindness, the state government might decide to provide some relief.

 What important interests and values should be considered when deciding whether to help victims recover from a national disaster? ☞

　　例如：假设某个州设立了一项计划，用来资助本地社区的防洪设施的建设。在这项计划中，如果本地社区用财产税来支付该计划费用的一半，州政府将会支付改善设施所需费用的另一半。如果我们假设：这项增加税收来修筑防洪设施以保护某个河岸边小镇的提案，一直遭到镇上选民的否决。就在某年春天，下过几场大暴雨后，河流涨潮漫过了河堤，洪水冲进了镇上，冲毁了成千上万的房屋和商店，镇上居民因此向州政府请求援助救灾。

　　一种狭隘的或有局限性的分配正义观念可能会要求州政府拒绝小镇居民的援助请求。然而做这样的决定，其结果将使更多人或更广泛地区受灾。因此，考虑到其他价值，例如"仁慈"，州政府会决定为该镇居民提供一些援助。

在决定是否要帮助一场国家灾难中的受害者时，应当考虑哪些重要的利益和价值？

Critical Thinking Exercise

USING INTELLECTUAL TOOLS

TO EVALUATE A LEGAL CASE The following case arose before Congress passed the Civil Rights Act of 1964. That act, and other federal laws and court decisions, now prohibit racial discrimination in employment and in public accommodations. Read the case and work in small groups to complete the chart that follows it. The chart contains the intellectual tools you have just studied. Be prepared to explain your position to the class.

Colorado Anti-Discrimination Commissionv. Continental Airlines, Inc.

Marlon D. Green, an African-American, had served as a pilot in the United States Air Force for several years. In 1957, when he was about to leave the Air Force, he wrote to several airline companies, including Continental Airlines, seeking employment as a pilot.

An executive of Continental Airlines told Green to fill out an employment application. They accepted his application and he took Continental's employment tests for pilots along with other applicants.

Green was one of the six people who passed the employment tests. He had more flying experience than the other five qualified applicants who were all white. Yet Green was not hired. He was put on the waiting list, while the other five applicants joined the company and entered the pilots' training program immediately. In the next two months, Continental accepted seventeen more white men into the training program. Green was still on the waiting list.

At this time Green filed a complaint with the Colorado Anti-Discrimination Commission. At the hearing held by the Commission, Green argued that Continental Airlines had refused to hire him solely because of his race. He argued that the airline company had violated the Colorado Anti-Discrimination Act of 1957. This act provided that it was unfair for any employer to refuse to hire any qualified applicant because of that person's race, creed, color, national origin, or ancestry.

重点思考练习

运用知识工具评估一个法庭判例

以下案例发生在美国国会通过 1964 年民权法案前夕。现在，包括 1964 年民权法案在内的各种联邦法律和法庭判决都禁止就业问题和公共场所中的种族歧视。阅读以下案例，以小组方式完成案例后的表格。该表格中包含了你们刚刚学过的知识工具。准备好与全班说明你们组的观点。

科罗拉多州反种族歧视委员会诉美国大陆航空公司案

一位非裔美国人马龙·D·格林曾经在美国空军服役数年，1957 年，他在退役前给几家航空公司（其中包括美国大陆航空公司）写信投递了简历，应聘飞行驾驶员职位。

大陆航空公司的一位主管让格林填写了一张求职申请表，他们接受了他的求职申请，这位主管还带他和其他求职者一起参加了大陆航空公司的机师职业测试。

格林是通过测试的 6 个人之一，他比其他 5 位求职者有更多的飞行经验，而这 5 位求职者都是白人。然而，格林却没有被聘用，他被列在候选名单上，其他 5 位求职者则进入了公司，并随即开始进行机师培训。在之后的两个月里，大陆航空公司招收了另外 17 名白人员工参加机师培训，格林此时却依然在候选名单上。

格林向科罗拉多州反种族歧视委员会投诉了此事。在委员会召开的听证会上，格林认为大陆航空公司拒绝聘用他的唯一原因是他的种族，他认为航空公司违反了 1957 年的科罗拉多州反种族歧视法案。该法案规定，任何雇主若因申请者的种族、信仰、肤色、国籍或民族而拒绝聘用任何合乎资格的申请者，是不公平的。

Continental Airlines officials argued that the hiring of Green would cause great problems. His presence in the cockpit of an airplane might create arguments, which could be a safety hazard. They also said they would have a problem housing and feeding a black pilot because of racial discrimination in some cities. Further more, the company was afraid that the pilots' union would reject Green. This rejection would cause labor problems for the company. Therefore, they argued that the airline company could legitimately refuse to hire Green.

Using the Lesson

1. Identify an issue of distributive justice in a newspaper or newsmagazine. Determine how the ideas of need, capacity, or desert were used in dealing with the issue. Be prepared to discuss the issue with your class.

2. Before1920, the laws of most states did not allow women to vote. Do you think these laws were based mainly on ideas of need, capacity, or desert? Explain your answer.

Since 1920, women have been guaranteed the right to vote by the Nineteenth Amendment to the U.S. Constitution. Do you think this provision of the Constitution is based mainly on ideas of need capacity or desert? Explain your answer.

3. Interview persons who are responsible for hiring decisions. Ask them to describe the considerations they use in choosing among candidates. Compare their ideas with those you have just studied.

4. Describe a situation in which someone made a decision about distributive justice that you think was unfair. Explain why you think the decision was unfair, and what you think the right decision would have been. Explain the considerations you used in reaching your position.

　　大陆航空公司的管理者则认为他们如果聘用了格林将产生许多问题：如果他出现在飞机驾驶舱，将引发机组人员之间的争吵，可能会带来某种安全隐患。同时，因为在某些城市中仍然存在种族歧视，公司要为一位黑人机师解决食宿问题也会很麻烦。另外，航空公司还担心飞行员联盟会拒绝格林的加入，这也会为公司带来一系列劳工问题。因此，航空公司认为自己可以合法地拒绝聘用格林。

知识运用

1. 在报纸或杂志的新闻报道中找出一个有关分配正义的问题。判断人们如何运用需求、能力或值得与否的考虑因素来解决这一问题。准备与全班讨论这个问题。

2. 在1920年以前，美国大多数州的法律都不允许妇女拥有投票选举权，你认为这些法律是否主要建立在对需求、能力或值得与否的考虑因素基础之上？说明你的答案。

   从1920年开始，美国联邦宪法第19条修正案使妇女的投票选举权得到了保障。你认为宪法的这一条款是否主要建立在对需求、能力或值得与否的考虑因素基础之上？说明你的答案。

3. 采访一些负责决定招聘事务的人，请他们描述自己在筛选求职者的过程中所用到的考虑因素，将他们的想法与你之前研究这一问题时的想法进行对比。

4. 举例并描述一个你认为并不公平的有关分配正义的决定，说明你认为这一决定不公平的理由，以及你认为什么决定才是正确的。说明你在得出这一结论时所用到的考虑因素。

Intellectual Tool Chart for Issues of Distributive Justice	
Questions	**Answers**
1. What benefit or burden is to be distributed?	
2. Who are the persons being considered to receive the benefit or burden?	
3. What important similarities or differences are there among the persons in terms of • need • capacity • desert	
4. Which of the similarities and differences listed	
5. Based on the similarities and differences you have	
6. What might be the advantages and disadvantages of doing what is fair? Would other values and interests be served by a different distribution of the benefit or burden?	
7. How do you think the benefit or burden should be distributed? Explain your position.	

有关分配正义问题的知识工具表	
问题	答案
1.要分配的利益或负担是什么?	
2.谁要获得利益或接受负担?	
3.人们之间在以下方面有哪些重要的相似或不同之处: 需求 能力 值得与否	
4.在决定谁应当获得利益或接受负担时,应当考虑以上哪些相似或不同之处?说明你的观点。	
5.基于以上你所选择考虑的相似或不同之处,什么是公平的分配利益或负担的方式?	
6.按照以上公平的方式进行分配的优势和劣势是什么? 如果按照不同的方式分配利益或负担,有可能兼顾其他价值或利益吗?	
7.你认为应当怎样分配利益或负担?说明你的观点。	

LESSON 4

How Should State Governments Distribute Financial Assistance?

> ### Purpose of Lesson
>
> In this lesson you use intellectual tools to decide who should be eligible to receive financial assistance. You will give your opinion on the issue and defend it. When you have completed this lesson, you should be able to explain how you have used the intellectual tools you have learned in evaluating, taking, and defending positions on the issue of distributive justice.

Who should be eligibile for state financial assistance?

Each year state governments distribute millions of tax dollars to people in the form of income subsidies and welfare payments. The basic principle involves providing assistance to people who are in need to enable them to maintain at least a minimal standard of living.

Although various states are different in terms of the types of persons eligible to receive government financial assistance, the following are some of the kinds of categories or groups of people commonly eligible:

- People who are too old to work and do not have enough income to support themselves.

- Adults who are blind and do not have enough money to support themselves.

- Adults who are so physically or emotionally disabled that they cannot earn enough to support themselves and have no other means of support.

- Families with young children who do not make enough money to adequately provide for their needs and those of their children.

- Adults who, for one reason or another, cannot find a job and have no other means of support.

第四课：政府应当如何分配福利救济金？

本课目标

在本课中你们将运用知识工具来决定谁应当有资格获得福利救济金。你们将针对这一问题发表并论证自己的看法。学完本课后，你们应当能够说明自己是如何运用所学到的知识工具来评估、选择和论证有关分配正义问题的观点的。

谁应当有资格获得福利救济金？

每年各州政府都会以收入补贴和福利金的形式将数百万美元的税款发放给人们。发放的基本原则是给那些需要帮助的人提供援助，使他们能至少维持一种最低标准的生活水平。在各州有资格领取政府福利救济金的人有很多种，以下是某些通常有资格领取政府福利救济金的民众群体或种类：

年纪太大、无法工作，没有足够收入维持生活的老人

- 眼盲的成年人，没有足够收入维持生活
- 身体或心理障碍的成年人，无法赚取足够的收入来维持自己的生活，并且没有其他方式的援助
- 有年幼儿童的家庭，没有足够收入维持家庭和孩子的需要
- 因为某种原因无法找到工作的成年人，并且没有其他方式的援助

- Mothers of young children who cannot work because they have to take care of their children and who do not have other means of support.

- Adults who, although they may be working, cannot earn enough money to support themselves and their families at a minimum level.

What do you think?

1. What considerations (need, capacity, desert) appear to have been used to establish these categories or groups?

2. Should people in each of the categories be eligible for financial assistance? Why?

3. What might be the consequences of providing financial assistance to all eligible people in these categories? Which consequences would be classified as advantages? Which would be disadvantages?

4. What values and interests underlie your position?

 How would you decide who should be eligible for state financial assistance? ☞

- 年幼儿童的母亲，因为要照顾孩子而无法工作，并且没有其他方式的援助
- 有工作的成年人，但没有足够收入维持自己和家庭的最低生活水平

你怎么看？

1. 将这些人分组或分类所依据的考虑因素是哪些？需求、能力还是值得与否？
2. 以上每一类人是否有资格申领政府福利救济金？为什么？
3. 如果给以上每一类人中具备资格的人发放福利救济金，会产生哪些结果？哪些结果是优势？哪些是劣势？
4. 什么价值和利益决定了你的看法？

如何判定谁符合州政府发放福利救济金的资格？

Critical Thinking Exercise

EVALUATING THE ELIGIBILITY OF APPLICANTS FOR STATE FINANCIAL ASSISTANCE

A number of applicants are applying for financial assistance, and you will help determine which ones are eligible by applying the principle of similarity and considerations of need, capacity, and desert and other values and interests. Your teacher will divide your class into six groups to role-play a hearing before the Governor's Assistance Eligibility Board. One group will play the role of the Eligibility Board, and will hear testimony from representatives of the other groups. Each of the other groups will be assigned to represent one of the five applicants described below, and will present arguments to the Board explaining why they should be eligible to receive benefits.

First, each group should read the descriptions of the five hypothetical cases described below. Next, the groups representing the applicants should prepare their arguments and select one or two spokespersons to present them to the Board. The Board should use the Intellectual Tool Chart for Issues of Distributive Justice on page 58 in making its decision. The groups representing the applicants should refer to the chart and prepare arguments focusing on need, capacity, desert, and other values and interests to present their applicant's best possible case. While the other groups are preparing their arguments, the Board should use the intellectual tool chart from Lesson 3 to reach some preliminary impressions about which applicants should be eligible to receive benefits, and select a chairperson to conduct the hearing.

重点思考练习

评估州政府福利救济金申请者的资格

有许多人都在申领州政府的福利救济金，你需要通过运用相似原理以及需求、能力和值得与否的考虑因素，来帮助你判断哪些人有资格获得救济金。老师会将你们班分成 6 组，举办一场"州长救济金资格评定委员会"的模拟听证会。其中一组将扮演资格评定委员会，听取其他组代表的团体所做的论证发言。其他每个组要分别扮演以下描述的五位申请者之一，并向委员会陈述发言，说明为什么自己组代表的申请人有资格领取福利。

首先，每个组应当阅读以下描述的五个假设案例。其次，代表申请人的小组应当准备自己的论据，并选出一到两位发言人向委员会进行陈述发言。委员会应当运用第 59 页的"解决分配正义问题的知识工具表"来做出决定。代表申请人的小组也应当参照该知识工具表，并准备自己的论据。论据要强调从需求、能力、值得与否和其他价值及利益方面，说明那些能最有力支持自己所代表的申请人的论点。

After the groups representing each of the applicants have presented their arguments, the Eligibility Board should reach a decision on which applicants are eligible for benefits, and explain its decisions to the class. The class as a whole should then discuss the "What do you think?" questions on page 72.

Group 1: Eccentric Creator

Boris Axelrod was by common standards eccentric in his habits. He slept all day and worked throughout the night on his creative projects. These included composing music, inventing various machines, and writing philosophical essays on the nature of love and patriotism, which he hoped to publish.

Boris was thrifty and liked gaudy secondhand clothes. He had not been successful at earning money with any of his creations, not because he lacked talent, but mostly because he did not understand business matters.

Boris's father left the family when Boris was young and had not been seen or heard from since. When his mother was alive, she supported Boris. After she died, Boris found it necessary to support himself. He had a mechanical mind and sometimes found work as a handyman, but he preferred night work and had difficulty getting it. Once he had a regular job as a night watchman, but he became so absorbed in composing a musical suite that he forgot to go to work, and he was unaware for two weeks that he had been fired.

Boris had no relatives and scarcely any friends. The few people who knew him said, "He'll never be able to hold a job." Finally, a neighbor suggested that he apply for state financial assistance.

 Which consideration–need, capacity, or desert–should be evaluated in deciding whether Boris Axelrod should receive state financial assistance?
☞

在其他组准备论据时，委员会小组应当运用第三课中的知识工具表对哪些申请者有资格领取福利金形成某些初步印象，并选出一位主席主持听证会。在各组代表申请人发表论据时，资格评定委员会应当针对申请人是否有资格领取福利救济金而做出决定，并向全班解释自己的决定。最后，全班应当一起讨论第 73 页"你怎么看？"这一部分的问题。

第一组：古怪的创作者

用常人眼光来看，鲍里斯・阿克塞尔罗德有些很古怪的习惯，他每天白天睡觉，晚上工作，创作各种创意作品，其中包括作曲、发明各种机器。他还撰写有关爱情和爱国主义的实质的哲学论文，并希望能最终发表这些文章。鲍里斯生活节俭，喜欢华丽的二手衣。他的创意作品并没能给他赚多少钱，并不是因为他缺乏天分，主要是他不懂商业运作。

鲍里斯的父亲在他很小的时候就离开了家，此后杳无音讯。他的母亲在世时可以供养鲍里斯，她去世以后，鲍里斯发现必须要想办法养活自己继续创作。鲍里斯的个人意识有些顽固，他有时候也会找到一份类似勤杂工的工作，但他喜欢在晚上工作，而这样的工作往往很难找。有一次，他得到了一个做夜间看守员的工作机会，但他很快就全神贯注地开始创作一部音乐剧组曲，于是忘记了要去上班，直到两个星期后他才意识到自己已经被解雇了。

鲍里斯几乎没有任何亲戚和朋友，少数认识他的人说："他永远都无法坚持做一份长期的工作。"后来，一个邻居建议他去申请政府的福利救济金。

在决定鲍里斯・阿克塞尔罗德是否应当获得政府福利救济金时，应当评估哪些考虑因素（需求、能力或值得与否）？

Group 2: Unskilled Worker

John Harwood and his wife, Louise, struggled continually to feed their eight children, aged one to twelve. Both parents were poorly trained and uneducated, which made it very difficult for them to find jobs. Louise was unable to work outside her home because child care was unaffordable.

John had applied at more than seventeen factories and at various community agencies, but there were no openings in manual labor categories. The Harwoods could not provide a minimal level of shelter, food, or other necessities for themselves or their children, so they applied for government financial assistance.

Group 3: Unemployed Engineer

Andrea Baer had been an engineer in the aerospace industry. She had worked for Aero Labs for seven years. As a result of a government cancellation of a contract, Aero Labs laid off several hundred employees, among them Andrea. Andrea's specialization was hydrology; she worked on designs for undersea missile launching devices. After losing her job, she spent several hundred dollars on a job resume and distributed it to prospective employers. She received a few vague responses and finally a job offer at a much lower salary than she had been making at Aero Labs. The offer came from a firm in another state, and her family was against moving from their home.

After several months, Andrea had used her twenty-six weeks of unemployment compensation and her personal savings. With great reluctance, she applied for state financial assistance to support her family.

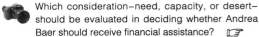 Which consideration–need, capacity, or desert– should be evaluated in deciding whether Andrea Baer should receive financial assistance? ☞

第二组：非熟练技术工人

约翰・哈伍德和他的妻子露易丝不断艰难工作养活他们的 8 个孩子，最小的只有 1 岁，最大的 12 岁。他们两个都没受过任何职业培训和教育，这也使他们很难找到工作。因为要在家照看孩子，露易丝不能离开家工作。

约翰已经申请了超过 17 家工厂和各种社区机构，但这些地方都没有单纯体力劳动的空缺。哈伍德夫妇无法为自己和孩子们提供最基本的住宿、食物或其他必需品，因此他们决定申请政府的福利救济金。

第三组：失业的工程师

安德烈・贝尔曾经是一名航空航天工程师，她为某个航空实验室工作了 7 年，后来因政府取消了与航空实验室的合同，实验室解雇了数百名员工，其中就包括安德烈。安德烈的专业是水文，负责设计水下导弹发射装置。在失去工作后，她花了几百美元写工作简历并分发到各个潜在雇主手里。她收到为数不多的几个模棱两可的答复，最后找到了一份比她在航空实验室的薪资低得多的工作。因为这家公司在另外一个州，而她的家人却不想离开这里。几个月后，安德烈已经花光了她的 26 周失业补偿金和个人积蓄，她极不情愿地开始申请政府福利救济金，以便获得援助。

在决定安德烈・贝尔是否应当获得政府福利救济金时，应当评估哪些考虑因素（需求、能力或值得与否）？

Group 4: Paraplegic Worker

Donald Pierce, whose legs were paralyzed at birth, moved about in a wheelchair. To maintain his health he visited his doctor frequently and received regular physical therapy.

Educated in his home through tutoring, Donald excelled in English and political science. Due to his interest in civic matters and current events, he began writing letters to the editor of his local newspaper. The editor of the newspaper recognized Donald's ability to analyze community problems and provide good ideas, He asked him to work part-time as a staff writer.

Which consideration-need, capacity, or desert-should be evaluated in deciding whether Donald Pierce should receive financial assistance?

Donald received the same pay as others for this type of work; however, because of his special needs, he could work only a few hours a week. Although Donald was able and willing to contribute to his own support, he still needed help and found it necessary to apply for state government financial assistance.

Group 5: Abandoned Children

Mary Jones was a 26-year-old mother of two who suffered from drug addiction. She had already been jailed for one year on a narcotics offense. While in jail she attended Narcotics Anonymous meetings and learned that addiction is a disease recognized by the American Medical Association. She vowed to stay away from drugs when she was released.

After getting out of jail, Mary and her husband George had a third child. This increased the pressures that they both felt and they again became involved in drugs. Mary's job did not pay enough to support her and George's drug habit as well as their other needs. As a result Mary wrote some bad checks and was seriously overdrawn at the bank.

The Joneses frequently left the children alone while they searched for money and drugs. Since the children were young they could not look after themselves. Neighbors often heard them crying and could see that they were dirty and improperly fed.

第四组：半身不遂的工人

唐纳德·皮尔斯出生时患了小儿麻痹症，双腿瘫痪，只能依靠轮椅行动。为了保证他的健康，他需要经常去医生那里接受定期物理治疗。

唐纳德聘请家教在家学习了英语和政治学，出于对公民事务和时事活动的兴趣，他开始给当地的新闻报社写信。报社的编辑们很认可唐纳德在分析社区问题和提供完善意见方面的能力，他们邀请他担任报社的兼职作者。

唐纳德在这份工作上领到与他人相同的工资。然而，因为他的特殊状况，他每个星期只能工作几个小时。尽管唐纳德能够也愿意贡献自己的力量，但他仍然需要帮助，并有必要申请州政府的福利救济金。

第五组：被遗弃的孩子

玛丽·琼斯是一位有两个孩子的 26 岁母亲，同时也是一位吸毒者，因为一宗毒品案，她已经被关在监狱中大约一年的时间。在监狱里，她参加了匿名戒毒集会，并了解到吸毒成瘾被美国医学协会认定为一种疾病。她从监狱中释放出来时发誓要远离毒品。

出狱后，玛丽和她的丈夫乔治又有了第三个孩子这让他们感到了巨大的压力，他们再次开始吸毒。玛丽的工作收入不足以满足她和乔治的毒瘾，也无法负担他们的生活需要。玛丽因此开始开空头支票，银行的账户也严重透支。

当琼斯夫妇出门寻找钱和毒品的时候，他们经常将孩子们单独留在家里。由于孩子们还年幼，无法照顾自己，邻居们常听到他们在房间里哭泣，并看到他们浑身脏兮兮，一日三餐也不定时。

One evening George became ill and lost consciousness from an overdose. Mary called an ambulance, but later that night he died. Believing that she was unable to care for her children and work at the same time, Mary applied for state government financial assistance.

What do you think?

1. Which ideas-need, capacity, desert-were most important in deciding which applicants should be eligible? Which ideas were least important? Why?

2. What might be some benefits and costs of deciding eligibility for benefits using the principle of similarity?

3. What values underlie your position on the eligibility of the five applicants?

Using the Lesson

1. Identify an issue of distributive justice in a newspaper or news magazine. Determine how the ideas of need, capacity, or desert were used in dealing with the issue. Be prepared to discuss the issue with your class.

2. Ask a school administrator to visit the class and explain school policies on the distribution of special educational opportunities. Discuss how the school policies take into account the ideas of need, capacity, and desert. .

3. Ask your teacher, a librarian, or an attorney to help you find a written account of the Supreme Court's decision in Fullilove v. Klutznick, 448 U.S. 448 (1980), San Antonio Independent School District v. Rodriguez, 411 U.S. 1 (1973), or another court case dealing with an issue of distributive justice. Read the facts in the case and the decision of the court, and summarize them for class discussion.

　　一天晚上，乔治病了，并因过量吸食毒品而失去了意识。玛丽叫来了救护车，但当晚乔治死了。玛丽认为她无法在独自照顾孩子的同时兼顾工作，于是她决定申请政府的福利救济金。

你怎么看?

1. 在决定哪些申请人有资格领取政府福利救济金时，哪一种考虑因素（需求、能力和值得与否）是最重要的？哪一种是最不重要的？为什么？

2. 运用相似原理决定领取福利救济金的申请人资格时，会产生哪些利益和损失？

3. 在判断 5 位申请人的资格问题上，你的看法里包含了哪种价值观？

知识运用

1. 在报纸或新闻杂志中找一篇文章，从中找出一个有关分配正义的问题。判断在解决这一问题时所用到的需求、能力和值得与否这些考虑因素。准备与全班讨论这一问题。

2. 邀请一位学校管理者来班上，说明学校在有关特殊教育机会分配方面的政策。讨论如何在制定学校政策时考虑需求、能力和值得与否的因素。

3. 请老师、图书管理员或一位律师帮助你们找到最高法院对以下案例所做的判决的书面文档：富利拉夫诉克卢茨尼克案（448 U.S. 448，1980），圣安东尼奥独立学区诉罗德里格斯案（411 U.S. 1，1973），或其他有关解决分配正义问题的案例。阅读以上案例描述和法院判决，并在班级讨论中进行总结发言。

LESSON 5

How Can We Achieve Distributive Justice in Public Education?

Purpose of Lesson

In this lesson you evaluate an issue of distributive justice raised by the financing of public education in the United States. Your class role-plays a legislative debate on the subject and votes to uphold or to change the present system. When you have completed the lesson you should be able to evaluate, take, and defend positions on the issue of distributive justice.

Term to Know

caucus

Critical Thinking Exercise

EVALUATING THE ROLE OF THE TAXPAYER IN PUBLIC EDUCATION

Some people have doubts about the fairness of the system most states use for collecting tax money to support public schools. An issue of distributive justice that is raised may be stated as follows: How should the burden of paying taxes to support public education be distributed? Any solution must involve consideration of distributive justice and other values and interests of our society.

第五课：在公共教育中应当如何实现分配正义？

本课目标

在本课中你们将评估一个由筹集美国公共教育经费而产生的分配正义问题。你们班将针对这一问题进行一场模拟法庭辩论，并针对要保持或是要改变现有的体制进行投票。学完本课后，你们应当能够评估、选择和论证有关分配正义问题的观点。

掌握词汇

党团会议

重点思考练习

评估纳税人在公共教育中的角色

多数州采用的是用财政税收来资助公立学校的体制，这种体制的公平性遭到了一些人的质疑，由此产生了一个有关分配正义的问题：缴纳税款以支持公共教育的负担应当如何分配？针对这一问题所做的任何决定，都必须考虑到分配正义，以及我们社会中的其他价值和利益。

Distribution of the Property Tax Burden

Throughout our country the property tax is the most common way local communities raise money to support public schools. Most property tax money comes from taxes placed on houses, apartment buildings, stores, factories, other commercial and industrial buildings, and on open land. In most states, people who own these types of property must pay a tax each year that is based on the property's market value. For example, if a person's house had a market value of $75,000, and if the tax rate for residential property was two percent of market value, then the tax to be paid would amount to $1,500 ($75,000 x .02) each year. Most of that tax money would support the local school system.

Homeowners must pay property taxes directly from their income or savings. Owners of apartments, stores, businesses, and industries usually pay property taxes from the income they receive from people who rent their property or who buy their goods and services. Thus, even people who do not own property pay property taxes indirectly through payments for rent, goods and services, or both.

This form of taxation raises some basic problems of distributive justice. In 1978, a tax revolt began in California. The people who started the revolt believed that the rates of property tax for homes and businesses were unfair. The state legislature passed a law to limit the amount of property tax that local governments could charge. This action caused a crisis in the support of public schools. It also has had repercussions throughout the nation as people began reexamining the ways they were being taxed and the fairness of the property tax and other means of taxation.

Who should have to pay taxes to support public schools? ☞

财产税负担的分配

在美国，财产税是地方社区集资支持公立学校的最常用的方式。大部分财产税款来自于对房屋、公寓楼、商店、工厂和其他商业或工业建筑以及空地征收的税收。在大多数州，拥有以上类型财产的人必须每年缴纳基于自己的不动产的市场价值之上的税款。例如，如果一个人的房子的市场价值是 75000 美元，不动产所在地的税率是市场价值的 2%，那么这个人每年需要缴纳的税款就是 1500 美元（75000 美元 x 0.02）。大部分财产税都将用于资助当地的教育系统。

房产所有者必须直接从自己的收入或存款中支付财产税。公寓、商店、企业和工厂的所有者，通常是用租住或购买其产品和服务的人支付给他们的收入来缴纳财产税的。因此，即便是那些没有自己房产的人也会通过支付租金、购买商品和服务而间接缴纳了财产税。

这种形式的财产税涉及了某些有关分配正义的基本问题。1978 年，加利福利亚州发生了抗税行动，发起这场行动的人们认为，该州房屋和企业的财产税率很不公平。随后，州议会通过了一项法律，限制了地方政府可以征收的财产税的额度，这项法令也导致了公立学校资金来源的危机。但是，当人们开始重新审视自己被征税的方式、财产税和其他税收方式的公平性时，这项法令也得到了全国范围内的反响。

谁应当纳税以资助公立学校？

A Problem in Taxation

Many people claim that how taxes are now collected to support public schools and other local government services is unfair and unreasonable. In particular, they argue that a family's tax burden should depend on the number of school-age children in the family. These claims raise questions about the basic principles and practices of taxation presently used by our government.

To understand and evaluate these claims, consider the following example:

The Browns, the Franks, the Davidsons and the Smiths are neighbors. Their houses have the same market value, and they each pay the same amount of property taxes. The Browns have no children. The Franks have two children who are now grown and attend college. The Davidsons have three children who attend public school, and the Smiths pay for their three children to go to a private school operated by their church.

What do you think?

1. What similarities or differences are there between the Browns, the Franks, the Davidsons and the Smiths in regard to their tax burden?

2. What similarities or differences are there between the Browns, the Franks, the Davidsons and the Smiths with regard to the benefits they receive from public schools?

3. How, if at all, can the present distribution of the tax burden between the Browns, the Franks, the Davidsons and the Smiths be justified in terms of similarities or differences in relation to any of the following considerations: need, capacity, or desert?

4. What other considerations might be taken into account to support the present distribution of the tax burden between the families?

5. What might be the advantages and disadvantages of the present distribution?

6. Taking into account your responses to the above questions, is the present distribution of the tax burden fair? Why? Is it desirable? Why?

7. What changes, if any, would you suggest to the distribution of the tax burden between the families? Why?

一个纳税问题

许多人认为当前用征税来资助公立学校和其他地方政府服务的方式是不公平、不合理的。他们特别指出，一个家庭的税收负担应当根据家里学龄儿童的人数来决定。针对美国政府目前所使用的征税体制来看，这种要求提出了现有体制在行为和基本原则方面的问题。

为理解和评估这些要求，思考以下范例：

布朗家、弗兰克家、戴维森家和史密斯家是邻居，他们的房子在市场价值上是一样的，各家也支付相同数目的财产税。布朗家没有孩子，弗兰克家有两个孩子，一个现在已经成年上了大学。戴维森家有三个在公立学校读书的孩子，同时，史密斯家出钱让自己的三个孩子上了当地教会办的一所私立学校。

你怎么看？

1. 布朗家、弗兰克家、戴维森家和史密斯家在对待各自的纳税负担方面有什么相似或不同之处？

2. 对于从公立学校获得的利益来看，布朗家、弗兰克家、戴维森家和史密斯家之间有什么相似或不同之处？

3. 根据三种考虑因素（需求、能力或值得与否）的相似或不同之处，怎样才能（如果可以的话）使布朗家、弗兰克家、戴维森家和史密斯家之间现在的纳税负担分配可以变得更公平？

4. 支持现在四家之间纳税负担的分配应当考虑哪些其他因素？

5. 现在的分配方式有什么优势和劣势？

6. 思考你对以上问题的回答，现在纳税负担的分配公平吗？为什么？这种分配是理想的吗？为什么？

7. 如果可以，你会建议应当对四家之间纳税负担的分配做什么改变？为什么？

Critical Thinking Exercise

TAKING AND DEFENDING A POSITION ON TAXATION TO SUPPORT PUBLIC SCHOOLS

In this exercise your class engages in a simulated debate in the state legislature on the subject of financing public education. Specifically, you will debate whether the system of financing public education should be changed to make a family's tax burden depend on the number of school-age children in the family. To conduct the exercise, your teacher will divide the class into four groups, and each group should prepare for the debate according to their instructions.

Group 1: Committee on Property Taxation

You are the members of the state legislature who have been asked to evaluate the fairness of the present system of property taxation. Report your recommendations for changing the system or for keeping it as it is to the entire legislature. Your group should do the following:

1. Select a chairperson to moderate your committee meeting.

2. Discuss the fairness of the present system of property taxation, focusing on the issue of whether a family's tax burden should depend on the number of school-age children in the family.

3. Discuss possible changes that might make the system of property taxation more fair.

4. Vote on whether to recommend changing the present system of property taxation or to recommend keeping it as it is.

5. Prepare a three-minute presentation (the majority report) to make to the entire legislature to support your recommendation.

6. If you wish, prepare a three-minute presentation (the minority report) to explain to the entire legislature the views of those members of the committee who oppose the committee's recommendation.

7. Select spokespersons to present the committee's reports to the legislature.

重点思考练习

针对纳税以支持公立学校的问题选择并论证一种观点

在本次练习中，你们班将参与一场州议会的模拟辩论会，内容是关于集资支持公共教育的方式。具体来说，你们将讨论是否应当改变目前集资资助公共教育的体制，转而使一个家庭的纳税负担取决于家里学龄儿童的数目。为了进行本次练习，老师将把你们班分成四个组，每个组都应当根据以下说明准备辩论。

第一组：财产税委员会

你们组代表州议会议员，民众要求你们评估现有的财产税制度的公平性。为了向州议会汇报你们有关改变或维持现有体制的建议，你们组应当完成以下几项任务：

1. 选择一位发言人主持你们委员会的会议。

2. 讨论现有财产税收制度的公平性，关注一个家庭的纳税负担是否应当取决于家中学龄儿童的数目问题。

3. 讨论什么改变可能会使财产税收制度变得更公平。

4. 投票决定是否要建议改变现有的财产税体制，或是建议维持现状。

5. 准备一个 3 分钟的发言(多数派报告)，说服整个议会支持你们的建议。

6. 如果你们愿意，准备一个 3 分钟的发言（少数派报告），向整个议会说明委员会当中反对最后决议的成员的意见。

7. 选出发言人向议会陈述你们委员会的报告。

Group 2: Urban Legislative Caucus

You are the members of the state legislature who represent people from the largest cities in your state. Your constituents include many families with low or moderate incomes and some wealthier families. Although some residential parts of your district have low property values, certain large commercial areas have high values and provide substantial property tax revenues. Your district includes some of the most crowded schools and some of the oldest schools in the state. Several schools in your district, however, have special programs that are not available in the suburban or rural schools in your state. Your group should do the following:

1. Select a chairperson to moderate your meeting.

2. Discuss how your constituents would view proposals to change the present system of property taxation, focusing on proposals to make the amount of taxes depend on the number of school-age children in a family.

3. Decide whether you would support any proposals to change the present system ofproperty taxation, given the interests of your constituents and your views on the issue.

4. Prepare arguments to support the positions you think you should take.

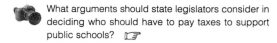

What arguments should state legislators consider in deciding who should have to pay taxes to support public schools? ☞

第二组：城市的立法党团会议

你们代表州议会中代表各大城市居民的议员，你们的选民包括许多中低收入家庭和一些富裕家庭，尽管你们的选区有部分住宅的价格很低，某些大型商业区却有很高的价值，并为本地区带来了可观的财产税收入。你们的地区包括某些人数最多的学校和某些州内历史最悠久的学校。然而，你们区有些学校的特别计划并不包括州内的郊区或农村的学校。

你们组应当完成以下几项任务：

1. 选出一位主席来主持你们组的会议。

2. 讨论你们的选民将会如何看待目前财产税体制的修改计划，这一更改将主要是使征收税款的数额根据家庭中学龄儿童的数目来决定。

3. 考虑到你们的选民的利益和你们自己对该问题的观点，决定你们组是否会支持任何对现有财产税体制的修改计划？

4. 准备论据支持你们认为自己会选择的观点。

在决定谁应当纳税以支持公立学校时，州议员应当考虑什么论据？

Group 3: Suburban Legislative Caucus

You are the members of the state legislature who represent people from the suburbs in your state. Your constituents include many families with moderate incomes and many wealthier families. Most residential neighborhoods in your district have high property values and generate substantial property tax revenues. Your district includes some of the most well-equipped schools in the state, and most of the schools in your district are new. Your group should do the following:

1. Select a chairperson to moderate your meeting.

2. Discuss how your constituents would view proposals to change the present system of property taxation. Focus on proposals to make the amount of taxes depend on the number of school-age children in a family.

3. Decide whether you would support any proposals to change the present system of property taxation, given the interests of your constituents and your views on the issue.

4. Prepare arguments to support the positions you think you should take.

Group 4: Rural Legislative Caucus

You are the members of the state legislature who represent people from the rural areas of your state. Your constituents include many families with moderate incomes and some poorer families. Most of the property in your district has low property values and generates little property tax revenues. Your district includes some of the most poorly funded schools in the state, and most of the schools in your district are old. Your group should do the following:

1. Select a chairperson to moderate your meeting.

2. Discuss how your constituents would view proposals to change the present system of property taxation. Focus on proposals to make the amount of taxes depend on the number of school-age children in a family.

3. Decide whether you would support any proposals to change the present system of property taxation, given the interests of your constituents and your views on the issue.

4. Prepare arguments to support the positions you think you should take.

第三组：郊区的立法党团会议

你们是州议会中代表州内郊区居民的议员。你们的选民包括许多中等收入家庭和许多富裕家庭。你们选区内的大部分居住区都有很高的价值，并贡献了相当可观的财产税收。你们的选区中有州内某些设施最完备的学校，同时你们地区大部分的学校都是新建的。

你们组应当完成以下几项任务：

1. 选出一位主席来主持你们组的会议。

2. 讨论你们的选民将会如何看待目前财产税体制的修改计划，这一更改将主要是使征收税款的数额根据家庭中学龄儿童的数目来决定。

3. 考虑到你们的选民的利益和你们自己对该问题的观点，决定你们组是否会支持任何对现有财产税体制的修改计划？

4. 准备论据支持你们认为自己会选择的观点。

第四组：农村的立法党团会议

你们是州议会中代表了州内农村居民的议员，你们的选民包括许多中等收入家庭和许多贫困家庭，你们的选区内大部分房产价值很低，并且没有多少财产税收入。你们地区包括了州内一些最缺乏财政支持的学校，而且你们区大部分的学校设施和校舍都很陈旧。

你们组应当完成以下几项任务：

1. 选出一位主席来主持你们组的会议。

2. 讨论你们的选民将会如何看待目前财产税体制的修改计划，这一更改将主要是使征收税款的数额根据家庭中学龄儿童的数目来决定。

3. 考虑到你们的选民的利益和你们自己对该问题的观点，决定你们组是否会支持任何对现有财产税体制的修改计划？

4. 准备论据支持你们认为自己会选择的观点。

Conducting a Legislative Debate

To conduct the debate, the spokespersons for the Committee on Property Taxation should give their reports first. Members of each legislative caucus should then present their views. If time permits, the committee members should have a chance to respond to the arguments presented by the other legislators. Following the debate, the class should vote on the proposal presented by the committee.

Using the Lesson

1. Should tax credits or vouchers be given to parents who send their children to private school? Proponents of such measures argue that parents who send children to private school reduce the cost of the public school system and should receive a tax credit to help offset the expense of private school. Opponents claim such measures could undermine the public school system, and that they amount to a tax subsidy mainly for wealthy families.

In 1993, Californians voted on such a voucher proposal. Do research to find out which groups supported or opposed the proposal, each group's arguments, and the outcome of the vote. Evaluate the issue and decide whether you would have voted for or against the voucher proposal. Report the results of your research and explain your position on the issue to the class. You may create a poster of other visual aid to enhance your report.

2. Do state lotteries provide a fair and effective way to increase funding for public education? Do research to find out how lotteries have affected funding for public education in one or more states and what arguments have been made for and against their use. Evaluate the issue and present a report explaining your views to the class.

举行一场议会辩论

辩论开始以后，财产税委员会的发言人应当首先做陈述发言。每个立法党团会议的成员应当随后陈述各自的观点。如果时间允许，委员会成员应当有机会回答其他议员提出的问题。在辩论后，全班应当对委员会提出的计划进行投票。

知识运用

1. 应当对那些送子女去私立学校的父母进行税收减免或颁发凭证吗？
   支持这些措施的人认为，把子女送到私立学校的父母减少了公立学校系统的支出，并应当获得税收减免，以有助于抵消一部分私立学校的费用。反对者认为，这些措施会破坏公立学校系统，并在实际上成了专为富裕家庭提供的税收补贴。
   1993 年，加利福尼亚州选民对这项税收优惠计划进行了投票。调查看看都有哪些团体支持或反对了这项提案，每个团体的观点是什么，以及这次投票的结果。评估这一问题并决定你是否会投票支持或反对这项税收优惠计划。向全班报告你的调查成果，并说明你对这个问题的看法。你可以制作一张海报或其他直观工具辅助你的报告。
2. 各州发行彩票是否是一种公平和有效的增加公共教育经费的方式？
   调查看看彩票业怎样影响了一个或多个州的公共教育经费来源，以及各州有什么支持或反对彩票业的观点。评估这一问题，并向全班陈述说明你的观点。

Unit Three: What Is Corrective Justice?

Purpose of Unit

This unit deals with corrective justice, that is with issues when you have completed this unit, you should be able of fair or proper responses to wrongs and injuries. In this to define corrective justice and explain its goals. You also unit you will learn the goals of corrective justice. You should be able to use the intellectual tools to evaluate also will earn a newset of intellectual tools that are useful issues of corrective justice and make thoughtful decisions in evaluating, taking, and defending positions on issues about how to respond to wrongs and injuries of corrective justice.

第三单元：什么是矫正正义？

单元目标

　　本单元讨论的是矫正正义，也就是如何公平或适当地回应错误和伤害的问题。在这一单元中你们将会学习矫正正义的目标。你们也会学习一组新的知识工具，有助于评估、选择和论证有关矫正正义问题的观点。

　　学完本单元后，你们应当能够定义矫正正义，并说明它的目标。你们也应当能够运用知识工具评估矫正正义问题，并对如何应对错误和伤害，做出明智和深思熟虑的决定。

 How do these photographs illustrate issues of corrective justice?

这些照片如何反应了矫正正义问题？

LESSON 6

What Are the Goals of Corrective Justice?

Purpose of Lesson

This lesson introduces you to the goals of corrective justice and examines the difference between wrongs and injuries. When you have completed the lesson, you should be able to define corrective justice, explain its goals, and identify wrongs and injuries in different situations.

Terms to Know

wrong	correction
Injury	prevention
deterrence	

What is corrective justice?

The Code of Hammurabi is the most complete extant collection of Babylonian laws. Developed during the reign of Hammurabi (1792-1750 BC), these 282 case laws include economic provisions dealing with prices, tariffs, trade, and commerce; family law including marriage and divorce; criminal law; and civil law dealing with issues such as slavery and debt. The code was intended for application to a wider realm than a single country.

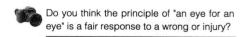 Do you think the principle of "an eye for an eye" is a fair response to a wrong or injury?

第六课：矫正正义的目标是什么?

本课目标

　　本课将向你们介绍矫正正义的目标，并研究错误和伤害之间的区别。学完本课后，你们应当能够定义矫正正义，说明其目标，并在不同的情况下明确错误和伤害。

掌握词汇

错误　　伤害　　制止　　矫正　　预防

什么是矫正正义?

　　《汉谟拉比法典》是现存最完整的巴比伦法律集。这部制定于汉谟拉比时期（公元前 1792 年至 1750 年）的法典，有 282 项判例法，包括涉及价格、关税、贸易和商业的经济条款，涉及婚姻和离婚的家庭法，刑事法律，涉及例如奴隶制和债务问题的民事法。法典原本的设计意图是将法典运用到超越单一国家的更广泛的地域。

你认为"以牙还牙"原则是否是对错误或伤害公平的回应?

Each of the following situations involves an issue of corrective justice. Corrective justice refers to the fairness of responses to wrongs or injuries. A wrong is conduct that violates a duty or responsibility imposed by laws, rules, customs, or moral principles. An injury is harm or damage to persons or property, or violation of a person's rights.

- Convicted of theft, Mustafa was taken into the public square where the executioner chopped off his right hand with a sword.

- While Paul was stopped for a red light, Sarah crashed into his car. The court ordered Sarah to pay $5,500 for damages to Paul's car and $8,376 for his medical bills.

- Three members of a gang beat and robbed a 60-year-old woman standing at a bus stop. The woman was hospitalized for two months and permanently crippled by the beating. The gang members were arrested and placed in Juvenile Hall for six months where they were given psychological counseling, released, and placed on probation for one year.

What do you think?

1. What is fair or unfair about each response to the wrong or injury described?

2. What values and interests, other than fairness, are important to weigh in choosing a proper response to a wrong or injury?

What is the need for corrective justice?

In all societies there are situations in which one individual or group wrongs or injures another. In some cases the wrong or injury may be accidental and in other cases intentional. Since the earliest civilization, human beings have felt that if someone commits a wrong or causes an injury to another, things should be set right in some way. Ideally, this would mean restoring things to the way they were before the wrong or injury occurred. In some cases this may be possible, but in most cases it is not. For example, one cannot restore a life. Since it is not always possible to restore things to the way they were before, people have developed other ways to respond to wrongs and injuries.

以下每段材料中都涉及了一个矫正正义问题。矫正正义指的是对错误和伤害回应的公平性。错误是指违背了由法律、规则、传统或道德原则规定的义务或责任的行为。伤害是指对个人或财产的损害，或对个人权利的侵犯。

- 被判犯了盗窃罪后，穆斯塔法被带到一个公共广场上，刽子手用剑斩断了他的右手。
- 虽然保罗在红灯前停了下来，但萨拉还是撞上了他的车。法庭要求萨拉支付保罗5,500美元的汽车赔偿，并支付保罗8,376美元的医疗费用。
- 一个犯罪团伙的三名成员在公共汽车站殴打并抢劫了一位60岁的妇女。老妇人住院两个月，并且因为被殴打而终生残疾。该犯罪团伙后来被逮捕并送到少管所拘留了6个月，同时接受了心理辅导，释放后还要继续接受一年的管教察看。

你怎么看？

1. 以上描述的每一种对错误或伤害的回应是公平的还是不公平的？
2. 在权衡选择一种对错误或伤害的适当的回应时，除了公平之外，哪些价值和利益也是很重要的？

什么是对矫正正义的需求？

在所有社会中都会发生个人或团体犯错，或是伤害其他个人或团体的情况。在某些情况下，这些错误或伤害可能是偶然的，也有些情况下是故意的。从远古文明开始，人们就感觉到如果有人犯了错或是伤害了其他人，这样的事情应当以某种方式得到矫正。理想状态下，这就意味着将事情恢复到错误或伤害发生前的状态。在某些时候，这样做是可能的，但大多数时候是不可行的。例如，人不能起死回生。因为不可能总是将事情恢复如昨，人们创造了其他方式去应对错误和伤害。

Corrective justice is concerned with fair or proper responses to wrongs and injuries. Proper responses to wrongs and injuries may vary widely. In some instances, one may ignore what has happened, forgive the person causing the wrong or injury, or use the situation to educate the person to prevent a repetition of the event. In other situations, one might wish to require a person to compensate in one way or another for a wrong or injury done to others. In some instances, courts of law may punish wrongdoers by fines, imprisonment, or even death.

The most desirable or proper response to a wrong or injury may not satisfy our need for corrective justice in some situations, but it may serve other purposes such as the wish to forgive or pardon a person or to deter or prevent further wrongs or injuries. For example, if a friend with little money accidentally broke something you owned, you might not want to ask the friend to replace the object or compensate you for the loss. You might expect an apology, however.

Corrective justice has one principal goal-the fair correction of a wrong or injury. Additionally, we may want to prevent or discourage future wrongful or careless conduct by teaching a lesson to the wrongdoer or by making an example of him or her. Thus, the purposes or goals of corrective justice are

- correction-providing a remedy or imposing a penalty to set things right in a fair way

- prevention-responding to wrongdoing in a way that will prevent the person from doing wrong again

- deterrence-discouraging people from committing wrongs and causing injuries, for fear of the consequences

Correction, deterrence, and prevention are essential to the very existence of society. Without efforts to serve these goals, disorder and chaos may result. Ensuring proper responses to wrongs and injuries is important not only with regard to criminal behavior and civil matters but also in families, schools, and other areas of the private sector. Of course it goes without saying that one must first determine who should be considered responsible for a wrong or injury before evaluating what the proper response would be.

　　矫正正义关注的是对错误和伤害公平或适当的回应。对错误和伤害适当的回应可能会有很多种：在某些情况下，人们可能会忽略已经发生的事，原谅那些制造错误或伤害的人，或用这样的事例去教育人们预防类似事情再次发生；在其他情况下，人们可能希望造成错误和伤害的人能以某种方式对受害者进行赔偿；另外还有些情况下，法院可能会处罚犯错者，施以罚款、入狱甚至死刑。

　　对错误或伤害最适宜或最恰当的回应，往往可能无法满足我们在某些情况下对矫正正义的需求，但它会实现其他目的：比如，人们希望原谅或赦免他人，人们希望制止或预防更多的错误或伤害。例如，如果一个手头并不宽裕的朋友不小心打碎了你的某件物品，你可能不会让他再去买个一模一样的赔给你，或是让他赔钱，不过，你会期望他为此而向你道歉。

　　矫正正义的主要目标就是公平地纠正某个错误或伤害，此外，我们也希望能够通过教育违法犯罪的人，或是为他们树立正确行为的典范，以此来预防或阻止日后的违法或粗心犯错行为。由此可知，矫正正义的目的或目标是：

　　矫正：为了以公平的方式矫正错误和伤害，提供一种补救措施或施以惩罚。

　　预防：以某种方式回应错误和伤害行为，预防人们再次犯错。

　　制止：出于对错误和伤害结果的恐惧，阻止人们犯错和造成伤害。

　　矫正、制止和预防，对社会的生存来说至关重要。如果没有为了实现这些目标所做的努力，社会将变得失序、混乱。确保对错误和伤害的适当反应，不仅对犯罪行为和公民事务来说是重要的，对家庭、学校和其他私人生活领域来说也是非常关键的。当然，毫无疑问地，人们必须首先判断谁应当为错误或伤害负责，然后才能评估什么样的回应是适当的。

What do you think?

1. Make a list of the most common responses to wrongs or injuries that you have observed.

2. What are some situations in which a response to a wrong or injury has been fair? Why was it fair?

3. What are some situations in which a response to a wrong or injury was unfair? Why was it unfair?

4. What might happen in a family, school, community, or nation if no attempts were made to provide fair responses to wrongs or injuries, or to deter or prevent them? Why?

5. In what types of situations might it be right to let a wrong or injury go uncorrected, but still do something to make sure such wrongs or injuries do not occur again?

 Do you think assigning community services to persons convicted of minor offenses is a fair response to a wrong? ☞

你怎么看?

1. 列出你所看到的最常见的对错误或伤害的回应。

2. 哪些情况下对错误或伤害的回应是公平的? 为什么是公平的?

3. 哪些情况下对错误或伤害的回应是不公平的? 为什么是不公平的?

4. 如果人们没有实施任何措施对错误和伤害进行公平的回应, 或是去制止和预防它们, 那么家庭、学校、社区或国家会发生什么事? 为什么?

5. 在哪些情况下, 最正确的方法是不去矫正错误或伤害行为, 而是做某些事情确保类似的错误或伤害不再发生?

你认为让犯轻微罪行的人去做社区服务是否是对错误的一种公平的回应?

How should we deal with issues of corrective justice?

Deciding how to respond to a wrong or injury may be simple in some situations, such as when a young child takes away the toy (property) of another child. Our sense of justice may be met by merely restoring the toy to the owner. Our interest in preventing such things from happening again may be met by informing the child that it is wrong to take another person's property without permission. It is hoped these actions will teach the child proper behavior.

In other situations, finding a fair response to a wrong or injury may be more difficult. Unfortunately, there is no simple formula for deciding on proper responses in difficult situations. There are a number of intellectual tools, however, that can be useful when making such decisions. They form the following procedure that you can use to make thoughtful decisions about how to respond to a wrong or injury:

1. Identify the important characteristics of the wrong and/or injury.

2. Identify the important characteristics of the person or persons causing the wrong or injury.

3. Identify the important characteristics of the person or persons who were wronged or injured.

4. Examine common responses to wrongs or injuries and their purposes.

5. Consider other values and interests and decide what the proper response(s) would be.

Each step and the intellectual tools it involves will be examined in detail in lessons 7 and 8. First, however, let's look at the difference between wrongs and injuries.

What is the difference between wrongs and injuries?

In examining issues of corrective justice it is important to understand the difference between wrongs and injuries. As you have learned, .

- A wrong is conduct that violates a duty or responsibility imposed by laws, rules, customs, or moral principles.

- An injury is harm or damage to persons or property, or violation of a person's rights.

应当如何解决矫正正义问题？

在某些情况下，决定如何应对某个错误或伤害可能很简单，例如，当一个孩子拿走了其他孩子的玩具（物品），只需要单纯地将玩具还给物主，我们对正义的感受就能得到满足，只要告诉孩子，不经过他人允许拿别人的东西是不对的，这样我们预防类似事情再次发生的想法也能得到满足。人们希望这些举动能教会孩子正确的行为方式。

在其他情况下，要找到对某种错误或伤害公平的回应方式可能就比较困难了。遗憾的是，没有简单、通用的公式帮助我们在不同情况下做出恰当的回应，然而，仍然有许多知识工具有助于我们做类似决定。这些知识工具组成了下述解决矫正正义问题的程序，你们可以运用这些工具来针对如何应对错误或伤害做出深思熟虑的决定：

1. 识别错误和（或）伤害的重要特征；

2. 识别造成错误或伤害的单个或多个人的重要特征；

3. 识别受到错误侵害或伤害的单个或多个人的重要特征；

4. 研究对错误或伤害的常见回应以及它们的目标；

5. 思考其他重要价值和利益，判断什么是适当的回应。

上述程序中的每一个步骤和包含的知识工具都在第七课和第八课中具体探讨。下面，我们将首先讨论错误和伤害之间的区别。

错误和伤害之间的区别是什么？

在研究矫正正义问题时，理解错误和伤害之间的区别是非常重要的。正如你们学过的：

· 错误是指违背了由法律、规则、传统或道德原则规定的义务或责任的行为。

· 伤害是指对个人或财产的损害，或对个人权利的侵犯。

In some cases, conduct may be wrong and also cause an injury, such as when someone robs a store and shoots the cashier. In other cases, conduct may be wrong but not cause an injury, such as when someone drives with a suspended license. There also may be injuries caused without wrongful conduct, such as when a football player is injured by a clean hit. The following exercise asks you to determine whether situations involve a wrong, an injury, or both.

Critical Thinking Exercise

EXAMINING WRONGS AND INJURIES

Work with a study partner. Read each of the following situations and then answer the questions at the end of the exercise. Be prepared to share your answers with the class.

1. Dozens of people died and hundreds of homes were destroyed when a campfire set by a transient got out of hand.

2. Valerie pushed Monica in the volleyball finals to save the point. Monica suffered a broke.

3. George drove his car through a red light. Fortunately, no accident occurred.

4. Will, a mechanic, forgot to tighten the wheels after he changed the tires. The left front wheel came off while the customer was driving and the car crashed into a parked truck.

5. The security guard shot at the bank robber, but missed. The bank robber took a hostage to ensure his escape. Later, the hostage was released.

What do you think?

1. In each situation, what were the wrongs, if any? What were the injuries, if any?

2. In which situations does your sense of fairness or justice make you want to respond in some way to set things right?

3. In those situations, what do you think would be a fair and just response?

4. What purposes or goals would be served by your proposed responses?

在某些情况下，人们的行为可能是错误的，并同时造成某种伤害，例如，当某个人抢劫了一家商店并枪击了收银员。在某些情况下，人们的行为可能会是错误的，但并没有造成伤害，例如，当某个人携带过期驾照开车。也有可能没有任何错误的行为，也会产生伤害，例如，一个足球运动员在运动中因正常的冲撞而受伤。以下练习要求你们判断某种情况中是否有错误的行为，或是造成了某种伤害，亦或两者皆有。

重点思考练习

识别错误和伤害

与一位同学一起阅读以下阅读材料，并回答练习后面的问题。准备与全班分享你们的答案。

1. 瞬变电流失控引发的大火导致数十人死亡，数百座房屋被烧毁。
2. 瓦莱丽在排球决赛中为了救一个球而推倒了莫妮卡，莫妮卡因此而骨折。
3. 乔治开着车闯了红灯，幸运的是，没有发生任何事故。
4. 机械师威尔在换完轮胎后忘记拧紧螺丝，顾客驾车时左前轮突然脱落，导致车主撞上了一辆停在路边的卡车。
5. 保安向银行劫匪射击却没有击中，银行劫匪随后劫持了一名人质以确保自己安全逃离，最后，人质安全获救。

你怎么看?

1. 在以上每一种情况中，哪些行为是错误的（如果有）？哪些造成了伤害（如果有）？
2. 在以上情况中，你的正义感或公平感是否使你希望能以某种方式回应这些错误或伤害，并让事情得到矫正？
3. 在以上情况中，哪些你认为会得到公平和正义的回应？
4. 你计划的回应方式有什么目的或目标？

Critical Thinking Exercise

EVALUATING AND TAKING A POSITION ON RESPONSES TO WRONGS AND INJURIES

The class should be divided into small groups to review the following situations. For each situation the group should answer the 'What do you think?" questions at the end of the exercise. Be prepared to share your answers with the class.

1. Leslie went into a department store and tried on a shirt. She really liked the way it looked, but she didn't have enough money to pay for it. Leslie decided to steal the shirt. She put it in her purse and walked out of the store. Suddenly, a security guard grabbed her by the arm. She was caught.

2. Arman drank too many beers while watching the football game with his friends. On the way home he failed to stop as the traffic light turned red. Arman's car smashed into the side of a small pickup truck, killing the passenger and seriously injuring the driver. Frank also suffered injuries, and is not expected to gain full use of his legs again.

3. Anita and her one-year-old daughter had just left the house. Suddenly, two men appeared at the side of the car and opened the door. "Get out." they shouted. "We're taking this car." Anita screamed, "My baby!" The men grabbed Anita, pulled her out of the car, jumped inside, and started to drive. Anita's arm was caught in the seat belt. She was dragged along the side of the car. The man who was driving wouldn't stop. He drove the car against a fence to brush Anita off the car. Anita was killed. The men stopped, put the baby on the side of the road and sped away. Four hours later they were caught.

What do you think?

1. What are the wrongs and injuries described?

2. Given the information you have, what do you think would be fair or proper responses to the wrongs and injuries described in each selection?

3. What purposes or goals are your responses designed to promote?

重点思考练习

针对如何回应错误和伤害，评估和选择一种观点

全班需分成小组来评估以下材料。针对每一种情况，各小组都要回答练习最后"你怎么看？"这一部分的问题。准备与全班分享你们组的答案。

1. 莱斯利走进一家百货商店，试了一件衬衫，她确实很喜欢这件衣服，但她没有足够的钱买下来。莱斯利决定要偷这件衬衫。她把衣服放到了自己包里，然后走出了商店。突然，保安抓住了她的胳膊，她被捉住了。

2. 阿尔曼在跟朋友们看足球比赛的时候喝了太多酒，在回家路上，他没能让车子在红灯前停住，将车撞到了路旁的一辆小型载货卡车，卡车内的乘客当场死亡，司机受了重伤。同车的弗兰克也受了伤，他的双腿也不可能再恢复正常功能了。

3. 阿妮塔和她一岁的女儿刚刚开车离开家，突然，有两个人出现在车边，并打开了她的车门。他们大叫："出来！我们要这车！"阿妮塔叫道："我的孩子！"其中一个人抓住阿妮塔，把她从车里拖出来，跳进车子并启动开走了车。阿妮塔的手臂被驾驶座的安全带绑住了，她被挂在车外一侧，随着车子拖行，开车的人也没有停车，反而将车子撞向路边的篱笆，试图摆脱阿妮塔。阿妮塔当即死亡。男人把车停下来，将车里的孩子放在路边，然后开车逃跑了。4个小时后，他们被逮捕了。

你怎么看？

1. 上述情况中哪些是错误，哪些是伤害？

2. 根据上述信息，对以上每一段阅读材料中描述的错误和伤害来说，什么是公平或适当的回应？

3. 你设计的这种回应希望达到什么目的或目标？

4. What additional information would you like to help you decide on a fair or proper response to the wrongs and injuries described? Why might this information be important?

Using the Lesson

1. Interview people responsible for dealing with wrongs and injuries as a part of their profession. You might consider police officers, lawyers, judges, probation officers, or school principals. Ask them to describe some situations they have handled. Find out their ideas on the best responses to wrongs and injuries.

2. Law number 125 of Hammurabi's code states: If anyone place his property with another for safe keeping, and there, either through thieves or robbers, his property and the property of the other man be lost, the owner of the house, through whose neglect the loss took place, shall compensate the owner for all that was given to him in charge. But the owner of the house shall try to follow up and recover his property, and take it away from the thief.

In your opinion is the Code's response to the injury fair? Why or why not?

4. 针对上述错误和伤害，在判断什么是公平或适当的回应时，你还需要什么其他辅助信息来帮助你做决定？为什么这种辅助信息是必要的？

知识运用

1. 采访某个工作中需要负责处理错误和伤害行为的人。你可以考虑采访警察、律师、法官、看守所警官或学校校长，请他们描述自己在处理这类问题时遇到的某些案例，从中找出他们认为对错误和伤害最好的回应是什么。

2. 《汉谟拉比法典》第 125 条法规规定：如果任何人将自己的财物放在别人家里妥善保管，那么无论是遇到小偷或是劫匪，对方家里和其他人的财物都丢失了，因为自己的疏忽大意，房屋的所有者应当赔偿所有那些将物品交给他保管的人们的损失。房屋的主人也应当随后追踪并从窃贼处寻回自己的财产。在你看来，这条法例对伤害的回应公平吗？为什么？为什么不？

LESSON 7
What Intellectual Tools Are Useful in Making Decisions About Issues of Corrective Justice?

Purpose of Lesson

This lesson introduces you to some intellectual tools which are useful in examining issues of corrective justice. When you have completed this lesson, you should be able to use these tools to evaluate, take, and defend positions on issues of corrective justice.

Terms to Know

proportionality	recklessness
extent	negligence
duration	probable consequences
impact	justification
offensiveness	remorse
intent	regret

What is the first step in evaluating issues of corrective justice?
STEP 1.

Identify the important characteristics of the wrong and/or injury.

a. What was the wrong or injury?

Since corrective justice deals with the fairness of responses to wrongs and injuries, identifying the wrongs and injuries in a particular situation is a logical first step in evaluating issues of corrective justice. Identifying the wrongs and injuries also is important because it helps us evaluate whether an injury was caused by wrongful conduct, that is, by the violation of a duty.

第七课：对矫正正义问题进行决策时应使用什么知识工具？

本课目标

　　本课将向你们介绍某些在研究矫正正义问题时有用的知识工具。学完本课后，你们应当能够运用这些工具来评估、选择和论证有关矫正正义问题的观点。

掌握词汇

比例	程度
持续时间	影响
恶劣性	故意
鲁莽	疏忽
可能的结果	辩护
悔恨	遗憾

评估矫正正义的首要步骤是什么？

步骤一：识别错误和（或）伤害的重要特征

1. 哪些是错误或伤害？

　　矫正正义解决的是对错误和伤害回应的公平性问题，因此在评估矫正正义问题时，逻辑上的首要步骤就是在某个特殊情况下识别哪些是错误和伤害。明确错误和伤害不仅是重要的，同时也可以帮助我们评估某种伤害是否源于某种错误的行为，即是否源于某种对责任的违背。

Whether or not an injury was caused by someone's violation of a duty makes a crucial difference in deciding what a fair or proper response would be.

Example: Suppose a young child dashed into the street and ,was run over by a car. In deciding on a fair or proper response, would it make any difference if the driver was driving carefully and obeying all traffic laws, or if the driver could not stop in time to avoid the accident because he or she was speeding?

b. How serious was the wrong or injury?

Evaluating the seriousness of the wrongs and injuries in a particular situation is important, because the response to a wrong or injury should be fair in relation to the seriousness of the wrong or injury.

We call this the principle of proportionality. This principle means that a response to a wrong or injury should be in proportion to the seriousness of the wrong or injury. This is what we mean when we say the punishment should fit the crime.

The principle of proportionality implies that the seriousness of a wrong or injury must be taken into account in deciding what response would be fair or proper.

 Why is it important to determine if an injury was caused by wrongful conduct?   ☞

　　明确伤害是否是由某个人违背了自己的责任（义务）造成的，这对决定什么是公平或适当的回应有至关重要的作用。例如，假设一个小孩突然冲到大街上，并被一辆车撞倒。在决定什么是公平或适当的回应时，如果司机是很专注地开车并遵守交通规则，或如果司机是因为驾驶超速而无法及时刹车避免车祸，将产生两种截然不同的判断。

　　2. 错误或伤害的程度有多严重？

　　评估某种特定情况下错误和伤害的严重性是非常重要的，因为，公平地回应错误或伤害与这种错误或伤害本身的严重性是相关联的。我们称之为比例原则（相称性原则）。这种原则意味着对错误或伤害的回应，应当与错误或伤害本身的严重程度成正比，这就是我们为什么会说：罪罚相当。比例原则（相称性原则）意味着我们在决定哪种回应是公平或适当的时候，必须考虑到这种错误或伤害的严重性。

判断某种伤害是否由错误的行为导致为什么是重要的？

Example: Suppose Michael was driving too fast on the freeway when he saw police lights flashing in his rear view mirror. Would it make any difference if the driver slowed down immediately and pulled over as soon as he could, or if he drove even faster trying to get away, running several cars off the road in the process?

As you can see, it is important to evaluate how serious a wrong or injury is when you are trying to decide what would be a fair or proper response. How can you make this evaluation? There are a number of ideas that you can use to evaluate the seriousness of a wrong or injury.

- **Extent**-How many people or things were affected?

- **Duration**-How long did the wrongful or injury-causing conduct last?

- **Impact**-How severe was the harm or damage? Will it be permanent?

- **Offensiveness**-How objectionable was the wrong in terms of your sense of right and wrong, human dignity, or other values?

 Why is it important to consider the seriousness of a wrong or injury in deciding what the response should be?   ☞

例如，假设迈克尔在高速公路上开车超速时，看到警察的灯在他的后视镜中反光。如果他立即降低车速并尽快停在路边，或者如果他开得更快了以便尽快脱身，并在逃逸的过程中撞翻数辆汽车，这两种情况的结果会有区别吗？

正如你们所看到的，要决定什么是公平、适当的回应时，评估某种错误或伤害的严重性是非常重要的。你们将如何进行这样的评估？在评估某种错误或伤害的严重性时，你们可以用到许多不同的考虑因素：

- **程度**：有多少人或事受到了影响？

- **持续时间**：产生错误或造成伤害的行为持续了多久？

- **影响**：伤害或损失有多严重？这将是永久性的吗？

- **恶劣性**：根据你的是非观念、人的尊严或其他价值观判断，这种错误有多令人反感？

为什么必须在决定应当如何回应时考虑错误或伤害的严重性？

Critical Thinking Exercise

EVALUATING THE SERIOUSNESS OF WRONGS AND INJURIES

Work with a study partner. Read the situations in "Two Foul Factories." Evaluate the seriousness of the wrongs and injuries each factory caused by answering the "What do you think?" questions. Be prepared to discuss your answers with the class.

Two Foul Factories

Suppose two factories have been charged with violating environmental laws dealing with the disposal of potentially harmful wastes.

Mondo Corporation has polluted the air of a large residential area where about 10,000 people live. The company has been allowing harmful pollutants to fill the air for five years. The pollutants can cause respiratory ailments such as emphysema, and may be a cause of cancer. The company has refused to do anything to control its emissions, despite verified reports of people in the area who have become severely ill.

Zenon Utility Co. is located on the outskirts of a city. It discharges air pollutants that are annoying, but do not threaten life. The pollutants have affected about 1,000 people living nearby who claim the smell from the power plant makes it unbearable to live in their homes. The plant has been discharging pollutants for two months. The company has made efforts to control the pollution caused by its operations, but its efforts do not satisfy the local residents.

 What factors would you consider in deciding the seriousness of wrongs or injuries caused by industrial pollution? ☞

重点思考练习

评估错误和伤害的严重性

与一位同学一起，阅读以下材料——"两家违规工厂"。通过回答材料后"你怎么看？"部分的问题，评估每家工厂的错误和造成的伤害的严重性。准备与全班讨论你们的答案。

两家违规工厂

我们假设有两家工厂被指控违反了有关潜在有害废物处理的环境保护法。

1. 盟多公司污染了一个大约有 10，000 人居住的大型社区的空气。该公司 5 年内连续将有害污染物排放到空气中，这些污染物将导致肺气肿等呼吸系统疾病，并有可能引发癌症。该公司拒绝采取任何措施来控制污染物排放，尽管经核实，这一地区已经确定出现了病情严重的病例报告。

2. 择农公共事业公司位于某个城市的郊区，该公司电厂排放的污染物令人难以忍受却并非危及生命。这些污染物影响了居住在附近的大约 1000 多位居民，他们认为电厂所排放出的气体味道实在太过难闻，使他们完全无法待在家里。电厂已经排放这种气体 2 个多月了，但该公司也正在努力采取措施，控制机器运行过程中的污染问题，但当地居民对此并不满意。

在判断工业污染导致的错误或伤害的严重性时，你会考虑哪些因素？

What do you think?

1. How extensive was each factory's wrong or injury? How many people or things were affected?

2. What was the duration of each factory's wrong or injury? How long did the wrongful or injury-causing conduct last?

3. What was the impact of each factory's wrong or injury? How severe was the harm or damage? Will it be permanent?

4. How offensive was each factory's wrong or injury? How objectionable was it in terms of your sense of right and wrong, human dignity, or other values?

Critical Thinking Exercise

EVALUATING THE NEED FOR PUNISHMENT

In the previous exercise you examined the intellectual tools that are useful for evaluating the seriousness of a wrong or injury. But issues of corrective justice cannot be resolved just by evaluating the seriousness of the wrong or injury. Other factors or considerations also need to be taken into account.

The class should be divided into small groups and each group should read "The Fire," and then discuss the 'What do you think?" questions. Be prepared to share your answers with the class.

The Fire

George and his friend Dan were seven years old. Both boys had played many times in the house, yard, and garage of their neighbor. They also had watched him bum leaves in a lot next door. When they asked if they could help him, he told them to keep away from the fire.

One day when the neighbor was out of town, the boys pulled aside a sheet of canvas that covered the entrance to his garage. They went inside to play, but after a while they felt cold. They noticed a charcoal grill in the garage and decided to build a fire to keep themselves warm. They moved the grill close to the garage's entrance and then went outside and gathered leaves to make a fire. Dan went home to get some matches.

你怎么看？

1. 上述两家工厂的错误或伤害影响的范围分别有多广？有多少人或事受到了影响？

2. 两家工厂的错误或伤害持续的时间分别有多长？造成错误或伤害的行为分别持续了多久？

3. 每家工厂的错误或伤害的影响是什么？伤害或损失有多严重？这些伤害或损失是永久的吗？

4. 每家工厂的错误或伤害有多恶劣？根据你的是非观念、人类尊严或其他价值观来判断，这种错误有多令人反感？

重点思考练习

评估对惩罚的需要

在之前的练习中，你们研究了有助于评估错误或伤害严重性的知识工具。但矫正正义的问题单靠评估错误或伤害的严重性是无法得到解决的，我们还需要考虑其他因素。

全班应当分成几个小组，每一组都要阅读以下材料——"火灾"，并讨论"你怎么看？"这一部分的问题。准备与全班分享你们的答案。

火灾

乔治和他的朋友丹都已经7岁了，两个男孩常常一起到邻居家里、院子里和车库里玩耍。他们曾经看到过邻居叔叔用火烧树叶，并问他是否需要帮忙，邻居叔叔说让他们离火远一点。

有一天，邻居出城了，两个男孩拉开了盖在车库门口的帆布罩。他们进到车库里面玩。过了一会儿两个人都觉得有点冷，他们看到车库里有一个炭火烤炉，决定生个火让自己暖和起来。他们将炉子移到车库的入口处，并跑到车库外面找树叶来生火，丹还回家拿了一些火柴来。

The boys lit the fire in the grill and stood with their backs to it trying to get warm. Then the canvas sheet caught on fire. They tried to put the fire out, but failed. The fire spread from the garage to the attached house and caused $28,000 in damages.

Both boys were of average intelligence. Both had been told by their parents not to play with matches and fire.

What do you think?

1. What factors or considerations suggest that George and Dan should be punished? Whatsuggeststhatthey should not be punished?

2. What other information would you like to have in deciding whether George and Dan should be punished? Why would this information be important?

3. What do you think would be a fair response to the wrongs and injuries described in this story?

4. Is the response you have suggested designed to correct the wrongs and injuries? How?

5. Is the response you have suggested designed to prevent further wrongs and injuries? How?

 What factors or considerations might be important in deciding how to respond to the wrongs and injuries described in this case? ☞

男孩们点燃了炉子里的火，背靠着炉子站着来试图取暖。很快，帆布罩着火了。他们试图扑灭它但失败了。火势迅速从车库蔓延到隔壁的房子，造成的损失高达 28，000 美元。

两个男孩都有一定的智商，都被父母告知过不可以玩火柴和明火。

你怎么看？

1. 哪些考虑因素表明乔治和丹应当受到惩罚？哪些表明他们不应当受罚？

2. 在决定乔治和丹是否应当受罚时，你希望参考其他哪些信息？为什么这些信息是重要的？

3. 你认为在这个故事的描述中，哪种对错误和伤害的回应是公平的？

4. 以上你提议的这种回应方式，是用来矫正错误和伤害的吗？如何矫正？

5. 以上你提议的这种回应方式，是用来预防更多的错误和伤害的吗？如何预防？

在决定如何回应以上案例中的错误或伤害时，哪些考虑因素是必要的？

What factors are important in deciding how to respond to a wrong or injury?

In "The Fire"exercise, you evaluated whether to respond to a particular wrong and injury by punishing the wrongdoers. You also identified some important things to consider in making such decisions. As you have learned, it is not always necessary to respond to a wrong or injury by punishing the wrongdoer. Other responses are possible, and in some situations other responses may be better than punishment.

In the first place, injuries which are not caused by the careless or wrongful conduct of another do not require a response to set things right. In some cases, we decide not to punish a wrongdoer because the wrong or injury is not very serious, and we do not want to take the time or effort to try to correct it.

In other situations, we decide not to punish a wrongdoer because we believe that punishment is not the best way to prevent similar conduct in the future. A better way to prevent future wrongful conduct would be to inform the wrongdoer that he or she has committed a wrong, or to provide treatment or education. We might think future wrongful conduct is unlikely even if the wrongdoer is forgiven or pardoned.

What reasons might we have for believing that punishment is not necessary to teach a lesson to the wrongdoer? In some cases, evaluating the wrongdoer's conduct may persuade us that the wrong or injury was not caused with wrongful intent or purpose. In some cases evaluating the nature or character of the wrongdoer may persuade us that the person should be given a chance to mend his or her ways. And in some cases evaluating the conduct of the person or persons who were wronged or injured may persuade us that the wrongdoer's conduct was justified or excused to some degree.

The following critical thinking exercise explains the next two steps in the procedure for evaluating issues of corrective justice. It introduces the intellectual tools you can use to evaluate the important characteristics of the person or persons who caused the wrong or injury, and the important characteristics of the person or persons who were wronged or injured.

决定如何回应某种错误或伤害时，哪些考虑因素是必要的？

在上述阅读材料《火灾》的练习中，你评估了是否通过惩罚犯错的人，作为对某种特定错误和伤害的回应，你们也识别了某些在做类似决策时应当考虑的重要的事情。正如你们学到的，为回应某种错误或伤害，并不总是需要通过惩罚做错事的人来完成，其他回应也是可行的。在某些情况下，其他回应可能比惩罚更好。

首先，并不是因为他人粗心或错误的行为而造成的伤害，不需要用矫正的方式回应。在某些情况下，我们决定不去惩罚犯错的人，因为这种错误或伤害并不严重，我们也不希望花费时间或精力去纠正它。

在其他情况下，我们决定不去惩罚犯错的人，因为我们相信惩罚并不是预防类似行为在未来发生的最好的方法。预防未来错误行为发生的最佳方式，应当是让犯错的人知道他们做了一件错事，或为他们提供治疗或教育。即使犯错的人得到了原谅或宽恕，我们会认为这种错误的行为以后不会再发生了。

为什么我们会认为惩罚并不足以起到教育犯错者的作用？在某些情况下，评估犯错者的行为可能会说服我们，错误或伤害并不是由错误的动机或目的引起的。在某些案例中，评估犯错者的本性或特征可能会说服我们，应当给予这个人改过自新的机会。同时，在许多情况下，评估一个或多个受到错误对待或受伤害的人的行为可能会说服我们，犯错者的行为在某种程度上是正确的或可以被原谅的。

下面的重点思考练习中，将说明评估矫正正义问题的程序中接下来的两个步骤，同时还将介绍多组知识工具。你们可以用这些工具来评估那些导致错误或伤害的一个或多个人的重要特征，以及评估受到错误对待或受伤害的人的重要特征。

Critical Thinking Exercise

IDENTIFYING IMPORTANT CHARACTERISTICS BY USING INTELLECTUAL TOOLS

Directions: After you have read each step in the following procedure, be prepared to

• discuss the usefulness of each step

• give examples of its application to situations you have experienced or observed

STEP 2.

Identify the important characteristics of the person or persons causing the wrong or injury.

Questions a-e in Step 2. should be answered before deciding what to do about the person or persons causing a wrong or injury.

a. State of mind: What was the person's state of mind at the time he or she caused the wrong or injury?

A person's state of mind is one of the most important things to consider when trying to find a fair response to a wrong or injury. To determine the person's state of mind, a number of things should be considered.

• **Intent:** Did the person act intentionally (on purpose) to bring about the wrong or injury?

• **Recklessness:** Did the person deliberately (or knowingly) ignore obvious risks of serious harm?

• **Carelessness:** Did the person act in a thoughtless manner, without paying enough attention to risks that were foreseeable?

• **Knowledge of Probable Consequences:** Did the person know, or have the capability of knowing, that what he or she was doing was wrong or likely to cause an injury?

• **Control:** Did the person have physical and mental control over his or her actions?

• **Duty or Obligation:** Did the person have a duty to act, or not act, in a certain way in order to prevent the wrong or injury?

重点思考练习

运用知识工具识别重要特征

阅读以下程序中的每一个步骤，然后准备：

· 讨论每一个步骤的作用

· 举例说明每一个步骤在你所经历或看过的情况中的运用

步骤二：识别造成错误或伤害的一个或多个人的重要特征

步骤二当中的问题 1 至 5，需要在决定如何处置造成错误或伤害的人之前回答。

1. 精神状态：在他造成错误或伤害的时候，这个人的精神状态如何？

当人们希望找到一种应对错误或伤害公平的回应时，一个人的精神状态是最重要的考虑因素之一。要决定某个人的精神状态，应当考虑的因素如下：

故意：某个人是否故意（有意）导致了错误或伤害？

鲁莽：某个人是否故意（有意）忽略了明显的严重伤害的风险？

粗心：某个人是否采取了轻率的行为方式，对可预见的风险缺乏足够的重视？

了解可能的结果：某个人是否了解，或有能力了解他所做的事情是错误的，或可能会造成伤害？

控制：某个人是否能从生理和精神上控制他的行动？

义务或责任：某个人是否有为了避免错误或伤害而采取行动或不行动的义务？

More Important Values and Interests: Did the person have any other important values, interests, responsibilities, or motives that might justify or excuse his or her actions?

Example: Consider the story of "The Fire" from the previous exercise. Would it make any difference if George and Dan set fire to the canvas sheet on purpose? Would it make any difference if they were older, and knew what might happen?

Example: Consider the case of someone speeding on the freeway. Would it make any difference if the driver was rushing an injured person to the hospital, or if he was exceeding the speed limit simply because he liked to drive fast?

b. Past history: Has the person committed similar wrongs or caused similar injuries in the past?

c. Character and personality traits: Is the person generally trustworthy, careful, considerate of other's rights, and non-violent?

d. Feelings of regret or remorse: Is the person sorry for his or her conduct, or unconcerned about the wrong or injury he or she caused?

e. Role: Did the person act alone or with others, as a leader or as a minor participant?

Example: Consider again the story of "The Fire" from the previous exercise. Would it make any difference if George and Dan had damaged homes by setting fires in the past? Would it make any difference if they were sorry or not sorry about the damage the fire caused? Would it make any difference if they had been encouraged by older children to start the fire?

What factors should a judge consider in deciding what sentence to impose?   ☞

更重要的价值和利益：某个人是否有任何其他更重要的价值、利益、责任或动机，可以用来证明的自己的行动或成为行动的理由？

例1：思考上个练习中有关"火灾"的故事，如果乔治和丹故意用火点燃帆布罩，结果会有什么不同吗？如果他们年龄更大一些，了解可能会发生的事，那结果会有什么不同吗？

例2：思考某个人在高速公路上超速驾驶的例子。如果司机是着急送一位伤者去医院，结果会有什么不同吗？或者如果他超速的原因仅仅只是因为他喜欢开快车呢？

2. 过去的经历：某个人过去是否犯过相似的错误，或是制造过相似的伤害？

3. 个性和人格特质：一般来说，某个人是否值得信任、细心谨慎、考虑到他人的权利以及无暴力倾向？

4. 感到遗憾或悔恨：某个人是否为自己的行为感到后悔，或者对自己造成的错误或伤害无动于衷？

5. 角色：某个人是单独行动，还是与他人一起？是领导者或者是次要参与者？

例：思考上个练习中有关"火灾"的故事，如果乔治和丹以前曾经放火毁坏过房屋，结果会有什么不同？如果他们对火灾造成的损失感到很后悔或者完全无动于衷，结果会有什么不同？如果他们是被年龄较大的孩子怂恿纵火的，结果又会有什么不同？

一个决定做出什么判决的法官应当考虑哪些因素？

STEP 3.

Identify the important characteristics of the person or persons who were wronged or injured.

Besides looking at the relevant characteristics of the person or persons causing the wrong or injury, there may be important characteristics about the person or persons who suffered the wrong or injury that should be considered. The following two questions are designed to focus your attention on this aspect of the issue.

a. Did the person or persons who were wronged or injured contribute to causing the wrong or injury?

b. What is the person's ability to recover from the wrong or injury?

Example: Consider again the story of "The Fire" from the previous exercise. Would it make any difference if the neighbor had been home, and had specifically told the boys they could bum leaves in the charcoal grill? Would it make any difference if the fire had destroyed the neighbor's irreplaceable family heirlooms?

What do you think?

1.Why might it be important to consider the wrongdoer's state of mind in deciding how to respond to a wrong or injury? Why might it be important to consider the justifications or excuses for the wrongdoer's conduct?

2.What arguments can you make to support the position that a person's past history, character, personality traits, and feelings of remorse or regret should be considered in deciding how to respond to a wrong or injury he or she caused? What arguments can you make to support the position that responses to wrongs and injuries should not depend on the nature or character of the wrongdoer, but should be the same for anyone who commits a particular wrong?

3.Are the three steps in the procedure you have studied in this lesson adequate to resolve issues of corrective justice, or should other considerations also be taken into account? Explain your answer.

步骤三：识别受到错误对待或受伤害的一个或多个人的重要特征

除了研究造成错误或伤害的一个或多个人的相关特征外，还应当考虑那些受到错误对待或受伤害的人的重要特征。以下两个问题将用来提醒你们关注问题的这一面：

1. 受到错误对待或受伤害的人是否也要对错误或伤害的发生负责？

2. 受到错误对待或受伤害的人从错误或伤害中复原的能力如何？

例：思考上个练习中有关"火灾"的故事，如果邻居之前在家的时候特别告诉过男孩们可以在炭火炉里烧树叶生火，结果会有什么不同？如果大火烧毁了邻居家不可复制的传家之宝，结果会有什么不同？

你怎么看？

1. 在判断如何回应错误或伤害时，考虑犯错者的精神状态为什么是有必要的？考虑犯错者行为的合理性或理由为什么是有必要的？

2. 你可以找到什么论据来证明：在判断如何回应错误或伤害时，应当考虑犯错者个人的过往经历、个性、人格特质以及对错误或伤害的遗憾与悔恨之意？你可以找到什么论据来证明：对错误和伤害的回应不应当以犯错者的天性和个性为依据，而应当对犯了某种特定错误的任何人一视同仁。

3. 你在本课中学习了程序中的前三个步骤，是否足以解决矫正正义问题？或者是否还应当考虑其他因素？说明你的答案。

Using the Lesson

1. Bring excerpts from newspapers to class, or descriptions of television news or entertainment programs, in which issues of corrective justice are raised. Explain to the class which intellectual tools were used to decide how to respond to the wrongs and injuries.

2. Working with your teacher, invite a judge or attorney to class to discuss how the intellectual tools you have studied are used in court cases.

3. Draw a cartoon to illustrate a situation involving an issue of corrective justice, specifically showing one or more of the intellectual tools you have studied.

知识运用

1. 从报纸、电视新闻或娱乐节目中找出一些涉及矫正正义问题的报道，简要描述这些问题，并向全班说明其中运用了哪一种知识工具来决定如何应对错误和伤害。

2. 与老师一起邀请一位法官或律师到班上来，讨论你们所学习的知识工具如何被运用在法庭判例中。

3. 画一幅漫画，说明某个涉及矫正正义的问题，特别要体现你们所学的一个或一个以上的知识工具。

LESSON 8

What Values and Interests Should We Consider in Deciding How to Respond to Wrongs and Injuries?

Purpose of Lesson

This lesson introduces you to the remaining two intellectual tools useful in examining issues of corrective justice. You learn some common responses to wrongs and injuries and the goals these responses serve. You also examine some values and interests that are important in deciding on proper responses to wrongs and injuries.

When you have completed the lesson, you should be able to explain the purposes served by common responses to wrongs and injuries. You also should be able to use the intellectual tools you have learned to evaluate issues of corrective justice in different situations.

Terms to Know

pardon / restore / compensate

What are the final steps in the procedure for examining issues of corrective justice?

So far, you have considered the first three steps in the procedure to be used in deciding issues of corrective justice: Step 1 -Identifying important characteristics of the wrong or injury; Step 2 -Identifying important characteristics of the person or persons causing the wrong or injury; Step 3 -Identifying important characteristics of the person or persons wronged or injured. Two steps remain in this procedure: Step 4 -Examining common responses to wrongs and injuries and their purposes; and Step 5 -Considering related values and interests to decide what would be the best response.

As you have learned, there are many possible responses to wrongs and injuries. To make sure you select the best response or responses, you should evaluate all the possibilities and examine related values and interests.

第八课：决定如何回应错误和伤害时应考虑哪些价值和利益？

本课目标

本课将向你们介绍在研究矫正正义问题中用到的其余两种知识工具。你们会学习某些常见的对错误和伤害的回应，以及这些回应所要实现的目标。你们也将研究在判断对错误和伤害适当的回应时需要考虑的某些价值和利益。

学完本课后，你们应当能够说明某些常见的对错误和伤害的回应所要实现的目标。你们也应当能够运用所学的知识工具来评估不同情况下的矫正正义问题。

掌握词汇

宽恕　　复原　　赔偿

研究矫正正义问题的程序的最后步骤是哪些？

到目前为止，你们已经按照决定矫正正义问题的程序的前三个步骤进行了思考：步骤一，识别错误或伤害的重要特征；步骤二，识别造成错误或伤害的一个或多个人的重要特征；步骤三，识别受到错误对待或受伤害的一个或多个人的重要特征。程序中接下来的两个步骤是：步骤四，研究对错误和伤害的常见回应以及它们的目标；步骤五，考虑相关价值和利益，判断什么是适当的回应。

正如你们所学到的，对错误和伤害可能有许多种回应方式。为确保你们选择了最佳的回应，就应当评估所有可能性，并研究相关的价值和利益。

STEP 4.

Examine common responses to wrongs and injuries and their purposes.

As mentioned earlier, the principal goal of corrective justice is to provide a fair or proper response to a wrong or injury, to set things right. Responses may be used not only to correct wrongs or injuries, but also to prevent those responsible from causing further wrongs or injuries, and to deter or discourage others from causing wrongs or injuries. In some cases, a response may be chosen to serve other values and interests, rather than to serve the goals of corrective justice. The following is a list of common responses to wrongs and injuries and a brief explanation of the purposes of each. Often more than one response may be chosen, and often more than one purpose may be involved.

a. We may inform or tell the wrongdoer that what he or she did was wrong or caused injury.

The purpose of this type of response is to prevent future wrongs and injuries by explaining to the wrongdoer how his or her conduct was wrong or caused injury. In these cases, the wrong or injury goes uncorrected, unless some other response is also chosen.

Example: After stopping a motorist with an out-of-state driver's license, the officer informed the driver that in this state making a right turn on a red light was illegal, but allowed the driver to proceed without giving him a ticket.

Example: Craig, age six, was playing with matches and started a small grass fire, which his parents put out. Later, a member of the fire department called on Craig and his parents and informed Craig of the danger he had created to himself and others and the damage he had caused by his wrongful conduct.

b. We may overlook or ignore a wrong or injury.

Sometimes we decide to overlook or ignore a wrong or injury because it is not worth the time and effort to try to correct it. Sometimes we may believe the wrongdoer is just trying to get attention. Ignoring the wrongful act may deter such conduct in the future. In these cases the wrong or injury goes uncorrected.

Example: When the J-M Company truck was delivering a new television set to Kevin's house, the driver accidentally ran over Kevin's prize rose bush. Although Kevin was upset, he chose to do nothing about it.

步骤四：研究对错误和伤害的常见回应以及它们的目标

如前所述，矫正正义的主要目标是对错误或伤害提供一种公平或适当的回应，使事情得以矫正。回应不仅可以用来纠正错误或伤害，也能预防人们犯更多的错或制造更大的伤害，以及制止其他人犯错或制造伤害。在某些情况下，人们会选择一种回应方式来满足其他价值和利益的需要，而不是服从矫正正义的目标。以下是一系列常见的对错误和伤害的回应方式，以及对每一种回应方式目标的简要说明。通常，人们可能会选择一种以上的回应方式，通常其中也包含了一种以上的目标。

1.　我们可以告知犯错者他所做的事情是错误的或造成了伤害。这种回应方式的目的是，通过向犯错者说明他的行为是错误的或造成了伤害，以此来预防未来的错误和伤害。在这种情况下，人们并没有对错误或伤害进行矫正，除非同时还选择了其他某些回应方式。

例1：交警拦下了一位携带外州驾驶执照的摩托车，交警告诉车手：本州的交规规定，红灯时右转是非法的，但他会允许摩托车手继续驾车，不会给他开罚单。

例2：六岁的克雷格因为玩火柴而将草地引燃，这场小火灾后来被他的父母扑灭。随后，消防部门的一位工作人员上门拜访了克雷格和他的父母，并告诉克雷格，他错误的行为会为他自己和其他人带来某些危险及伤害。

2.　我们会忽视或忽略某种错误或伤害。有时候我们决定忽视或忽略某种错误或伤害，因为它们并不值得我们用时间和精力去纠正。有时候我们会认为犯错的人只是希望吸引他人的注意。忽略这种错误的行为可能反而会起到制止类似的行为的作用。在这种情况下，人们不会对错误或伤害进行矫正。

例1：负责递送新电视机到凯文家的J-M公司的卡车司机不小心撞毁了凯文最心爱的玫瑰花丛，尽管凯文有点郁闷，但他什么也没说。

Example: Mrs. Johnson was a nursery school teacher. One of her younger students repeatedly clapped his hands while she read a story to the class. Mrs. Johnson generally ignored his behavior.

c. We may forgive or pardon the wrongdoer for a wrong or injury.

Sometimes we decide to forgive or pardon wrongful acts in the hope that this will cause the wrongdoers to regret their actions and mend their ways. Sometimes we decide to forgive or pardon a wrongdoer out of the belief that he or she has already suffered enough; we understand that everyone makes mistakes and we would want others to forgive our mistakes. In these cases the wrong or injury goes uncorrected.

Example: When Thomas accidentally fell against Paul, causing him to sprain his ankle, he apologized and indicated how sorry he was. Paul told him not to worry; he realized it had been an accident and he forgave Thomas completely.

Example: Sue loaned $1,000 to her friend, Mike. Mike agreed to repay Sue over a period of one year. Mike lost his job and was unable to repay the loan. Instead of pursuing the matter in court, Sue decided not to make Mike repay her.

d. We may punish the wrongdoer for a wrong or injury.

One purpose of punishment is corrective justice, that is, to avenge or get even for a wrong or injury. Punishment also may prevent future wrongs and injuries by teaching the person a lesson. It also may deter others from wrongdoing by setting an example.

Example: When Martin and Lorenzo started fighting in class, the principal suspended them from school for five days.

Example: Convicted of burglarizing two homes, Sylvia, Marie, and Sam were sentenced to six months in jail.

例 2：约翰逊夫人是一所幼儿园的老师，在她给全班朗读一篇课文时，她班上年纪最小的学生不断拍手鼓掌，约翰逊夫人通常都会忽视他的行为。

3. 我们会原谅或宽恕犯错者的错误或伤害。有时候我们决定原谅或宽恕错误的行为是期望这样会使犯错者为自己的行为感到后悔并改过自新。有时候我们决定原谅或宽恕犯错者，通常是认为他已经得到应有的惩罚。我们能理解所有人都会犯错，我们也希望他人能原谅我们的过错，在这种情况下，人们并没有对错误或伤害进行矫正。

例 1：当托马斯不小心撞倒保罗害他扭到了脚，托马斯向保罗赔礼道歉，并表示自己相当懊悔。保罗告诉他不要担心，他认为这只是一个意外，他已经完全原谅了托马斯。

例 2：苏借了 1000 美元给她的朋友麦克，麦克说一年后还给苏，但麦克后来失业了，无法偿还这笔欠款。苏并没有到法院起诉麦克，相反，她决定麦克不用还她这笔钱了。

4. 我们可能会因为某种错误或伤害而惩罚犯错者。惩罚的目的之一就是矫正正义，即为一件错事或一种伤害而进行惩罚或报复。惩罚也可以通过给犯错者一个教训来预防未来的错误和伤害，它也能通过树立典型而阻止其他人做错事。

例 1：马丁和洛伦佐在班上打架，校长罚他们停学 5 天。

例 2：因为两次入室盗窃，希尔维亚、玛丽和山姆 3 人被判 6 个月监禁。

e. We may require the wrongdoer to restore or give back something he or she has taken.

When a wrongdoer has taken things that can be returned to their owner, we may require the wrongdoer to restore or give back the items in order to set things right. Requiring a wrongdoer to restore what he or she has taken also may serve to prevent or deter future wrongs and injuries.

Example: When David was convicted of fraud in the purchase of the Hausers' home, the judge required him to return the property deed to them.

Example: When the security officer caught Jason spray painting the side of the gym, he had to spend the next Saturday repainting the wall he had decorated.

What might be a fair and proper response to the wrongs and injuries caused by graffiti artists who paint the property of others without permission? ☞

5. 我们会要求犯错者复原或归还某些他们拿走的东西。当一个犯错者拿走的某些物品可以退还给物主时，我们会要求犯错者复原或归还这些物品，以便纠正错误。要求犯错者复原他们拿走的东西也能起到预防或制止未来再发生类似错误和伤害的作用。

例1：大卫在购买豪泽尔家的房屋时涉嫌欺诈，法官要求他归还房产证。

例2：一位保安发现杰森在健身房的墙面上涂鸦，杰森必须用下星期六的时间重新将这面墙恢复原貌。

对于未经他人允许涂鸦艺术家喷涂他人房屋所造成的错误和伤害，什么回应可能是公平、适当的？

f. We may require the wrongdoer to compensate or pay for a wrong or injury.

In many cases a wrong or injury cannot be undone in the sense that the items taken, damaged, or destroyed cannot be restored or put back. In such cases, we may require the wrongdoer to compensate for the loss by paying money or giving something of value to the wronged or injured person. Requiring a wrongdoer to compensate or pay for a wrong or injury also may serve to prevent or deter future wrongs and injuries.

Example: After borrowing a book from the library, Mr. Bums lost it. He had to pay the price of a new book to compensate for the one he had lost.

Example: A driver's family sued an automobile manufacturer for damages when one of its cars exploded, killing the driver. After a trial, the jury awarded $1 million to the driver's wife to compensate for the loss of her husband. The court made the manufacturer pay this amount to the driver's wife.

 Do you think monetary awards are appropriate to compensate for losses that cannot be restored? ☞

6. 我们会要求犯错者为错误或伤害进行赔偿或支付。在许多时候，某些错误或伤害在某种意义上不可能被撤销，也就是说，被拿走、损伤或破坏的事物不可能得到复原或还原。在这样的情况下，我们会要求犯错者通过支付金钱或其他有价物品的方式，赔偿受错误伤害的人受到的损失。要求犯错者为错误或伤害进行赔偿和支付，也能起到预防未来错误和伤害的作用。

例1：伯恩斯先生丢了一本从图书馆借的书，他必须按照原书的价钱支付费用，以赔偿他丢失的那本。

例2：一家汽车制造厂商生产的汽车爆炸，司机当场死亡，司机家属起诉了该汽车公司。经审理，法官判决汽车制造商应赔偿司机的妻子100万美元，以弥补她失去丈夫的巨大伤害。

为弥补那些不能再被复原的损失，你认为金钱赔偿是否合适？

g. We may provide treatment or education to the wrongdoer.

Providing treatment or education to wrongdoers is not intended to correct the wrong or injury they caused. Its purpose is to prevent them from causing further wrongs or injuries by giving them the knowledge and skills to become self-sufficient and responsible members of society.

Example: In Topeka, Kansas, all persons sentenced to prison receive tests and treatment from psychiatrists and other mental health experts. Studies show that these prisoners are 25 percent less likely to return to prison after release than prisoners who do not receive treatment.

Example: Carlo was driving too fast and got a ticket for speeding. The court allowed Carlo to attend driving school instead of paying a fine because it was his first offense.

 How might education serve the goals of corrective justice? ☞

7. 我们会对犯错者进行治疗或教育。对犯错者进行治疗或教育并不是要试图纠正他们犯的错误或造成的伤害，而是要通过教给他们知识和技能，使他们变成社会中负责任的、自立的成员，预防他们造成更多的错误或伤害。

例1：在美国堪萨斯州的托比卡，所有被判入狱的人都要接受精神病医生及其他精神健康专家的检查和治疗。研究表明，比起没有接受治疗的犯人，这些人在释放后再犯入狱的比率减少了25%。

例2：卡罗开车开得太快了，他因为超速收到一张罚单。考虑到他是初犯，法庭允许卡罗参加驾驶学校的培训以代替罚款。

教育如何为实现矫正正义的目标服务？

What do you think?

1. What are some situations in which you might decide not to punish someone for committing a wrong or causing an injury? What other responses would you choose in these situations? Why?

2. In your opinion, what should be the response if someone carelessly injures another person or damages another person's property? What should be the response if the injury or damage was caused on purpose?

3. If an adult has committed a wrong in the past and he or she has been warned not to do it again, what should be the response if the person commits the wrong again? Would your answer be different if the wrongdoer were an infant? A teenager? Explain your answers.

STEP 5.

Consider related values and interests and decide what the proper response would be.

As you have learned, the basic goal of corrective justice is to set things right in a fair way when a wrong or injury has occurred. Often, we also wish to prevent similar wrongs or injuries from happening because we want to live in an orderly and just society. Thus, we should consider the goals of correction, prevention, and deterrence in deciding on responses to wrongs and injuries. To ensure that the responses are fair, we should consider the principle of proportionality.

We also should consider other values and interests. On the one hand, we might want to satisfy our sense of human dignity and respect for life. On the other hand, we might want retribution.

It is often difficult to weigh all these considerations, some of which might be contradictory. Sometimes we choose a response to serve the goals of corrective justice, and sometimes we design a response to serve other values and interests. In deciding what the proper response(s) would be, you should consider the following:

a. What responses would correct the wrong or injury?

Our need for corrective justice might be satisfied by responses that set things right in one way or another, such as those that require a person to give back something taken from another person, compensate a person for a loss, or those that place a burden or punishment on a wrongdoer.

你怎么看?

1. 在哪些情况下你会决定不去惩罚那些犯错或制造了伤害的人?在这些情况下你还会选择哪些其他回应错误或伤害的方式?为什么?

2. 在你看来,如果有人无心伤害了其他人或损坏了他人的物品,应当如何回应?如果伤害或损坏是故意造成的,应当如何回应?

3. 如果一个成年人过去犯了错,他也已经被警告不再这么做,如果他再次犯错,应该如何回应?如果犯错者是个婴儿,你的答案会不同吗?如果是青少年呢?说明你的答案。

步骤五:考虑相关价值和利益,判断什么是适当的回应

正如你们学过的,矫正正义的基本目的是当错误和伤害发生时以一种公平的方式纠正错误。通常,我们也希望能预防相似的错误和伤害再次发生,因为我们希望生活在一个有序和公平的社会。因此,在决定如何回应错误和伤害时,我们应当考虑矫正、预防和制止的目标。为确保回应是公平的,我们应当考虑比例原则(对称性原则)。

同时,我们也应当考虑其他价值和利益。一方面,我们会希望满足自己对人类尊严和对生命尊重的感受。另一方面,我们会想要对错误和伤害进行惩罚。

要权衡所有这些考虑因素通常是很困难的,某些因素可能是相互冲突的。有时我们选择某种回应方式,以满足某个矫正正义的目标;有时我们会设计出某种回应方式以满足其他价值和利益。在判断什么是最适当的回应时,你们应当考虑以下因素:

1. 什么回应方式可以纠正错误或伤害?

我们对矫正正义的需求可以通过以某种方式纠正错误的回应来满足,例如那些需要犯错者归还他人物品、赔偿他人损失的回应,或者那些给犯错者规定责任、惩罚犯错者的回应。

However, it is important to remember that a response may be chosen to serve other values and interests, rather than to serve the goals of corrective justice.

Example: If a friend were to break something of yours by accident, you might not ask or allow her to replace it or pay for it.

b. How might a response deter or prevent future wrongs or injuries?

In many situations, one of the main reasons for selecting a particular response to a wrong or injury is that the response probably will prevent the wrongdoer from committing such actions in the future and will deter other people from committing such actions.

Example: Sending someone who has committed a crime to prison removes the person from society. It is hoped that when the person is released, he or she will refrain from such actions in the future. Others, who value their freedom, may be deterred from wrongdoing because they do not wish to be imprisoned.

c. How might a response affect distributive justice?

Distributive justice requires that like cases be treated alike. Cases that are different in important ways should be treated differently.

Example: Suppose two persons with similar backgrounds and criminal records were caught stealing. Both were tried and convicted. If one of the persons was sentenced to prison and the other was placed on probation, the response might be considered a violation of distributive justice.

d. How might a response affect human dignity?

An important belief held by many people is that all persons, no matter what their actions, should be treated with dignity-as persons of value with basic rights, deserving respect as human beings. For example, responses that are cruel should not be used no matter how offensive a person's crime may be.

e. How might a response affect promotion of the value of human life?

Human life has a basic worth or value that should be protected. Some people say that the death penalty conflicts with this value, even when it is imposed for taking the life of another person. Others argue that the death penalty deters potential murderers and promotes the value of human life.

但同时也要记住，我们宁愿选择另外某种回应方式以满足其他价值和利益，而不是满足矫正正义的目标。

例如，如果一个朋友不小心打碎了你的物品，你不会要求她或者让她再去买一个或者为此付钱。

2．回应方式如何制止或预防未来的错误或伤害？

在许多情况下，针对某种错误或伤害选择某种特定回应方式的主要原因之一，是这种回应方式能够预防犯错者未来再做出类似的行为，也能够制止其他人犯类似的错误。

例如，把犯罪者送进监狱，是将他与社会隔离。人们希望当这个人被释放时，他能克制自己不再犯类似的错误。另一方面，珍惜个人自由的人，也会因为不想坐牢而不去犯错。

3．回应方式会如何影响分配正义？

分配正义要求：同样的事情，得到同等对待；在重要方式上不同的事情，应当被区别对待。

例如，假设有相似背景和犯罪记录的两个人因偷窃而被捕。两个人都接受了审判并被判有罪。如果其中一个人被判入狱服刑，而另外一个则被判缓刑察看，这种回应方式会被看作是违背了分配正义。

4．回应方式会如何影响人类尊严？

许多人都有一种重要的信仰，那就是所有人，无论他们做了什么，都应当被有尊严地对待，被当作人类来尊重，这是人的基本权利和价值。

例如，无论一个人的罪行有多么恶劣，都不应当用残忍的回应方式对待。

5．回应方式如何提高人类生命的价值？

人类生命有一种基本的应当被保护的价值。一些人认为，即便是为了惩罚那些剥夺了他人生命的人，死刑是与这种价值相冲突的。另外有一些人认为，死刑阻止了潜在的杀人犯，并提高了人类生命的价值。

f. What responses are practical given the resources available?

Individuals and society-the public-need to make efficient use of their time, energy, and property when making responses to wrongs and injuries. The costs of various responses must be considered and, in some instances, a response that sets things completely right may prove too costly.

Example: Under our system, society pays for the costs of gathering evidence against criminal wrongdoers, trying them in a court, and, if they are found guilty, sometimes placing them in a prison or other institution. However, society usually does not pay the victim for any losses he or she may have suffered as a result of criminal wrongdoing.

g. How might a response affect freedom?

Our society, like many others, places a high value on individual liberty, choice, movement and expression. In selecting a response, one should consider the value of freedom-both of the wrong doer and of the rest of society,

h. How might a response affect proportionality?

A fundamental consideration in judging whether a response is fair is whether it is in proportion to the seriousness ofthe wrong or injury.

Example: The response to a cold-blooded murder should be more serious than the response to stealing a bicycle. This is what we mean when we say the punishment should fit the crime.

i. How might a response satisfy the desire for revenge?

Since ancient times, humans have included in their ideas of justice the desire for revenge. In Greek mythology, Nemesis was the goddess of vengeance. Today some people believe revenge should not be a consideration in selecting or evaluating responses. Others, however, believe the desire for revenge is natural and can be considered in allowing society to get even as a part of setting things right.

Example: In 1625, Sir Francis Bacon wrote "Revenge is a kind of wild justice, which the more man's nature runs to, the more ought law to weed it out."

6. 如果有可用的资源，什么回应方式是实际可行的？

在对错误和伤害进行回应时，个人和社会（公众）需要有效利用自己的时间、精力和财富。必须考虑到各种不同的回应所需要付出的代价，在某些情况下，某种要把错误完全纠正过来的回应方式可能会证明代价太高。

例如：在美国的体制中，为对抗犯罪而收集犯罪证据、进行法庭审判、以及将被定罪的人送进监狱或其他机构的所有费用都是由社会支付的。然而，社会通常并不对受害者支付他们因罪犯的错误而受到的损失。

7. 回应方式如何影响自由？

与其他国家一样，我们的社会对个人自由、选择、行动和表达都赋予了很高的价值。在选择回应方式时，我们都应当考虑犯错者和社会中其他人同等的自由价值。

8. 回应方式如何影响比例原则？

在判断某种回应方式是否公平时，最重要的是要考虑这种回应方式是否与错误或伤害的严重性成正比。

例如，对一个冷血杀手的回应方式就应当比对一个偷自行车的人的回应更严厉。这就是我们所说的"罪罚相当"。

9. 回应方式如何满足复仇的欲望？

从远古时代开始，人类就在自己有关正义的观念里包含了对复仇的欲望，希腊神话中就有一位复仇女神叫涅墨西斯。今天，有些人认为，在选择或评估回应方式时，人们不应当考虑要复仇。而其他人仍然相信，复仇的欲望是自然的，允许社会"报复"可以看作是纠正错误的一种方式。

例如，1625 年弗朗西斯·培根爵士这样写道："复仇是一种野蛮的正义，人的本性越是倾向它，就越应该用法律消除它。"

What do you think?

1. How might consideration of values and interests help ensure the fairness with which wrongs and injuries are corrected?

2. What problems might arise if values and interests were not considered in deciding how to respond to wrongs and injuries?

3. How might a response that satisfies the desire for revenge conflict with the values of human dignity or human life? How should this conflict be resolved? Why?

Critical Thinking Exercise

EVALUATING AN ISSUE OF CORRECTIVE JUSTICE BY USING INTELLECTUAL TOOLS

Read the following story based on Crime and Punishment by Fyodor Dostoevsky (1821-1881) and work in small groups to complete the intellectual tool chart on pages 154,156. After completing the chart, answer the "What do you think?" questions on page 152. Be prepared to share your answers with the class.

The Murder of Aliona Ivanovna

Rodion Raskolnikov left his family's home in the countryside of Russia to move to St. Petersburg to study at the university. His family was poor, but struggled to send him a little money so he could continue his studies. Raskolnikov lived in a tiny, dark room and ate sparingly. He found it increasingly difficult to concentrate on his studies. His own poverty did not disturb him, but he kept thinking about the sacrifices of his family.

What factors should you consider in deciding the seriousness of the wrongs and injuries committed by Roskolnikov? ☞

你怎么看?

1. 对价值和利益的考虑因素如何有助于保障纠正错误和伤害的正义性?

2. 如果在决定如何回应错误和伤害时不考虑价值和利益因素,会产生什么问题?

3. 当复仇的欲望与人类尊严或人类生命相冲突时,回应方式将如何满足人们复仇的欲望?这种冲突应当如何解决?为什么?

重点思考练习

运用知识工具评估一个矫正正义的问题

阅读以下根据费奥多尔·陀思妥耶夫斯基(1821-1881)的小说《罪与罚》改编的故事,分成小组完成第 155、157 页的知识工具表。填完表后,回答第 153 页的"你怎么看?"这一部分的问题。准备与全班分享你们的答案。

《谋杀阿廖娜·伊万诺芙娜》

拉斯柯尔尼科夫离开了他在俄罗斯乡村的家,搬到了圣彼得堡去大学学习。他的家庭虽然很贫困,但仍艰辛地给他寄很少的钱以维持他的学业。拉斯柯尔尼科夫住在一间又小又黑的房间里,节衣缩食。他发现自己越来越无法集中精神学习,他自身的贫困并没有困扰他,但他却一直想着他的家人为他所做出的牺牲。

在判断拉斯柯尔尼科夫所犯的错误和带来的伤害的严重性时,应当考虑哪些因素?

The young student dreamed of committing the perfect crime. This crime would free his family from poverty and struggle. But it would be more than a crime for money. It would be a crime that would change life for the better, a crime for which Raskolnikov would be thanked.

Raskolnikov resolved to kill Aliona Ivanovna, an elderly pawnbroker who had given many students money in exchange for family heirlooms. The woman had become rich from the poverty of students like Raskolnikov. Yet, she forced her stepsister Lizaveta, a kindly, but slowwitted woman, to work hard to add to the household income. In Raskolnikov's mind, the pawnbroker was a person who did not deserve to live. He believed that Lizaveta and the world would be better off if the pawnbroker died.

Raskolnikov went to the apartment of Aliona Ivanovna and Lizaveta at a time when he knew that Lizaveta would be working in the marketplace. He pretended to the pawnbroker that he had a silver cigarette case to pawn. When she turned her back to him, he struck her with an ax. Once he was sure that she was dead, he began to rob the apartment.

Suddenly, Lizaveta returned home. She was so terrified when she saw the dead body of her stepsister that she could hardly speak or move. Raskolnikov realized that Lizaveta would identify him as the murderer of the pawnbroker. Before Lizaveta could scream or run out of the apartment, he killed her with the ax.

 What might be a fair and proper response to the wrongs and injuries in this story? Which goals of corrective justice would the response serve?   ☞

这位年轻的学生幻想着进行一次完美的犯罪，可以将他的家人从贫困潦倒中解救出来，并且并不仅仅是单纯为了钱而犯罪。这次犯罪是为了用生命交换更好的生活，拉斯柯尔尼科夫将会因为这次犯罪而得到感谢。拉斯柯尔尼科夫决定谋杀阿廖娜·伊万诺芙娜，一个上了年纪的高利贷当铺老板娘。有很多学生来找她用家族的传家宝换钱，这个老妇人从许多像拉斯柯尔尼科夫这样的学生手上赚了很多钱，变得越来越富有。然而，她却强迫她的继妹莉扎薇塔，一位善良但反应迟钝的女人辛苦工作以增加增加家庭财富。在拉斯柯尔尼科夫的心目中，当铺老板娘是不应该活着的人，他认为如果她死了的话，莉扎薇塔和世界都会变得更好。

拉斯柯尔尼科夫去阿廖娜·伊万诺芙娜和莉扎薇塔的家里，他知道莉扎薇塔此时正在店里工作，他假装跟阿廖娜说他有一个银质烟盒要当。当她转过身背对着他时，他用一把斧头袭击了她。当他确定她已经死了以后便开始抢劫公寓。突然，莉扎薇塔回家了，她看到了自己继姐的尸体，感到非常恐惧，甚至无法言语和行动。拉斯柯尔尼科夫意识到莉扎薇塔会指认他是谋杀老板娘的凶手，在莉扎薇塔尖叫着逃离公寓前，他也用斧子砍死了莉扎薇塔。

对这个故事里描述的错误和伤害，一种公平和适当的回应应该是什么？这种回应方式将实现哪种矫正正义的目标？

He ran out of the apartment and back to his room where he hid the ax. Soon he began to feel guilty about the murders and hinted to friends that he knew who the murderer was. When the police questioned Raskolnikov, he gave them information that led them to identify him as the murderer. Before police could arrest him however Raskolnikov confessed to both murders.

What do you think?

1. What would be the proper response(s) to the wrongs and injuries described in the story?

2. If Rodion Raskolnikov were to receive separate responses for the two murders, should the response in the killing of Aliona Ivanovnabe more severe than the response to the killing of Lizaveta? Why or why not?

3. Are the responses you suggested designed to correct the wrong or injury?

4. Are the responses you suggested designed to prevent further wrongs or injuries?

Using the Lesson

1. Imagine that you live in czarist Russia at the time of the Ivanovna murders. Choose one of the following titles and write a newspaper editorial on the Raskolnikov case and the response you think should have been made to it.

- Who's the Real Victim?
- A Travesty of Justice
- In the Interest of Civil Order
- An Eye for an Eye
- True Confessions
- Violence Against Women

2. Do research to find out how different societies respond to one of the following crimes, and present a report to the class describing what you learn:

- murder
- robbery
- theft of government property

他跑出公寓回到自己的房间里将斧头藏了起来。很快，他就开始对杀人罪行感到悔恨，他向朋友们透露他知道谁是杀人凶手。当警察讯问拉斯柯尔尼科夫时，他也给他们提供了讯息，使他们直接确认了自己就是杀人凶手。在警察逮捕他之前，拉斯柯尔尼科夫就坦白自己犯了两宗谋杀案。

你怎么看?

1. 对故事中描述的错误和伤害来说，适当的回应应当是什么？

2. 如果拉斯柯尔尼科夫的两宗谋杀罪行得到了不同的两种回应，谋杀阿廖娜·伊万诺芙娜的会比杀死莉扎薇塔的更严重吗？为什么？为什么不会？

3. 你所提议的回应方式是用来纠正错误或伤害的吗？

4. 你所提议的回应方式是用来预防未来的错误或伤害的吗？

知识运用

1. 假设你生活在沙俄时代伊万诺芙娜谋杀案发生的年代，选择以下其中一个题目，写一篇有关"拉斯柯尔尼科夫案"的新闻评论，以及你认为应当对此事做出的回应。

   - 谁是真正的受害人？
   - 正义的曲解
   - 为了公民秩序的利益
   - 以眼还眼，以牙还牙
   - 真诚的忏悔
   - 伤害妇女的暴行

2. 调查不同社会如何回应以下罪行，向全班报告并说明你的发现

   - 谋杀
   - 抢劫
   - 偷窃政府财物

Intellectual Tool Chart for Issues of Corrective Justice	
Questions	**Answers**
1. Identify the wrong or injury: a. What was the wrong or injury? b. How serious was the wrong or injury? Consider: • extent • duration • impact • offensiveness	
2. Identify important characteristics of the person or persons causing the wrong or injury: a. What was the person's state of mind at the time he or she caused the wrong or injury? Consider: • intent • recklessness • carelessness • knowledge of probable consequences • control or choice • duty or obligation • important values, interests, or responsibilities b. What facts about the person's past history are relevant in deciding upon a fair response? c. What facts about the person's character are relevant in deciding upon a fair response? d. What feelings did the person express after causing the wrong or injury? e. What was the person's role in causing the wrong or injury?	
3. Identify important characteristics of the person or persons who were wronged or injured: a. Did the person or persons contribute to causing the wrong or injury he or she suffered? b. What is the person's ability to recover from the wrong or injury?	

矫正正义问题的知识工具表	
问题	答案
一、识别错误或伤害： 　1.哪些是错误或伤害？ 　2.错误或伤害的程度有多严重？请考虑： 　　程度 　　持续时间 　　影响 　　恶劣性	
二、识别造成错误或伤害的一个或多个人的重 　　要特征： 　1.犯错或制造伤害的时候，这个人的精神状 　　态如何？请考虑： 　　故意 　　鲁莽 　　粗心 　　了解可能的结果 　　控制或选择 　　义务或责任 　　重要的价值、利益或责任 　2.在决定如何公平回应时，这个人的过去经历 　　中有哪些事实与之相关？ 　3.在决定如何公平回应时，这个人的个性中有 　　哪些事实与之相关？ 　4.在犯错或制造伤害之后，这个人表达了哪些 　　感受？ 　5.这个人在犯错或制造伤害中扮演了什么角 　　色？	
三、识别受到错误对待或伤害的一个或多个人 　　的重要特征： 　1.这个（些）人是否也要对他遭受的错误或 　　伤害负责？ 　2.这个人从错误或伤害中复原的能力如何？	

Intellectual Tool Chart for Issues of Corrective Justice	
Questions	**Answers**
4. Examine common responses to wrongs and injuries and their purposes: a. Should we inform the person that what he or she did was wrong and injurious? Why? b. Should we overlook or ignore the wrong or injury? Why? c. Should we forgive or pardon the person for causing the wrong or injury? Why? d. Should we punish the person for causing the wrong or injury? Why? e. Should we require the person to restore what was taken or damaged? Why? f. Should we require the person to compensate for causing the wrong or injury? Why? g. Should we provide treatment or education to the wrongdoer? Why?	
5. Consider related values and interests and decide what the proper response would be: a. What responses would correct the wrong or injury? b. What responses would deter or prevent future wrongs or injuries? c. What responses would promote distributive justice? d. What responses would preserve human dignity? e. What responses would promote the value of human life? f. What responses are practical given the resources available? g. What responses would protect freedom, both of the wrongdoer and of other members of society? h. What responses would be in proportion to the seriousness of the wrong or injury? i. What responses might satisfy the desire for revenge?	
6. Explain the reasons for your decision.	

矫正正义问题的知识工具表

问题	答案
四、研究对错误或伤害的常见回应以及它们的目标：	
1.我们是否应当告知犯错者他所做的事情是错误的或造成了伤害？为什么？	
2.我们是否应当忽视或忽略这种错误或伤害？为什么？	
3.我们是否应当原谅或宽恕犯错或带来伤害的人？为什么？	
4.我们是否应当因为某种错误或伤害而惩罚犯错者？	
5.我们是否应当要求这个人复原那些被拿走或被损害的东西？为什么？	
6.我们是否应当要求人们为错误或伤害进行赔偿？为什么？	
7.我们是否应当对犯错者进行治疗或教育？为什么？	
五、考虑相关价值和利益，判断什么是适当的回应：	
1.什么回应方式可以纠正错误或伤害？	
2.哪些回应方式会制止或预防未来的错误或伤害？	
3.哪些回应方式会促进分配正义？	
4.哪些回应方式会保护人类尊严？	
5.哪些回应方式会促进人类生命的价值？	
6.根据现有的资源，什么回应方式是实际可行的？	
7.哪些回应方式会保护自由，不仅是犯错者的，还包括社会其他成员的？	
8.哪些回应方式会与错误或伤害的严重性成正比？	
9.哪些回应方式会满足复仇的欲望？	
六、说明你所做的决定的理由。	

LESSON 9

What Would Be Proper Responses to These Wrongs and Injuries?

Purpose of Lesson

In this lesson you use the intellectual tools you have studied in this unit in a final exercise. When you have completed the lesson, you should be able to use these intellectual tools to evaluate, take, and defend positions on issues of corrective justice.

Critical Thinking Exercise

EVALUATING, TAKING, AND DEFENDING A POSITION

Read the fictional "A Scandal in City Government," then do the following:

• Identify the wrongs and injuries caused by some of the officials of the Bay City government.

• Use the intellectuall tool chart at the end of this lesson to develop positions on desirable responses.

Your teacher may ask you to report your positions independently or may divide the class into groups to role-play meetings of a mayor's task force. The task force has the responsibility of investigating the scandal and recommending action. Instructions to the mayor's task force follow the fictional newspaper article.

第九课：什么是对错误和伤害的适当的回应？

本课目标

在本课中，你们会在最后一次练习中运用在本单元学习的知识工具。学完本课后，你们应当能够运用这些知识工具评估、选择和论证有关矫正正义问题的观点。

重点思考练习

评估、选择和论证观点

阅读虚构的故事——"市政府里的丑闻"，然后：

· 识别海湾市政府的某些官员所造成的错误和伤害

· 运用本课末尾的知识工具表，针对什么是最理想的回应方式形成自己的观点

老师会让你们独立陈述自己的观点，或者将全班分成小组模拟举行市长的工作小组会议。工作小组有责任调查此次丑闻并建议采取什么行动。在下述虚拟报纸文章后是有关市长的工作小组的工作说明。

A Scandal in City Government

Widespread Corruption Uncovered In Bay City

A Gazette Exclusive

Bay City-The Gazette has learned of widespread corruption on the part of Bay City officials. Dozens of incidents involving bribe-taking and illegal payoffs to city inspectors have been documented. City departments involved include: the Fire Department, the Building Code Office, and the Health Commission. Also implicated are a number of state-licensed building contractors.

In order to investigate the rumors of corruption, the Gazette provided funds and authorized reporter Myrta Ramirez to purchase a rundown snack shop. She completed a few repairs, but left many serious building and health code violations. Then, the reporter contacted Robert Manning, a state-licensed building contractor.

Ms. Ramirez asked Mr. Manning if he could arrange the necessary inspections to satisfy the city's building, health, and safety codes. Mr. Manning told her that he would be glad to run things through the city if she first paid him his fee. After Ms. Ramirez paid Mr. Manning a sizable amount in cash, he gave her some of his business cards. He explained that whenever an inspector came to the premises, she should put $100 in an envelope along with his business card and give it to the inspector. If you do that, you won't be hassled, he promised.

The first inspector to come to the shop was from the Fire Department. Ms. Ramirez gave her an envelope and she checked its contents. Then, ignoring a number of serious fire hazards, the inspector filled out a department form stating that the snack shop was safe for occupancy.

Ms. Ramirez followed the same procedure each time an inspector came to the shop. Each supplied the needed verification once he or she was given an envelope. Not one of these city employees conducted a thorough inspection or ordered Ms. Ramirez to make any changes in the conditions of the shop.

After the events described above, the Gazette invited the heads of each of the departments involved to meet Ms. Ramirez at the snack shop. Each department head was asked to make a thorough examination of the shop for code violations. They made detailed inspections and noted a total of thirty-eight serious code violations. The department heads who participated in the inspection agreed that the snack shop constituted a serious hazard to public health and safety.

市政府里的丑闻

《海湾市普遍存在的腐败现象曝光》

本报独家报道。海湾市。本报了解到海湾市部分官员中普遍存在着腐败现象，包括收受贿赂、非法行贿市政检查员等数十起事件都被记录在案，其中涉及的市政府部门包括：消防局、建筑规范办公室以及健康委员会，同时也牵涉到许多州政府授权的建筑承包商。

为了调查有关腐败的传言，本报通讯社资助并授权记者迈塔·拉米雷斯买下了一家破旧的小吃店。她对店面做了一点整修，但留下了许多严重违反建筑和健康规范的地方。接着，记者联系了一个州政府授权的建筑承包商罗伯特·曼宁。

拉米雷斯小姐问曼宁先生是否能安排对小吃店进行必要的审查以满足本市的建筑、健康和安全规范要求。曼宁先生告诉她，他会很乐意为她在这个城市打点一切，如果她先付给他一些费用。拉米雷斯小姐付给曼宁先生一大笔现金，他给了她一些自己的名片，并解释说，不管什么时候检查员来店里，她应该把100美元放在一个信封里，连同他的名片一起交给检查员。他保证，如果她这样做，就不会有什么麻烦。

第一个来店里的检查员是消防局的。拉米雷斯小姐给了检查员一个信封，检查员看了看信封里面的东西，接着，无视许多严重的火灾危险，检查员填写了一张部门表格，说小吃店可以安全运营。

拉米雷斯小姐对每个来店里的检查员都采用了相同的步骤，递给他们每个人的信封里都提供了必需的东西。这些市政府的雇员们没有一个对店面进行彻底的检查，也没有一个人要求拉米雷斯小姐改善商店的经营条件。

上述事件发生后，本报邀请以上每个相关部门的领导与拉米雷斯小姐在小吃店会面。每一位部门领导都被要求对小吃店的店面是否违反规范进行了全面的检查。他们进行了仔细的调查，并记录了共计38项严重触犯安全规范的地方。参与调查的部门领导都同意小吃店对公共健康和安全构成了严重威胁。

Meeting of the Mayor's Task Force

Within a week after publication of the story about corruption in Bay City government, the mayor appointed a task force to examine the problem and make recommendations about what responses the mayor's office or other government agencies should make to the wrongs. If your class is divided into groups for this lesson, each group should act as at ask force and complete the following steps:

• Read the witness summaries.

• Fill out the intellectual tool chart on pages 172、174、176.

• Recommend a response for each of the persons described in the witness summaries.

• Be prepared to explain recommended responses to the entire class.

The witness summaries were taken from transcripts of hearings held by the mayor's task force.

市长的工作小组会议

海湾市政府腐败的新闻刊登后一个星期内，市长任命了一个工作小组研究这一问题，并针对市长办公室或其他政府机构应当如何回应本部门的错误提出建议。如果你们班要分组完成本课的学习，每一组都应当扮演一个工作小组，完成以下步骤：

· 阅读证词提要
· 填写第 173、175、177 页的知识工具表
· 为证词提要中描述的每个人建议一种回应方式
· 准备向全班说明你们组所提议的回应方式

以下证词提要摘自市长工作小组举行的听证会笔录。

Don R. Duchinsky, Department Head, Building Code Office. Testimony taken February 5, morning session.

Mr. Duchinsky is thirty-seven years old and divorced. He has worked for the city for seventeen years. He has held his present position for the last eight years. His salary is $40,000 per year.

Mr. Duchinsky has a good civil service record and his superior rated him "excellent" in his last personnel evaluation. He has no prior criminal record.

In his testimony, Mr. Duchinsky stated, "I knew nothing about the alleged acts of people in my office. Maybe I should have known, but I didn't."

Then Mr. Duchinsky was reminded that last year the mayor had asked him to look into complaints about bribe-taking by building code inspectors. The department head shrugged his shoulders and said, "I asked a few of my people about it. They said no one was taking bribes. When you've been in city government as long as I have, you learn not to ask too many questions.

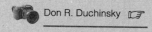 Don R. Duchinsky ☞

多恩·R·德钦斯基，建筑规范办公室主任，证词记录时间：2月5日早上

德钦斯基先生是一位 37 岁的离婚男人。他为这座城市工作了 17 年，8 年前开始做现在这份工作。他的工资是每年 4 万美元。

德钦斯基先生有一份良好的公民服务纪录，在他最后的个人评估中，他的上司

多恩·R·德钦斯基

给了他"优秀"的评价。他没有任何前科和犯罪纪录。在他的证词里，德钦斯基先生说："我对外界谣传的我办公室的下属的行为一无所知。也许我应该对此有所了解，但我的确不知道。"有人提醒德钦斯基先生，市长去年曾请他深入调查有关建筑规范检查员收受贿赂的投诉。这位部门领导耸耸肩膀说："有关这件事我问过几个我的下属，他们说没有人收受贿赂。要是你在市政府的时间跟我一样长，你就会学会不要问太多问题。"

Robert Manning, Contractor. Testimony taken February 4, afternoon session.

The witness is fifty-two, married, and the father of four children aged eleven to twenty-six. He has been the possessor of State Contractor's License #15683-A for almost twenty-five years.

Mr. Manning acknowledged that he has personal assets in excess of $1 million, but would not give details as to how he acquired them.

State records indicate that Mr. Manning was suspended from contracting activities in 1980 for six months. The suspension resulted from supplying faulty building materials on a contract. He has no prior criminal or professional violations.

In giving testimony, Mr. Manning admitted that he acted as described in the news article, but seemed surprised at the uproar resulting from the Gazette series. He expressed the belief that his conduct was not in any way unusual. "It's just Bay City," he said. "I've been a contractor here for more than twenty years and that's how things have always been done and always will be."

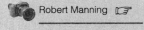 Robert Manning ☞

罗伯特·曼宁，建筑承包商，证词记录时间：2 月 4 日下午

罗伯特·曼宁

证人 52 岁，已婚，育有 4 个从 11 岁到 26 岁的子女。他拥有州政府承包商执照第 #15683-A 号已经将近 25 年了。曼宁先生知道他的个人资产已超过了 100 万美元，但不愿意透露他是如何获得这些资金的细节。州政府的档案显示：1980 年曼宁先生曾被暂停承包业务 6 个月的时间，暂停的原因是提供了与合同不符以及有问题的建筑材料。他并没有任何前科和犯罪记录或职业违规记录。

在提供证词时，曼宁先生承认他的确是像新闻报道里写的那样做的，但他看起来很惊讶本报的系列报道引发的轩然大波。他认为自己的行为没有什么地方是不正常的："这就是海湾市，"他说，"我在这里做承包商已经超过 20 年了，事情一直是这样做的，并将一直继续这样下去。"

Jeanine Lepere, Bay City Fire Officer. Testimony taken February 5, morning session.

Officer Lepere is twenty-three years old and the mother of two children. She has been an inspector with the Fire Department for two years. Her personnel record with the department is very good. She has no prior criminal record, but was once suspended from Bay City High for two weeks for cheating on an exam.

In her testimony, Officer Lepere admitted that she had taken bribes. "Look," she said, "I know it's wrong. When I started with the department, I never took a bribe, Then I saw the other inspectors taking them and nobody seemed to care. I'm alone and I've got two kids to think about, and a Fire Department salary doesn't go very far. So I figured that if I took a few bribes my kids would have decent clothes to wear."

During the February 6 morning session, Officer Lepere delivered a letter to the task force. The letter stated that she would testify about bribe-taking by other inspectors if the task force would recommend that she not be prosecuted.

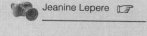 Jeanine Lepere ☞

吉奈恩・莱佩尔，海湾市消防局公务员，证词记录时间：2月5日早上

公务员莱佩尔 23 岁，是两个孩子的母亲。她在消防局担任检查员已经两年了。她在部门的个人记录非常好，她没有任何前科和犯罪记录，但曾经因为在海湾市高中的一次考试中作弊而被暂时停学两个星期。

在她的证词中，公务员莱佩尔承认了自己收受贿赂。她说："你们看，我知道这是错的。当

吉奈恩・莱佩尔

我开始在这个部门工作的时候，我从没有收过贿赂，后来我看到在其他检查员收取贿赂后似乎也没什么人在乎，我一个人要带两个小孩，消防局的工资并不多。因此我想，如果我收一点点贿赂，就能让我的孩子们可以有更好的衣服穿。"

在 2 月 6 日早上的证词记录中，公务员莱佩尔向工作小组递交了一封信，信中说，如果工作小组能保荐她不被起诉，她愿意为其他检查员收取贿赂的行为做证。

What do you think?

1. What responses did your group recommend for each person described in the witness summaries?

2. Did all the groups agree on the same responses for the wrongs and injuries described in the Gazette article?

3. How fair are the suggested responses? Justify.

4. Will the responses suggested correct the wrongs or injuries?

5. Will the responses suggested prevent further such wrongs or injuries?

Using the Lesson

1. Invite a representative of a government "watchdog" agency to class to discuss actual cases similar to the one presented in this lesson. Ask the representative what responses his or her agency looks for in such situations.

2. Do research to find out the responses to one of the following government scandals.

• 1972 Watergate scandal

• Late 1980s Iran-Contra scandal

Report what you learn to the class.

3. Identify a problem of corrective justice in your school, community, or state. Present a report to your class explaining the problem, how it involves corrective justice, and what other values and interests might be involved. Use the intellectual tool chart from Lesson 8 to develop a position on the issue or explain why you are unable to develop a reasonable position on the basis of the facts available to you.

你怎么看?

1. 针对上述证词提要中描述的每个人,你们组建议怎么回应?

2. 对本报系列报道中描述的错误和伤害,是否所有组都同意做出同样的回应?

3. 大家所提议的回应方式如何保证公平?请说明。

4. 大家所提议的回应方式会纠正错误或伤害吗?

5. 大家所提议的回应方式会预防未来类似的错误或伤害吗?

知识运用

1. 邀请一位政府"监察"机构的代表到班上,讨论与本课阅读材料类似的实际案例。询问代表在这样的案例中他的机构会做出什么回应。

2. 从以下政府丑闻中选出一个来进行调查,找出针对该案例的回应:
   · 1972 年水门丑闻
   · 20 世纪 80 年代末伊朗门丑闻
   向全班报告你的发现。

3. 在你的学校、社区或州里找出一个有关矫正正义的问题。向全班发表你的报告,说明这一问题,并描述这一问题如何涉及了矫正正义,以及说出这问题中可能涉及的其他价值和利益。运用第八课的知识工具表,基于可用的事实材料,形成你对这一问题的观点,或说明你为什么无法对这一问题形成一种合理的观点。

Intellectual Tool Chart for Issues of Corrective Justice			
1. Identify the wrong or injury:	Don R. Duchinsky	Robert Manning	Jeanine Lepere
a. What was the wrong or injury? How serious was the wrong or injury? b. How serious was the wrong or injury? Consider • extent • duration • impact • offensiveness			
2. Identify important characteristics of the person or persons causing the wrong or injury: a. What was the person's state of mind at the time he or she caused the wrong or injury? Consider: • intent • recklessness • carelessness • knowledge of probable consequences • control or choice • duty or obligation • important values, interests, or responsibilities b. What facts about the person's past history are relevant in deciding upon a fair response? c. What facts about the person's character are relevant in deciding upon a fair response? d. What feelings did the person express after causing the wrong or injury? e. What was the person's role in causing the wrong or injury?			

矫正正义问题的知识工具表

	多恩·R·德钦斯基	罗伯特·曼宁	吉奈恩·莱佩尔
一、识别错误或伤害： 1. 哪些是错误或伤害？ 2. 错误或伤害的程度有多严重？请考虑： 程度 持续时间 影响 恶劣性			
二、识别造成错误或伤害的一个或多个人的重要特征： 1.犯错或制造伤害的时候，这个人的精神状态如何？请考虑： 故意 鲁莽 粗心 了解可能的结果 控制或选择 义务或责任 重要的价值、利益或责任 2.在决定如何公平回应时，这个人的过去经历中有哪些事实与之相关？ 3.在决定如何公平回应时，这个人的个性中有哪些事实与之相关？ 4.在犯错或制造伤害之后，这个人表达了哪些感受？ 5.这个人在犯错或制造伤害中扮演了什么角色？			

Intellectual Tool Chart for Issues of Corrective Justice			
3. Identify important characteristics of the person or persons who were wronged or injured: a. Did the person or persons contribute to causing the wrong or injury he or she suffered? b. What is the person's ability to recover from the wrong or injury?	Don R. Duchinsky	Robert Manning	Jeanine Lepere
4. Examine common responses to wrongs and injuries and their purposes: a. Should we inform the person that what he or she did was wrong or injurious? Why? b. Should we overlook or ignore the wrong or injury? Why? c. Should we forgive or pardon the person for causing the wrong or injury? Why? d. Should we punish the person for causing the wrong or injury? Why? e. Should we require the person to restore what was taken or damaged? Why? f. Should we require the person to compensate for causing the wrong or injury? Why? g. Should we provide treatment or education to the wrongdoer? Why?			
5. Consider related values and interests and decide what the proper response would be: a. What responses would correct the wrong or injury? b. What responses would deter or prevent future wrongs or injuries? c. What responses would promote distributive justice?			

矫正正义问题的知识工具表			
三、识别受到错误对待或伤害的一个 　　或多个人的重要特征：	多恩·R·德钦斯基	罗伯特·曼宁	吉奈恩·莱佩尔
1.这个（些）人是否也要对他遭受 　的错误或伤害负责？			
2.这个人从错误或伤害中复原的能 　力如何？			
四、研究对错误或伤害的常见回应以 　　及它们的目标：			
1.我们是否应当告知犯错者他所做 　的事情是错误的或造成了伤害？ 　为什么？			
2.我们是否应当忽视或忽略这种错 　误或伤害？为什么？			
3.我们是否应当原谅或宽恕犯错或 　带来伤害的人？为什么？			
4.我们是否应当因为某种错误或伤 　害而惩罚犯错者？			
5.我们是否应当要求这个人复原那 　些被拿走或被损害的东西？为什 　么？			
6.我们是否应当要求人们为错误或 　伤害进行赔偿？为什么？			
7.我们是否应当对犯错者进行治疗 　或教育？为什么？			
五、考虑相关价值和利益，判断什么 　　是适当的回应：			
1.什么回应方式可以纠正错误或伤 　害？			
2.哪些回应方式会制止或预防未来 　的错误或伤害？			
3.哪些回应方式会促进分配正义？			

Intellectual Tool Chart for Issues of Corrective Justice			
d.What responses would preserve human dignity? e.What responses would promote the value of human life? f. What responses are practical given the resources available? g.What responses would protect freedom, both of the wrongdoer and of other members of society? h. What responses would be in proportion to the seriousness of the wrong or injury? i. What responses might satisfy the desire for revenge?	Don R. Duchinsky	Robert Manning	Jeanine Lepere
6. Explain the reasons for your decision.			

矫正正义问题的知识工具表			
4.哪些回应方式会保护人类尊严?	多恩·R·德钦斯基	罗伯特·曼宁	吉奈恩·莱佩尔
5.哪些回应方式会促进人类生命的价值?			
6.根据现有的资源，什么回应方式是实际可行的?			
7.哪些回应方式会保护自由，不仅是犯错者的，还包括社会其他成员的?			
8.哪些回应方式会与错误或伤害的严重性成正比?			
9.哪些回应方式会满足报复的欲望?			
六、说明你所做的决定的理由。			

Unit Four: What Is Procedural Justice?

Purpose of Unit

This unit deals with procedural justice, that is, with the fairness of procedures or ways of doing things. You will learn why procedural justice is important and the intellectual tools useful in evaluating, taking, and defending positions on issues of procedural justice. When you have completed this unit you should be able to define procedural justice and explain its importance. You also should be able to use the intellectual tools presented to make thoughtful decisions about issues of procedural justice.

第四单元：什么是程序正义？

单元目标

本单元讨论的是程序正义问题，即以公平的程序或公平的方式行事。你们将会学习为什么程序正义是重要的，以及评估、选择和论证有关程序正义问题的观点时所需要运用的知识工具。

学完本单元后，你们应当能够定义程序正义，并说明它的重要性。你们也应当能够运用本课学到的知识工具，对有关程序正义的问题做出深思熟虑的决定。

How do these photographs illustrate issues of procedural justice?

这些照片如何反应了程序正义问题？

LESSON 10
Why Is Procedural Justice Important?

Purpose of a Lesson

This lesson introduces you to the subject of procedural justice. You learn a definition of procedural justice and why it is important. When you have completed the lesson, you should be able to define procedural justice, explain its importance, and identify issue involving procedural justice from your owm experience.

Terms to Know

procedural justice

due process of law

Critical Thinking Exercise
EXAMINING ISSUES OF PROCEDURAL JUSTICE

Work with a study partner. For each of the following situations, answer the "What do you think?" questions. Be prepared to share your answers with the class.

Someone accuses you of having done something wrong and punishes you immediately without giving you an opportunity to tell your side of the story.

You and several friends have decided to go to the movies. When you arrive at one friend's home to discuss which show the group should see, you are irritated to find that the group has already decided to see a film in which you have no interest, without waiting for your opinion.

A city council holds a hearing to decide how to spend $5 million of tax money. Notice of the hearing is published so that interested individuals and groups from the community may attend the meeting and express their opinions on the use of the tax funds.

第十课：为什么程序正义是重要的？

本课目标

本课将主要向你们介绍程序正义的内容。你们会学习程序正义的定义，以及为什么它是重要的。学完本课后，你们应当能够定义程序正义，说明它的重要性，并在你们个人的经历中识别涉及程序正义的问题。

掌握词汇

程序正义

正当法律程序

重点思考练习

研究程序正义问题

与一位同学一起，阅读以下每个阅读材料，并回答"你怎么看？"这一部分的问题。准备好与全班分享你们的答案。

某人投诉你做了某些错事，并立刻惩罚了你，没有给你任何机会为自己辩解。

你和几个朋友决定去看电影，当你到其中一个朋友的家里打算跟大家讨论要看什么影片的时候，你发现大家没等你发表意见就已经决定去看一部你完全不感兴趣的电影，你被激怒了。

市政厅举行了一次听证会，以决定如何使用 500 万美元税款。市政厅将听证会的通告张贴了出来，以吸引社会中有兴趣的个人和团体来参加听证会，并表达他们自己对财政税收使用方面的观点。

The authorities tortured a suspected terrorist for five days before she confessed to having participated in several bombings which killed a number of people.

What do you think?

1. What procedure was used to gather information or to make a decision?

2. What was fair or unfair about the procedure that was used? Explain your answers.

What are the goals of procedural justice?

Each of the above situations involves an issue of procedural justice.

Procedural justice refers to the fairness of how certain things are done. More specifically, procedural justice refers to the following:

• the fairness of how information is gathered

• the fairness of how decisions are made

It does not refer to the fairness of the decisions themselves.

The goals of procedural justice are the following:

• to increase the chances that all information necessary for making wise and just decisions is gathered

• to ensure the wise and just use of information in the making of decisions

• to protect the right to privacy, human dignity, freedom, and other important values and interests such as distributive justice and corrective justice; and to promote efficiency

当局连续 5 天酷刑折磨了一个涉嫌参与数起死伤多人的炸弹袭击事件的恐怖分子，直到她招供。

你怎么看？

1. 为了做决策或者为了收集信息，应当使用什么程序？
2. 人们使用的程序是公平的还是不公平的？说明你的答案。

程序正义的目标是什么？

以上每一种情况中都涉及了一种程序正义问题。

程序正义是指如何做某件事的公平性，具体来说，程序正义指的是：

- 信息收集方式的公平性
- 制定决策方式的公平性

它并不是指决策本身的公平性

程序正义的目标如下：

- 为制定明智和公正的决定，增加收集所有必需信息的机会
- 确保决策过程中信息得到明智和公正的使用
- 保护隐私权、人类尊严、自由和其他重要价值与利益，例如分配正义和矫正正义，提高效率。

Why is procedural justice considered important?

Scholars and others who have studied procedural justice often claim that it is the keystone of liberty or the heart of the law. Observers of world affairs have sometimes claimed that the degree of procedural justice present in a country is a good indicator of the degree of freedom, respect for human dignity, and other basic human rights in that country. A lack of procedural justice is often considered an indication of an authoritarian or totalitarian political system. Respect for procedural justice is often a key indicator of a democratic political system.

People who are not familiar with the subject often place less importance on procedural justice than on other values or interests. To the average person it is sometimes difficult to believe that how information is gathered and how decisions are made are as important as the outcome. Some might claim, for example, that how the Congress or the president or the courts make their decisions is not as important as what decisions they make. It is more difficult to be concerned about how the police gather evidence or what procedures are used in a trial than it is to be concerned about making right decisions and punishing guilty persons.

Although the principal focus in this unit is on the activities of local, state, and federal government agencies, it is important to understand that procedural justice is also important in private matters such as information gathering and decision making in the home, school, community, business, and industry.

What do you think?

1. What situations have you observed in your home, school, and community in which issues of procedural justice have arisen?

2. Why might adherence to the goals of procedural justice be important in the private sector?

3. What might be the differences in adherence to the goals of procedural justice among democratic, authoritarian, and totalitarian political systems? What examples can you give from recent or historical events?

程序正义为什么重要?

学者们和其他研究程序正义的人经常说,程序正义是自由的基石或法律的核心。全球事务的观察家们有时会说,一个国家自由的程度、对人类尊严和其他基本人权的尊重程度的最佳指标之一,是程序正义的程度。缺乏程序正义通常被看作是一种威权主义或极权主义的政治体制的表现,对程序正义的尊重通常是民主政治体制的一种关键指标。

对程序正义不熟悉的人们经常会更重视其他价值和利益,而不是程序正义。普通人很难相信,信息收集和制定决策的方式与结果同样重要。例如,有些人会认为,国会或总统或法院的决策方式并不如他们所做的决策重要。比起做出正确的决定和惩罚罪犯来说,警察收集证据的方式或审判时使用的是哪种程序,就更难引起人们的关注了。

尽管本单元主要关注地区、各州和联邦政府机构的活动,但程序正义在私人事务中也同样非常重要,例如在家里、学校、社区、公司和工厂收集信息和做出决定。

你怎么看?

1. 在你家、学校和社区中,你观察到哪些现象中涉及了程序正义问题?
2. 为什么在私人领域里坚持程序正义的目标是很重要的?
3. 在民主、威权和极权政治体制中坚持程序正义的目标会有什么不同结果?从最近发生的或历史上的事件中你能举出哪些例子来说明?

Why are law enforcement agencies and the courts responsible for using fair procedures?

Most societies have found it necessary to give certain officials the authority to gather information about suspected crimes and to arrest persons suspected of breaking laws. They also have found it necessary to give authority to certain officials to hold hearings to decide whether or not a person is guilty of a crime or to settle conflicts among people. In the United States, people working in our law enforcement agencies and our courts usually carry out these activities.

We give great power over human life and property to people working in agencies of government. Therefore, we need a set of rules to limit that power and define how to use it. One set of these rules prohibits the government from taking a person's life, liberty, or property without due process of law. In most situations this means that the government cannot act against a person without giving the person a fair hearing. Due process also requires law enforcement agencies to respect important values such as privacy, human dignity, fairness, and freedom when they gather information and arrest people.

Why do we require the police to use fair procedures?   ☞

执法机构和法院为什么有责任使用公平的程序？

大多数社会都认为有必要赋予某些官员权威，以收集嫌疑犯的信息并逮捕那些涉嫌触犯法律的人。他们同样也发现有必要给予某些官员权威，以召开听证会决定某个人是否有罪或调解人们之间的冲突。在美国，这些行动通常由执法机构和法院的工作人员来执行。

我们将有关人类生命和财产的重要权力赋予那些在政府机构工作的人，因此，我们需要一套规则来限制他们的权力，并对应当如何使用这些权力做出界定。其中一套规则是：在缺乏法律正当程序的情况下，禁止政府剥夺个人的生命、自由和财产。在大多数情况下，这意味着未经公平的审判和听证，政府不能对个人采取不利的行动。正当程序也要求执法机构在收集信息和逮捕嫌犯时尊重某些重要的价值，例如隐私、人类尊严、公平和自由。

为什么我们需要警察使用公平的程序？

Some of the rules of procedural justice that must be followed by law enforcement agencies and courts come from laws and regulations adopted by Congress, state legislatures, and other government agencies.

Other important rules of procedural justice are set forth in the United States Constitution and Bill of Rights. For example, they include the following:

AMENDMENT IV(Bill of Rights, 1791)-The right of the people to be secure in their persons, houses, papers, and effects, against unreasonable searches and seizures, shall not be violated, and no warrants shall issue, but upon probable cause, supported by oath or affirmation, and particularly describing the place to be searched, and the persons or things to be seized.

AMENDMENT V (Bill of Rights, 1791) -No person shall be held to answer for a capital, or otherwise infamous crime, unless on a presentment or indictment of a Grand Jury, except in cases arising in the land or naval forces, or in the militia, when in actual service in time of war or public danger; nor shall any person be subject for the same offense to be twice put in jeopardy of life or limb; nor shall be compelled in any criminal case to be a witness against himself, nor be deprived of life, liberty, or property, without due process of law; nor shall private property be taken for public use, without just compensation.

AMENDMENT VI (Bill of Rights, 1791) -In all criminal prosecutions, the accused shall enjoy the right to a speedy and public trial, by an impartial jury of the state and district wherein the crime shall have been committed, which district shall have been previously ascertained by law, and to be informed of the nature and cause of the accusation; to be confronted with the witnesses against him; to have compulsory process for obtaining witnesses in his favor, and to have the assistance of counsel for his defense.

Why is it important to monitor the executive and legislative branches of government?

We often pay more attention to issues of procedural justice that arise from the activities of law enforcement agencies and the judicial branch than to those that may arise from the activities of other parts of our government. The reason for this attention may be that crimes and trials receive more publicity than the activities of the executive or legislative branches of government.

执法机构和法院必须尊重的某些程序正义的规则来自国会、州议会和其他政府机构批准的法律和规章制度。

《联邦宪法》与《权利法案》中规定了其他一些重要的程序正义规则。例如：

第四修正案（1791 年权利法案）：人民的人身、住宅、文件和财产不受无理搜查和扣押的权利，不得侵犯。除依照合理根据，以宣誓或代誓宣言保证，并具体说明搜查地点和扣押的人或物，不得发出搜查和扣押状。

第五修正案（1791 年权利法案）：无论任何人，除非根据大陪审团提出的报告或起诉，不得受判处死罪或其它不名誉罪行之审判，惟发生在陆、海军中或发生在战时或出现公共危险时服现役的民兵中的案件，不在此限。任何人不得因同一犯罪行为而两次遭受生命或身体的危害；不得在任何刑事案件中被迫自证其罪；不经正当法律程序，不得被剥夺生命、自由或财产；不给予公平赔偿，私有财产不得充作公用。

第六修正案（1791 年权利法案）：在一切刑事诉讼中，被告享有以下权利：由犯罪行为发生地的州和地区的公正陪审团予以迅速而公开的审判，该地区应事先已由法律确定；得知被控告的性质和理由；同原告证人对质；以强制程序取得对其有利的证人；取得律师帮助为其辩护。

为什么监督政府的行政和立法机构是很重要的？

我们通常更关注执法机构和司法机构的活动中产生的程序正义问题，对政府其他部门的活动中出现的程序正义问题则不太关注。这可能是因为，相比政府的行政或立法机构的活动来说，犯罪和审判通常更容易引起广泛的关注。

It is important to watch the activities of the executive and legislative branches of government in our communities, states, and nation. These branches of government also have authority to gather information and make decisions that have a great effect on our everyday lives. For example, they can declare war, control trade, collect taxes, and decide how to spend tax money.

Because the authority granted all government agencies is so great, and because the decisions they make are so important, it is essential that they use proper procedures to gather information and make decisions. The use of proper procedures is necessary not only to increase the chances that decisions will be wise and just, but also to ensure public support of those decisions.

 Why is it important for Congress to follow proper procedures when making decisions that affect the well–being of citizens? ☞

但更重要的是，我们要监督社区、各州和国家的行政与立法机构的活动。这些政府部门也有收集信息和做出决策的权威，对我们的日常生活有很重要的影响。例如，他们可以宣战、管理贸易、征收税费并决定如何使用税收。

因为人们授予所有政府机构的权威是如此庞大，也因为他们所做出的决策是如此重要，确保政府机构运用适当的程序收集信息和做出决策，是至关重要的。运用适当的程序是必需的，这不仅可以增加做出明智、公正决策的机会，也可以确保公众对这些决策的支持。

为什么国会在影响公民福利的事务上遵照适当程序来制定决策是很重要的？

What do you think?

1. Each constitutional amendment quoted establishes procedures that law enforcement agencies and the courts should use in gathering information about people suspected of crimes, wrongs, or injuries, and in the use of that information in decision making. In what ways does each rule appear to foster the goals of procedural justice?

2. What decisions made by members of legislative or executive branches of local, state, or federal government have had a significant impact on your life, liberty, or property?

3. What situations have you experienced or observed in which the adherence to fair procedures by members of legislative or executive branches of government has led to increased trust in government?

Is procedural justice always important?

An innocent person's conviction through the use of unfair procedures offends virtually everyone's sense of justice. On the other hand, what about situations where the accused person is guilty of serious wrongdoing? Does it really matter what procedures are used in their cases? Or is it more important to prevent them from doing wrong again?

The view that the ends justify the means was championed centuries ago by Niccolo Machiavelli (1469-1527). In The Prince, Machiavelli argued that if your goal is a good one, such as the creation of a free republic, it does 'not matter what you do to achieve it. In his words, 'The act accuses, the result excuses."

The Founders of our nation knew from their experience the oppression that can occur without procedural justice. The British government considered our patriots to be traitors. They branded them as criminals and put a price on their heads. British government officials illegally searched the homes of many citizens. They also transported many of them out of the country for secret trial, often by a judge alone without benefit of a trial by Jury.

 What problems might arise from Machiavelli's belief that if your goal is a good one, it does not matter what you do to achieve it ? What does this have to do with procedural justice?

你怎么看？

1. 以上摘录的每一项宪法修正案都建立了执法机构和法院应当使用的程序，他们在收集涉嫌犯罪、犯错或制造伤害的人的信息，以及收集用来制定决策的信息时使用这些程序。那么，以上每一项修正案以什么方式促进了程序正义的目标？

2. 地区、各州或联邦政府的立法或行政部门人员做出的哪些决策对你的生命、自由或财产有至关重要的影响？

3. 你经历过或看到过哪些案例中政府的立法或行政部门人员坚持公平的程序，使人们加强了对政府的信任？

程序正义一直这么重要吗？

通过不公平的程序判定一个无辜的人有罪，这实际上触犯了每个人的正义感。另一方面，如果通过不公平的程序判定被起诉的人的确犯有严重的罪行，又会怎么样？在对这些犯错者的审判中使用什么程序真的很重要吗？还是预防他们再次犯错更重要？

数个世纪前尼科洛·马基雅维利（1469-1527）提倡了"只要目的正当，可以不择手段"的观点。在《君主论》中，马基雅维利认为，如果你的目标是好的，例如建立一个自由的民主国家，那么通过什么方式去达到这样的目标并不重要。用他的话说就是："当行为指控他时，行为的结果却应宽恕之。"

美国的立国者从自身经历中了解到，如果没有程序正义就会发生压迫。当时的英国殖民政府认为美国的这些爱国者是叛徒，并判定他们为罪犯，悬赏追捕他们。英国殖民政府官员还非法搜查了许多公民的住宅，将许多公民遣送出国进行秘密审判，审判中通常只有一位法官，没有任何陪审团。

马基雅维利的这一观点——"如果你的目标是好的，通过什么方式来实现这一目标并不重要"可能会出现什么问题？这一观点与程序正义有什么关联？

Based on experiences like these, the Founders wanted to limit the power the government exercises over individual citizens. Therefore, when they formed their own nation, they looked for ways to make sure that the government they created would not be able to unfairly search, arrest, question, try, and imprison citizens.

The Founders wanted to create a system or procedure to ensure that, at all times, ordinary citizens would retain control over their government. They wanted to limit the power of government over the individuals the a society based on Machiavelli's philosophy? Why government was created to serve.

What do you think?

1. Would procedural justice be considered important in a society based on Machiavelli's philosophy? Why or why not?

2. What would be the advantages of a society based on Machiavelli's philosophy? What would be the disadvantages?

3. Which system of government, one based on Machiavelli's philosophy or one based on the Founders' philosophy, would be better able to suppress crime? Which system of government would be better able to suppress political dissent? Which system would be more sure to secure individual liberty and freedom?

Using the Lesson

1. Find examples of issues of procedural justice reported in the press or on television. Describe these issues to your class. Discuss the fairness of the procedures people used to gather information and make decisions in these situations.

2. Read the entire Bill of Rights and the Fourteenth Amendment. Identify the provisions that deal with the procedures the government uses to gather information and make decisions. How do these provisions ensure that people will receive a fair hearing? How do they ensure the protection of important values such as privacy, human dignity, and freedom?

　　基于这样的经历，美国的立国者们希望限制政府行使管理公民个人的权威。因此，当他们决定组建自己的国家时，他们努力寻找方法来确保自己建立的国家不能对公民进行不公平的搜查、逮捕、讯问、审判和监禁。

　　美国的立国者们希望建立一种体系或程序来保证在任何时候普通公民可以行使支配自己政府的权力。创建政府的目的就是为了服务公民个人，他们希望能对政府控制个人的权威加以限制。

你怎么看？

1. 以马基雅维利的理论为基础的社会里，程序正义是否重要？为什么？为什么不？

2. 一个以马基雅维利的理论为基础的社会有什么优势？有什么劣势？

3. 以马基雅维利理论为基础的社会，与以美国立国者的理论为基础的社会，哪一种政府体制能更好地阻止犯罪？哪一种政府体制能更好地压制政治分歧？哪一种政府体制能更好地保障个人自由？

知识运用

1. 在新闻或电视报道中找出有关程序正义的问题，向全班同学描述这些问题，并讨论在这些问题中人们收集信息和做出决策时所使用的程序的公平性。

2. 阅读《权利法案》和《联邦宪法》第十四修正案全文，找出其中有关政府收集信息和做出决策所使用的程序的条款。这些条款怎样确保了人们得到公平听证的机会？这些条款如何保护了重要的价值，例如隐私、人的尊严或自由？

LESSON 11

How Can You Evaluate Procedures to Determine If They Are Fair?

Purpose of Lesson

This lesson reviews the goals of procedural justice and introduces you to three sets of intellectual tools useful in dealing with issues of procedural justice. When you have completed the lesson, you should be able to explain the usefulness of these tools. A fourth set of intellectual tools will be examined in the next lesson.

Terms to Know

comprehensiveness   reliability
notice   impartiality
predictability   detection of error
flexibility

How can you examine issues of procedural justice?

At this point in your study you should be aware that the goals of procedural justice are the following:

- to increase the chances that all reliable information necessary for making wise and just decisions is gathered

- to ensure the wise and just use of the information in making decisions

- to protect important values and interests such as the right to privacy, human dignity, freedom, distributive justice and corrective justice; and to promote efficiency

You can use these basic goals for evaluating procedures to decide if they are fair. The goals are so general, however, they might be difficult to use in specific situations. Therefore, four steps or sets of intellectual tools are provided to determine whether the procedures used by an agency of government or other group are fair.

第十一课：如何评估程序以判断它是否公平？

本课目标

本课将讨论程序正义的目标，并向你们介绍用来解决程序正义问题的三组知识工具。完成本课后，你们应当能够解释这些工具的用途。下一课将学习第四组知识工具。

掌握词汇

完整性	通知
可预测性	灵活性
可靠性	不偏不倚
发现错误	

如何研究程序正义问题？

学到这里，你们应当已经明确了程序正义的目标是：

· 为制定明智和公正的决定，增加收集所有必需信息的机会。

· 确保决策过程中信息得到明智和公正的使用。

· 保护重要价值与利益，例如：隐私权、人类尊严、自由、分配正义和矫正正义以及提高效率。

你们可以运用这些基本目标来衡量程序是否公平，但这些目标是很宽泛的，在某些特定情况下，人们会很难用到它们。因此，我们将采用以下四个步骤或四组知识工具，来判断某个政府机构或其他团体所使用的程序是否公平。

This lesson provides the first three steps for examining issues of procedural justice. The next lesson presents the fourth step. As you apply these steps to situations presented in this unit, and later to other situations, you will discover that not all the tools are useful in every case.

Critical Thinking Exercise

IDENTIFYING INTELLECTUAL TOOLS TO USE IN INFORMATION GATHERING

You may accomplish this exercise during a class discussion of the steps led by your teacher, or you may examine the steps in small groups and then discuss your responses with the entire class.

Read each step in the procedure. Answer the questions in each step as they apply to the examples provided. Then discuss the usefulness of each step and give examples of how it might apply to situations you have experienced or observed.

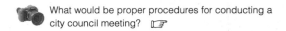
What would be proper procedures for conducting a city council meeting?

本课将介绍研究程序正义的前三个步骤，下一课将介绍第四个步骤。当你们将这些步骤运用到本单元所使用的案例和以后的事例中时，你们会发现并不是所有知识工具都能适用于每一个案例。

重点思考练习

识别信息收集时所使用的知识工具

你们可以按照老师指导的步骤通过课堂讨论来完成本次练习，或者你们可以分成小组来学习这些步骤，再与全班一起讨论你们的答案。

阅读程序中的每一个步骤，将其运用到案例中，并回答其中的问题。讨论每一个步骤的用途，举例说明每个步骤可以怎样运用到你经历过和看见过的事情中。

召开市政厅会议的适当程序是什么？

STEP 1.

Identify the purposes of the information gathering procedures.

What information is being sought? Why is this information needed?

Example: A policewoman driving past a bank heard an alarm and saw a person looking frightened leave the bank in a great hurry. She stopped the person and searched him.

Example: A city council held public hearings before deciding what kinds of recreational facilities to build in a public park

STEP 2.

Evaluate the procedures used to gather information.

Do the procedures ensure that all reliable information necessary for making a wise and just decision is gathered?

To answer this question, the procedures should be evaluated in terms of the following considerations:

a. Comprehensiveness. Are the procedures comprehensive or complete? That is, do the procedures ensure that all information necessary to make a wise and just decision will be gathered from all interested persons?

Example: Although Sir Walter Raleigh was granted a trial for conspiring to commit treason, the court did not allow him to present his side of the story.

Example: Often committees of Congress will hold hearings in Washington, D.C. on subjects they think might require new laws, such as medical care or air travel safety. Interested people and groups can participate in these hearings if they travel to Washington, D. C. to make their presentations.

b. Notice. Do the procedures provide adequate notice or warning of the time and the reason for the hearing to allow interested persons to prepare adequately?

Example: The authorities did not tell Kelly what the charges against her were or when her trial would occur.

Example: When the city council decided to hold a public hearing on a zoning issue, they advertised the hearing widely in the city during the previous two months.

步骤一：识别信息收集程序的目标

人们要寻找的信息是什么？为什么需要这些信息？

例1：一位女警察驾车经过一家银行时听到警铃响，一个看上去很慌乱的人，匆忙从银行走出来，她拦住了这个人，并对他进行了搜身。

例2：市政厅召开了公共听证会，讨论要在一个市立公园里修建哪一种娱乐设施。

步骤二：评估收集信息时使用的程序

这些程序是否确保收集到了做出明智、公正决定所需的所有可靠信息？

为了回答这一问题，我们应当根据以下考虑因素来评估程序：

1. 完整性。程序是否完全或完整？也就是说，为做出明智、公正决定，程序是否能确保从所有与事件有利害关系的人当中收集到所需的所有信息？

例1：尽管沃尔特·雷利爵士因为涉嫌阴谋策划叛国而被准予接受审判，但法院不允许他为自己申诉辩护。

例2：国会的各个委员会通常会在华盛顿特区召开听证会，讨论主题是那些他们认为有必要制定新法律的议题，例如医疗护理或空中旅行安全等。有兴趣的民众和团体，如果他们愿意来到华盛顿并陈述自己的观点都可以参加这些听证会。

2. 通知。这些程序是否对召开听证会的理由和时间进行了充分的通知或告示，以便让所有有兴趣参加听证会的人做好充分的准备？

例1：当局不会告诉凯莉将以什么罪名起诉她，也不会告诉她什么时候对她进行审判。

例2：某市政厅决定召开一个公共听证会讨论城市区划问题，他们提前两个月在市里进行了广泛的宣传。

c. Effective Presentation. Do the procedures allow interested persons to present effectively the information they wish decision-makers to consider?

Example: Until the Supreme Court's 1963 decision in Gideon v. Wainwright, criminal defendants who could not afford an attorney did not receive a lawyer to help them present their side of the story at trial, except in capital cases.

Example: Today, people accused of crimes who do not have enough money to hire lawyers often receive a public defender at taxpayers' expense. Public defenders sometimes have so many people to help they may have only ten to fifteen minutes to prepare for a hearing.

Clarence Earl Gideon (1910–1972). What do you think are the costs and benefits of the Supreme Court's decision in Gideon v. Wainwright? ☞

3.　有效表达。这些程序是否允许有兴趣参加听证会的人，都能有效地陈述他们希望决策者考虑的信息？

例1：请不起律师的刑事案件被告在审判中无法获得律师为他们辩护，除非是在涉及死刑的案件中。这一情况直到最高法院1963年，"吉迪恩诉温赖特案"的判例后才得以改变。

例2：现在，被起诉有罪的人如果没有足够的钱聘请律师，通常会接受纳税人资助的公共辩护律师为他们辩护。有时公共辩护律师有太多的人要帮助，导致他们可能平均只有10到15分钟的时间准备一个听证会或审判。

克拉伦斯·厄尔·吉迪恩 (1910–1972)。你认为最高法院对"吉迪恩诉温赖特案"的判决有哪些利弊得失？

d. Predictability and Flexibility. Are the procedures sufficiently predictable-established in advanceand flexible-able to change or adapt to promote justice?

Example: The court made up the procedures used in Alicia's trial as it proceeded. **Example:** Although Sarah's name had been placed on the agenda to speak at a meeting of her community group, she was late to the meeting because she had a flat tire. She arrived just before the meeting was about to close. When she explained what had happened, the chairperson allowed her to speak to the group even though she had missed her place on the agenda.

e. Reliability. Do the procedures ensure that the information gathered is reliable or trustworthy? **Example:** The court did not allow Sir Walter Raleigh to cross-examine the person who had accused him of treason.

Example: The court permitted an eyewitness to testify about what he saw when a bridge collapsed. However, he was not permitted to testify about the cause of the collapse because he did not have a college degree in architecture or structural engineering.

STEP 3.

Evaluate the procedures used to make a decision.

Do the procedures ensure that the information gathered will be used wisely and fairly?

To answer this question, the procedures should be evaluated in terms of the following considerations:

a. Impartiality. Do the procedures ensure impartiality-lack of bias or prejudice-in the making of decisions?

Examples: One of the judges at Sir Walter Raleigh's trial was Raleigh's sworn enemy. In the past, it was common for judges to be paid from fines they imposed on people they had found guilty of breaking laws.

b. Public Observation. Do the procedures allow interested members of the public to observe how information is being used in making decisions?

Example: The police secretly arrested Maria in the middle of the night and the authorities tried her in the jail without a jury. No one in her village knew what was happening other than the judge, police, and the witness testifying against her.

4. 可预测性与灵活性。这些程序是否具备充分的可预测性（是否是提前建立的）和灵活性（能够为促进正义而进行改变或调适）？

例1：法庭在审判艾丽西亚的过程中才建立了审判程序。

例2：尽管萨拉的名字已经被安排在她的社区小组会议的发言议程中，她却因为车轮爆胎而迟到了。当她赶到会场时，会议已经快结束了。但在她解释了自己所发生的事情后，小组组长允许她继续发言，尽管她已经错过了议程上原定的发言时间。

5. 可靠性。这些程序是否确保了收集的信息是可靠的或值得信赖的？

例1：法院不允许沃尔特·雷利爵士交叉询问控告他犯叛国罪的人。

例2：法院允许一位目击证人对他所目睹的大桥倒塌时的情况做证，然而，因为证人并没有任何建筑或结构工程学方面的学位，法院不允许他对大桥垮塌的原因提出证词。

步骤三：评估用来制定决策的程序

这些程序是否确保了收集的信息将得到明智、公正的使用？

为了回答这个问题，这些程序必须根据以下考虑因素来评估：

1. 不偏不倚。这些程序是否在制定决策的过程中确保不偏不倚——没有成见或偏见？

例1：参与对沃尔特雷利爵士审判的其中一位法官是雷利不共戴天的仇敌。

在过去，通常法官的报酬来自于他们判定违法犯罪的人所缴纳的罚款。

2. 公众观察。这些程序是否允许有兴趣的公众观察制定决策过程中信息的使用方式？

例1：警察半夜秘密逮捕了玛丽亚，没有任何陪审团，当局判她入狱。她居住的村子里没有人知道发生了什么事，除了法官、警察和对她提出不利证词的证人。

Example: The Sixth Amendment to the Constitution of the United States provides all persons accused of crimes the right to apublic trial.

c. Provision for the Detection and Correction of Errors. Do the procedures allow interested persons to review what was done to detect-discover-and correct errors?

Example: Gary was executed immediately after he was convicted. He had no opportunity to appeal the decision in his case.

Example: No one kept a record of a city council meeting when they decided that the applicant should receive a contract to build a new school.

What do you think?

1. Should members of government agencies be allowed to gather information about persons in any way they wish? Why or why not? What values and interests might be endangered?

2. How might the considerations of comprehensiveness, notice, effective presentation, predictability, flexibility, and reliability help you evaluate the fairness of information-gathering procedures?

3. How might the considerations of impartiality, public observation, and provision for the detection and correction of errors help you evaluate the fairness of decision-making procedure?

Using the Lesson

1. Find examples of issues of procedural justice reported in the press or on television. Describe these issues to your class. Discuss the fairness of the procedures people used to gather information and make decisions in these situations.

2. Read the entire Bill of Rights and the Fourteenth Amendment. Identify the provisions that deal with the procedures the government uses to gather information and make decisions. How do these provisions ensure that people will receive a fair hearing? How do they ensure the protection of important values such as privacy, human dignity, and freedom?

例2：《联邦宪法第六修正案》规定，所有被控犯罪的人都有权利接受公开审判。

3. 发现和纠正错误的措施。这些程序是否允许有兴趣的人核查已经完成的事项，以便发现（察觉）并纠正错误？

例1：盖里被判有罪后立刻被处以死刑。他完全没有任何机会对自己案件的判决提起上诉。

例2：在市政会议上，当他们决定一位申请者获得一项建设一所新学校的合约的时候，没有任何人对此做了会议记录。

你怎么看？

1. 是否应当允许政府机构的职员用任何他们希望的方式来收集个人信息？为什么？为什么不？这样做会威胁哪些价值和利益？

2. 上述考虑因素（完整性、通知、有效表达、可预测性和灵活性以及可靠性）如何帮助你们评估信息收集程序的公平性？

3. 上述考虑因素（不偏不倚、公众观察、发现和纠正错误的措施）如何帮助你们评估制定决策程序的公平性？

知识运用

1. 在新闻媒体或电视节目中找出程序正义问题的案例，向全班说明这些问题。讨论这些案例中人们用来收集信息、制定决策的程序的公平性。

2. 阅读《权利法案》和《联邦宪法》第四修正案全文，从中找出有关政府用来收集信息和制定决策的程序上的规定。这些规定如何确保了人们将会得到一个公平的听证会？它们怎样确保保护了某些重要的价值，例如隐私、人类尊严和自由？

LESSON 12

What Values and Interests Should You Consider in Determining Whether Procedures Are Fair?

Purpose of Lesson

In this lesson you examine the fourth set of intellectual tools to be used in dealing with issue of procedural justice. You apply the tools you studied in this unit to evaluate the procedures used in a fictional case, "The Count of Monte Cristo."

When you have completed this lesson, You should be able to use a chart containing all the tools you have learned to develop and support positions on the fairness of procedures used in various situations.

Why should you consider values and interests?

Steps 1-3 that you have just studied are not enough to enable you to decide an issue of procedural justice. A procedure may be very useful and effective in enabling members of government or others to gather information or evaluate that information, but it may be unfair when it endangers important values and interests. Thus, one also must take into account certain values and interests in deciding whether a procedure is fair. The fourth step, given below, focuses your attention on this subject.

Critical Thinking Exercise

IDENTIFYING INTELLECTUAL TOOLS TO USE IN CONSIDERING VALUES AND INTERESTS

This exercise may be accomplished during a class discussion of the fourth step led by your teacher or you may examine the fourth step in small groups and then discuss your responses with the entire class.

Read each part of the fourth step of the procedure. Answer the questions in each part as they apply to the examples. Then discuss the usefulness of each part and give examples of how it might apply to situations you have experienced or observed. Then answer the 'What do you think?" questions.

第十二课：判断程序是否公平时考虑哪些价值和利益？

本课目标

在本课中你们将会学习用于解决程序正义问题的第四组知识工具。你们会运用在本单元中所学的知识工具来评估小说《基督山伯爵》中所使用的程序。

学完本课后，你们应当能够运用一个包含了所有知识工具的表格来帮助你们，针对不同情况下所使用的程序的公平性问题，形成并论证自己的观点。

为什么应当考虑价值和利益？

前一课中学过的步骤一、二和三，并不足以帮助你们对程序正义问题做出决定。一个程序也许在帮助政府或其他机构成员收集或评估信息方面很有用也很有效，但当它威胁到其他重要价值和利益的时候就是不公平的了。因此，在判断一个程序是否公平的时候，人们也必须考虑某些价值和利益。以下将介绍的第四个步骤，就要求你们集中关注这一问题。

重点思考练习

识别在考虑价值和利益时要用到的知识工具

本次练习可以由老师带领大家一起针对步骤四进行课堂讨论来完成，或者你们可以分成小组来分别研究步骤四，然后与全班一起讨论各自的答案。

阅读程序中步骤四的每个部分，并将其分别运用到课文的案例中，并回答每个部分当中的问题。讨论每个部分的用途，并举例说明它可以怎样运用到你经历过或看到过的事情当中。回答"你怎么看？"这一部分的问题。

STEP 4. Consider Related Values and Interests.

Do the procedures protect related values and interests?

To answer this question, consider the following:

a. Privacy and Freedom. Do the procedures violate the right to privacy or freedom? Example: Today at all air terminals throughout the country, security people screen passengers and x-ray their luggage and may search them if necessary.

Example: Right before the Revolutionary War, British soldiers received the right to search colonists' homes at any time to discover evidence of smuggling or other illegal activities. Today, police officials must persuade a judge that they will likely find evidence in order to get a warrant authorizing the search of someone's home. The warrant does not authorize the search of other homes or places.

Example: During the Civil War, President Lincoln suspended the right to habeas corpus in certain areas. As a result, people could be jailed indefinitely without the authorities charging them with a specific crime or trying them.

 How did President Lincoln's suspension of habeas corpus conflict with other important values and interests? ☞

步骤四：考虑相关价值和利益

这些程序是否保护了相关价值和利益？

为回答这个问题，请考虑：

1. 隐私和自由。这些程序是否侵犯了隐私权或自由权？

例1：今天，全国所有的机场航站楼里，安保人员都会检查游客并用 X 光扫描他们的行李，如果需要还会对他们进行搜查。

例2：在革命战争之前，英国士兵被授予了在任何时间搜查殖民者住所，搜寻走私或其他非法活动证据的权利。今天警官必须说服一位法官他们将会找到证据，以便获得搜查某人房屋的授权令，这项搜查令不会授权警官搜查其他房屋或地点。

例3：在南北战争期间，林肯总统暂时中止了某些地区的人身保护权利，因此，在没有当局控告他们犯有某种特定罪行或审判他们的情况下，人们可能被无限期投进监狱。

林肯总统暂停人身保护权的命令如何与其他重要价值和利益相冲突？

b. Human Dignity. Do the procedures violate basic ideas about the right of all persons to be treated with dignity no matter what their beliefs or actions may be?

Example: In some countries, authorities torture people suspected of crimes to gain information from them.

Example: In our country, persons involved in certain kinds of cases may request that the court close their trials to the public.

c. Distributive Justice. Do the procedures violate basic principles of distributive justice?

Example: At a recent city council meeting on an issue of importance to the community, one group was given thirty minutes to make its presentation, while other groups had only ten minutes each.

Example: Earlier in our nation's history, the government permitted only white males to vote and serve on the Jury.

d. Practical Considerations. Do the procedures satisfy reasonable practical considerations?

Example: After the defendant had interrupted the trial with several outbursts, the judge warned him that he would be removed from the courtroom if he disrupted the trial again.

Example: Martha took her neighbor, Sam, to Small Claims Court to try to get him to pay $35 for damage his dog had done to her lawn. She asked another neighbor to testify on her behalf, but the neighbor refused, saying that although he thought she was right, he did not want to take the time off from work. Martha believed that she would not get a fair hearing unless she could compel the neighbor to testify.

What do you think?

1. What is the purpose of considering the values of privacy, freedom, human dignity, and distributive justice in evaluating issues of procedural justice?

2. Why might it be important to take practical considerations into account in evaluating issues of procedural justice?

3. How might an efficient way of gathering information violate important values and interests?

2.　人类尊严。这些程序是否违反了某些基本观念，即无论人们的信仰或行为如何，所有人都应有权被有尊严地对待。

例1：在某些国家，当局为从他们嘴里获得信息，酷刑对待涉嫌犯罪的人。

例2：在美国，涉嫌参与某类案件的人可能会要求法庭不公开审理他们的案件。

3.　分配正义。这些程序是否违反了分配正义的基本原则？

例1：在最近一次有关社区重要问题的市政厅会议中，某个团体有30分钟的时间进行陈述发言，而其他团体却分别只有10分钟时间。

例2：美国历史早期，政府只允许白人男性投票和担任陪审员。

4.　务实的考虑。这些程序是否符合理性和务实的考虑？

例1：在被告数度暴怒中断审判之后，法官警告他，如果他再干扰审判，就会将他逐出法庭。

例2：玛莎将她的邻居山姆带到小额赔偿法庭，试图让他支付35美元以弥补他的狗给她的草坪带来的损失。她请另一位邻居为她做证，但邻居拒绝了，他觉得即便自己认为她是正确的，却不希望花时间请假出庭。玛莎认为除非她能迫使这位邻居去做证，否则她不会得到公平的听证会。

你怎么看?

1.　在评估程序正义问题时，考虑隐私、自由、人类尊严、分配正义等价值的目的是什么？

2.　在评估程序和正义问题时，为什么考虑务实因素非常重要？

3.　一种收集信息的有效方式，会如何违背重要价值和利益？

Critical Thinking Exercise

EVALUATING PROCEDURES WITH INTELLECTUAL TOOLS

Read the following adaptation of the Count of Monte Cristo, by novelist Alexandre Dumas (1802-1870). Although it is a fictional account, Dumas based his novel on the actual experiences of political prisoners in 19th century France. Work in small groups or with a study partner to complete the intellectual tool chart on p. 230. Be prepared to discuss your answers with the rest of the class.

The Imprisonment of Edmond Dantes

The Captain's Request

It was the winter of 1815. A three-masted ship sailed the Mediterranean Sea, bound for Marseilles. In his cabin below, the captain lay dying of a brain fever. He sent for his first mate, young Edmond Dantes, and made a last request. "My dear Dantes," said he, "swear to do what I am going to tell you, for it is very important."

"I swear," replied Dantes.

"After my death, you will be captain. Stop at the Isle of Elba and give this letter to Napoleon. Perhaps he will give you another letter. If he does, deliver it, as I would have had I lived."

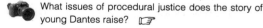

What issues of procedural justice does the story of young Dantes raise?

重点思考练习

用知识工具评估程序

　　阅读以下根据著名小说家亚历山大·大仲马（1802 — 1870）的《基督山伯爵》改编的材料。虽然这是一部虚构的作品，但大仲马是基于19世纪法国政治犯的实际经历创作了这部小说。分成小组或与一位同学一起完成第231页的知识工具表。准备与全班其他同学讨论你们的答案。

《囚禁爱德蒙·唐太斯》
船长的请求

　　那是 1815 年的冬天。一艘三桅帆船航行在地中海上，驶往马赛。在船舱下面，船长因为得了脑膜炎而发着高烧，奄奄一息地躺着。他叫来了他的大副，年轻的爱德蒙·唐太斯，并对他做了最后的请求。"我亲爱的唐太斯"，他说："发誓按照我跟你说的去做，因为这是非常重要的事情。"

　　"我发誓。"唐太斯回答。

　　"我死后，你将成为船长。把船停在厄尔巴岛，将这封信交给拿破仑。或许他会给你另外一封信，如果他这样做了，把信传出去，就像我活着的时候会做的那样。"

年轻的唐太斯的故事中体现了什么程序正义问题？

"I will do it, Captain, but will he see me?"

"Here is my ring," said the captain. "Send it to him, and he will see you." Two hours later the captain was delirious, and the next day he died.

The captain's request bothered Dantes. Napoleon, who had once ruled France, had been defeated and sent into exile on the Isle of Elba, where he was in fact a prisoner. However, there were still many people in France who loved Napoleon and wanted him to come back to rule.

Others thought that these people were traitors to the king of France, and the government imprisoned and executed many of them. To be suspected of liking Napoleon or feeling sorry for him was dangerous in France at that time. Dantes knew this, but he believed that the last request of a dying man should be obeyed, so he did as he had been told. He was only nineteen and had not served under Napoleon. In fact, he had almost no knowledge of politics at all; he felt sure that no one could accuse him of being loyal to Napoleon.

After delivering the letter, Napoleon gave him another one to deliver to a man named Nortier in Paris. Dantes then sailed for Marseilles, where he was to deliver the ship's cargo and marry a beautiful, young girl named Mercedes.

Unknown to Dantes, several men were plotting his downfall. One was jealous that Dantes, a young boy of nineteen, was now captain of the ship. Another was in love with Mercedes and hated Dantes for taking her from him. They sent a letter to the police that said Dantes had seen Napoleon and was carrying a letter to revolutionaries in Paris.

The Arrest of Dantes

Music, laughter, and bright costumes filled the room. The servants had prepared a plentiful feast and set the tables. It was the marriage party of Edmond Dantes and Mercedes. Friends and families of the happy pair filled the room. After the feast all were to go to the church for the marriage ceremony.

"Shall we go?" asked the sweet, silvery voice of Mercedes. "Two o'clock has just struck, and you know we are expected soon."

"To be sure, to be sure!" cried Dantes eagerly. "Let us go right now! "

"我会这么做的，船长，但他会见我吗？"

"这是我的戒指，"船长说，"把这枚戒指给他看，他会接见你的。"两个小时后，船长昏迷不醒，隔天他就死了。

船长的请求困扰着唐太斯。曾统治过法兰西的拿破仑，战败后被流放到了厄尔巴岛，在那里他实际上是一名囚徒。然而法国现在仍然有许多人爱戴拿破仑，并希望他能回到法国继续他的统治。

其他一些人却认为这些人是法国国王的叛徒，政府因此而囚禁并处死了许多人。在当时的法国，如果被人怀疑对拿破仑有敬爱之意或是为他感到惋惜都是非常危险的。唐太斯了解这一切，但他认为自己应当完成一个垂死的人的最后请求，因此他做了船长嘱咐他的事。当时他只有19岁，从未在拿破仑手下工作过。实际上，他对政治一无所知。他确信，没有人可以指责他效忠于拿破仑。

在将船长的信交给拿破仑后，拿破仑给了唐太斯另一封信，请他交给巴黎一个名叫诺瓦蒂埃的人。唐太斯随后将船驶回了马赛，他在那里将船上的货物卸下，并即将迎娶他美丽年轻的未婚妻美西蒂丝。

唐太斯不知道的是，许多人都在密谋整垮他。有一个人是因为嫉妒唐太斯，他才19岁，现在却成了一艘船的船长。另一个人是因为爱慕美西蒂丝，嫉恨唐太斯要娶她为妻。他们给警察局写了一封信，说唐太斯去见了拿破仑，并带着一封信要交给巴黎的革命党人。

唐太斯被捕

音乐、笑声和光鲜的华服充满了整个房间，仆人们准备了丰盛的食物，并正在布置桌台。这是为爱德蒙·唐太斯和美西蒂丝准备的婚宴，这对幸福眷侣的朋友们和家人们都聚集在房间里，宴会结束后，大家都将去教堂参加婚礼仪式。

"我们可以走了吗？"美西蒂丝那甜美、银铃般的声音问道："两点钟声刚刚敲过，你知道我们说好很快要到宴会现场的。"

"是的是的，没错！"唐太斯大声地说："我们现在就出发吧！"

At this moment they heard the dread sound of marching feet. Nearer and nearer came these sounds of terror. Three loud knocks of a sword hilt against the door increased the fears of the festive party.

"Open the door," said a loud voice, "in the name of the law." An officer and five soldiers entered the room. "Who is Edmond Dantes?"

Dantes stepped forward

"Edmond Dantes," replied the officer, "I arrest you in the name of the law!"

"Me?" replied Edmond, "For what reason?"

"I cannot tell you, but you will be told at your first examination."

After shaking hands with all of his friends, Dantes surrendered to the officer. He turned to his family and to Mercedes. "Don't worry, there is some little mistake; depend upon it. They shall set me free as soon as they discover it."

"Goodbye, goodbye, Edmond!" cried Mercedes from the balcony.

"Goodbye, sweet Mercedes! We shall soon meet again!"

The Interrogation

At the police station Monsieur de Villefort questioned Dantes. Villefort also was to marry that day, but when he heard of the arrest of this man charged with being a traitor and a friend of Napoleon's, he left the house of his bride. Villefort was in favor with the king, but he knew he had to be very careful to maintain this position. His father had been a supporter of Napoleon and even now was suspected of plotting against the king. Villefort would have nothing to do with his father and had even changed his name to further separate from him. He was a prosecutor for the king, and he knew that if he did not succeed in condemning anyone suspected of being loyal to Napoleon, he himself would be suspected.

His first glance at Dantes softened his heart. He saw that Edmond was intelligent, courageous, and honest. As Dantes told him the story of the dying captain's request and of his ignorance of politics, Villefort could not help but believe him.

"Ah!" said Villefort, "this seems to be the truth. If you are guilty of anything, it is in not acting wisely. And considering that you acted on your captain's orders, I cannot hold you guilty."

就在这时，他们听到令人恐惧的士兵行进的脚步声。这声音越来越近，听上去令人恐惧不安。房门上响起了一把剑叩门的声音，一共三下，整个宴会的气氛越来越让人害怕。

"开门！"一个响亮的声音喊道："我们是来执行法院的命令的！"一位警官和五个士兵走了进来。"谁是爱德蒙·唐太斯？"

唐太斯走上前。

"爱德蒙·唐太斯，"警官说，"我以法律的名义逮捕你！"

"我？"爱德蒙问："为什么？"

"我不能告诉你，但你第一次被审问的时候就会知道的。"

在与他的朋友们一一握手告别后，唐太斯走向了那名警官并转身他对家人和美西蒂丝说："别担心，只是一些小误会，放心，他们一旦查明真相很快就会放了我的。"

"再见了，再见了，爱德蒙！"美西蒂丝在阳台上哭喊着。

"再见了，亲爱的美西蒂丝，我们很快会再见的！"

审问

在警察局，维尔福伯爵审问了唐太斯。维尔福那天本来也要结婚，但当他听说这个人因为被指控为叛国以及作为拿破仑的朋友而被捕，他离开了家和自己的新娘。维尔福是倾向于法国国王的，但他知道他必须非常谨慎地维持现在的地位。他的父亲曾经是拿破仑的支持者，直到现在仍被怀疑阴谋反抗国王。维尔福希望与自己的父亲撇清关系，甚至还更改了自己的名字以彻底断绝关系。作为国王的检察官，他知道如果他不能成功证明那些被怀疑效忠于拿破仑的人有罪，他自己就会遭到怀疑。

当他第一眼看到唐太斯时，他心软了。他发现爱德蒙是一个有智慧的、勇敢和诚实的人。当唐太斯告诉他垂死的船长的最后嘱托和他对政治的一无所知时，维尔福无法不相信他。

"啊！"维尔福说："看来这是事实，如果你有错，也只能是行为不够明智。考虑到你是奉了船长的命令，我不能证明你有罪。"

"I am free, then, sir?" cried Dantes joyfully.

"Yes, but first give me the letter you were to deliver to Paris."

"You have it already, for it was taken from me by the officers. It was on your desk."

"Stop a minute," said Villefort, as Dantes took his hat and gloves. "To whom is it addressed?"

"To Monsieur Nortier in Paris."

If a thunderbolt had struck the room, Villefort could not have been more shocked. He sank into his chair, drew out the fatal letter, and looked at it with an expression of terror.

"Monsieur Nortier of Paris," he said, growing paler.

"Yes," said Dantes, "do you know him?"

"No!" replied Villefort, "a faithful servant of the King does not know traitors."

"It is a conspiracy then?" asked Dantes. "I knew nothing about it."

"Yes, but you know the name of the person to whom this letter was addressed."

"I had to read the address to know to whom to give it."

"Have you shown this letter to anyone?"

"To no one, on my honor."

Villefort fell back in his chair. "Oh, if the king learns that Nortier is my father, I am ruined," he murmured. "Dantes, I can no longer free you right away. I must talk to the judge. But look how I will help you. The main thing against you is in this letter. "Villefort went to the fireplace and cast the letter into the flames . "You see, I destroy it."

"Oh!" exclaimed Dantes, "you have saved me!"

"Do you trust me now?" asked Villefort.

"In every way," replied Dantes.

"Then listen to my advice. Don't tell anyone of the letter, no matter what happens, and all will be well."

"I will swear not to," said Dantes.

"那么，我是自由的了，先生？"唐太斯高兴地喊道。

"是的，但是你得先把你要带去巴黎的信交给我"。

"已经给您了，警官早就从我身上把信拿走了，就在您的桌子上。"

"等等，"正当唐太斯去拿他的帽子和手套的时候，维尔福说："这封信是写给谁的？"

"给巴黎的诺瓦蒂埃先生。"

当时，即使是一道闪电击中了房间，维尔福都不会如此震惊。他倒在椅子里，将那封伪装的信取出来，带着恐惧的神色看着它。

"巴黎的诺瓦蒂埃先生！"他说，脸色愈发苍白了。

"是的！"唐太斯答道："您认识他？"

"不！"维尔福回答："一个对国王忠诚的奴仆是不会认识叛徒的。"

"那么说，这是阴谋了？"唐太斯问，"我对此一无所知。"

"是的，但你知道这封信的收信人的名字。"

"我必须知道地址才能知道要交给谁。"

"你有没有将这封信给任何人看过？"

"没有，我以名誉发誓。"

维尔福又跌坐进他的椅子里。"噢，如果国王知道诺瓦蒂埃是我的父亲，我就毁了！"他低声说："唐太斯，我无法立刻放你自由了，我必须要与法官讨论。但我会看看怎样能帮到你，对你不利的事情都在这封信里。"维尔福走近壁炉，将信丢进了火中。"你看，我把它销毁了。"

"喔！"唐太斯喊道："您拯救了我！"

"你现在信任我了吗？"维尔福问。

"是的，完全。"唐太斯回答。

"那么听我的建议，无论发生什么事，都千万别告诉任何人关于这封信的事，一切都会没事的。"

"我发誓我不会说的。"唐太斯说。

Dantes Learns His Fate

Villefort rang a small bell. A policeman appeared. Villefort whispered some words in his ear, and the policeman nodded.

"Follow him," said Villefort.

That night four armed guards took Dantes in a carriage through the streets of the town. The carriage stopped at the port, and twelve more soldiers came out of the darkness.

"Can all this be for me?" Dantes thought.

He was taken to a boat and seated between armed guards. The oarsmen pulled and the boat skimmed over the dark waters of the bay.

"Where are you taking me?" asked Dantes.

"You will know soon enough," answered a guard.

Wild and strange thoughts ran through Dantes' mind. Were they going to leave him on some distant point? There were no ships in the harbor. They had not tied him, and this seemed to mean that they were going to let him go. Besides, Villefort had told him that as long as he did not mention the letter, or the name of Nortier, he would be free. He waited silently, staring through the darkness. He could see a light in the house where Mercedes lived.

If he were to shout she could hear him. He thought how silly the guards would think him if he were to shout like a madman.

He turned to the nearest policeman and said, "Friend, I beg you, as a Christian, to tell me where we are going. I am Captain Dantes, a loyal Frenchman, though accused of treason. Tell me where you are taking me, and I swear upon my honor I won't resist."

"I see no harm in telling you now. You are from Marseilles and a sailor, and you still don't know where we are going?"

"On my honor, I have no idea."

"Look around you then."

Dantes rose to his feet and looked forward. He saw the black and frowning rock on which stands the Chateaud'lf. It was a gloomy fortress more than three hundred years old, now used as a prison. To Dantes it looked like a hangman's scaffold.

唐太斯了解了自己的命运

维尔福拉响了铃，一位警官走进来，维尔福在他耳边低声说了几句，警官点了点头。

"跟他走！"维尔福说。

当晚，四个武装宪兵将唐太斯带上了一辆马车，穿过镇上的街道，马车停在了港口，又有12名宪兵从夜幕中出现。

"难道他们都是为了我吗？"唐太斯想。

他被带到一艘小船上，并坐在武装宪兵中间。桨手用力地划着船，小船行进在夜色笼罩的水面上。

"你们要把我带到哪里去？"唐太斯问。

"你很快就知道了。"一名宪兵回答。

唐太斯心中闪过一些可怕和奇怪的念头。难道他们打算在某个偏僻的地方放走他？港口并没有大船，他们并没有把他绑起来，这似乎是意味着他们会放他走。而且，维尔福告诉过他，只要他不提那封信，或诺瓦蒂埃的名字，他就会得到自由。他安静地等待着，瞪着眼前的一片黑暗，他能看到远处美西蒂丝房间的灯光。

如果他大声喊出来，她就能听到自己的声音。他想，如果他像个疯子一样大喊大叫，宪兵们会怎么想呢。

他转向那个靠他最近的宪兵说："朋友，我以一个基督徒的身份请求你，请告诉我我们要去哪里？我是唐太斯船长，一个忠诚的法国人，虽然我被控叛国，请告诉我你们要带我去哪里？我以我的人格担保我不会反抗。"

"现在我告诉你也无妨，你是从马赛来的水手，还不知道我们要去哪里吗？"

"我向你发誓，我一点也不知道。"

"那么看看你周围。"

唐太斯站起来，向前望去。他看到黑森森的岩石上耸立着的是伊夫堡。这座三百多年历史的阴森恐怖的古堡现在是一座监狱，对唐太斯来说，这看上去就象是刽子手和断头台。

"Why are we going there?" cried Dantes.

The policeman smiled.

"I am not going to that prison. It is used only for political prisoners. I have not done anything! Are there any judges or courts at the Chateaud'If?"

"No, only a warden, soldiers, and good thick walls."

"You think that I am to be imprisoned there?"

"It looks like it."

"Without a trial?"

"You've had a trial."

Dantes tried to leap overboard but the quick action of the police stopped him. The boat touched shore, and they took him to a cell. Dantes did not fight. He was like a man in a dream. "It is late," said the jailor. "Here is bread, water, and fresh straw, and that is all a prisoner can wish for. Good night."

Dantes was alone in darkness and silence. With the first light of day the jailor returned. He found Dantes in the same position, as if fixed there, his eyes swollen with weeping. He had passed the night standing and without sleep.

The jailor went to Dantes and put a hand on his shoulder..

"Haven't you slept?" he asked.

"I don't know," replied Dantes.

"Are you hungry?" he continued.

"Do you want anything?"

"I want to see the warden."

"That is impossible."

"Why?"

"It is against the rules. Someday you may see him, if we let you walk around, but he may not listen to you."

"But," asked Dantes, "how long will I have to wait?"

"我们为什么要去那儿？"唐太斯喊道。

宪兵笑了。

"我不是要去这座监狱吧！这是只用来关押政治犯的地方，我没有做任何事！伊夫堡有任何法官和法庭吗？"

"没有，只有监狱长、宪兵和又重又厚的墙壁。"

"你觉得我会被关在这儿吗？"

"看起来是这样的。"

"什么审判都没有？"

"你已经被审判过了啊。"

唐太斯正打算跃入海中的刹那，被宪兵迅速阻止了。小船抵岸后，他们将他带进了一间牢房。唐太斯并没有反抗，他就像一个梦游的人。"天已经晚了，"狱卒说："这儿有面包、水和新鲜稻草，一个犯人能希望得到的就这些了。晚安。"

唐太斯孤独地在黑暗中静默。第二天的第一道光照进囚室的时候，狱卒回来了。

他发现唐太斯站在昨天那个位置，一动也不动，好像钉在那儿，他的眼睛都哭肿了。他就这样站在这里一整夜都没有睡。

狱卒走向唐太斯，把手放在他肩膀上。

"你没有睡吗？"他问。

"我不知道，"唐太斯答。

"你饿不饿？"他又问。

"我不知道。"

"你想要什么吗？"

"我要见监狱长。"

"那是不可能的。"

"为什么？"

"因为这违反了规定。如果我们让你去散散步，总有一天你会见到他的，但他不会听你说的。"

"但是，"唐太斯问："我要等多久？"

"Ah! A month! Six months! A year."

Post script: Edmond Dantes remained in the Chateaud'lf for fourteen years before making his escape.

Using the Lesson

1. Read the Bill of Rights. Identify the provisions that would have prevented the violations of procedural justice that occurred in the case of Edmond Dantes.

2. Watch television programs involving law enforcement officers, private detectives, or courts. Evaluate the fairness of the procedures used by applying the intellectual tools you have studied.

 Do you think the procedures used to convict young Dantes adequately serve the goals of procedural justice? What changes would you make? ☞

"啊！一个月！六个月！一年！"

后记：直到最后逃脱，爱德蒙·唐太斯在伊夫堡整整待了 14 年。

知识运用

1. 阅读《权利法案》，找出某些条款，可以用来预防爱德蒙·唐太斯案件中所出现的违背程序正义的情况。

2. 收看一些有关执法人员、私人侦探或法庭的电视节目，运用你所学到的知识工具，评估案例中涉及的程序的公平性。

你认为用来证明年轻的唐太斯有罪的程序是否实现了程序正义的目标？你会对此做出什么改变？

Intellectual Tool Chart for Issues of Procedural Justice	
Questions	**Answers**
1. What information is being sought? Why is this information needed?	
2. Do the procedures ensure that all reliable information necessary for making a wise and just decision is gathered? Consider: a. comprehensiveness b. notice c. effective presentation d. predictability and flexibility e. reliability	
3. Do the procedures ensure that the information gathered will be used wisely and fairly in making a decision? Consider: a. impartiality b. public observation c. detection and correction of errors	
4. Do the procedures protect important values and interests? Consider: a. privacy and freedom b. human dignity c. distributive justice d. practical considerations	
5. Do you think the procedures adequately serve the goals of procedural justice? What changes (if any) would you make?	
6. Explain your position.	

程序正义问题的知识工具表	
问题	答案
1.要寻找的信息是什么？为什么需要这些信息？	
2.这些程序是否确保收集了做出明智、公正的决策所需的所有可靠信息？请考虑： 1）完整性 2）通知 3）有效表达 4）可预测性与灵活性 5）可靠性	
3.这些程序是否确保了所有收集的信息都将被明智、公正地用于制定决策？ 1）不偏不倚 2）公众观察 3）发现和纠正错误	
4.这些程序是否保护了重要的价值和利益？请考虑： 1）隐私和自由 2）人类尊严 3）分配正义 4）务实的考虑	
5.你认为这些程序是否足以实现程序正义的目标？如有必要，你认为需要进行哪些更改？	
6.说明你的观点	

LESSON 13

Were the Procedures Used in This Case Fair?

Purpose of Lesson

Now you may apply the intellectual tools you have studied in this unit to a historical case. You evaluate the procedures used to prosecute and uphold the conviction of Sacco and Vanzetti for murder and armed robbery in the 1920s. You role-play a governor's clemency board hearing on whether to recommend that the defendants' death sentences be carried out.

When you have completed this lesson, you should be able to evaluate, take, and defend positions on the fairness of procedures used in this case.

Critical Thinking Exercise

EVALUATING AND TAKING A POSITION ON PROCEDURAL JUSTICE IN A HISTORICAL CASE

Using the intellectual tools you have learned in this unit, tackle the following problem of procedural justice.

Below is an abridged account of the historical facts surrounding the trial of Nicola Sacco and Bartolomeo Vanzetti. This case, which took place in the 1920s, attracted enormous attention around the world. Although the defendants were tried for murder, many suspected they were actually on trial for their political beliefs. The procedures of the trial raised many questions.

After reading about the case, work with a study partner to complete the procedural justice intellectual tool chart on page 230, applying it to the Sacco and Vanzetti situation. What arguments would you make to the governor for or against a stay of execution? Discussion questions follow the story.

第十三课：这个案例中使用的程序公平吗？

本课目标

现在你们可以将自己在本单元中学到的知识工具运用到一件历史案件中。你们将会评估用来为20世纪20年代萨科和万泽蒂谋杀与武装抢劫案中进行起诉和辩护的程序。你们将模拟一次州长的赦免委员会听证会，对是否要提议对被告施以死刑做出决定。

学完本课后，你们应当能够针对这件案例中所使用的程序的公平性，评估、选择和论证相关观点。

重点思考练习

针对一宗历史案件中涉及的程序正义问题，评估和选择一种观点

运用你在本单元中学到的知识工具，解决下述程序正义问题。

以下是围绕有关尼古拉·萨科和巴托洛梅奥·万泽蒂的审判的历史事实的描述节选。这宗案件发生在 20 世纪 20 年代，吸引了全世界的关注。尽管被告被控谋杀，许多人怀疑他们实际上是因为政治信仰而被审判，这次审判所使用的程序引发了许多问题。

阅读有关这一案例的描述，与一位同学一起完成第 231 页的"程序正义知识工具表"，将它运用到萨科和万泽蒂的案例中。你会提出什么论据来说服州长支持或反对延期执行死刑？讨论故事后面提出的问题。

The Case of Sacco and Vanzetti

The Crime

On April 15, 1920, the $15,776.51 payroll for the Slater and Morrill shoe factory in South Braintree, Massachusetts was brought to the factory's office. The money was put into pay envelopes and the envelopes were placed in two steel boxes.

At 3 p.m. the paymaster and his guard were carrying the money down the street to the factory when they saw two men leaning on a fence. Suddenly, one of the men stepped forward, pulled a gun, and shot the guard. The guard staggered, fell, and was shot again. The paymaster ran, but was hit in the back by two bullets.

Just then, a dark car drove up with several men inside. The killers threw the money boxes into the car, jumped in, and sped away. As the car drove off, someone in it shot the guard again. The guard died there. The paymaster died the next day.

The Investigation

At the time of the crime, the police were investigating a similar incident in another town. Both cases involved gangs with dark cars. Witnesses to both crimes said they thought the criminals were Italian.

Shortly after the armed robbery, the police found a car being repaired at a garage that seemed to fit the description of the getaway car. The car belonged to an Italian named Mike Boda. On the evening of May 5, 1920, Boda and three other men came to pick up the car. The owner of the garage, who had been alerted by the police, told them that they had not completed the repairs.

Boda and one of the men then left on a motorcycle. Witnesses saw the other two men get on a streetcar. After they were gone, the garage owner's wife called the police. They arrested the two men who got on the streetcar in the trap set for Boda. However, Boda disappeared and was never seen again.

Neither of the two men arrested had police records. When they were arrested, both were carrying loaded guns. They gave their names as Nicola Sacco and Bartolomeo Vanzetti. Both were Italians, and both were aliens.

When apprehended on the streetcar, police did not tell Sacco and Vanzetti why they were arrested. Neither man spoke English very well, nor did they understand that they had certain constitutional rights.

《萨科和万泽蒂案》

罪案

1920 年 4 月 15 日，马萨诸塞州南布伦特里的斯莱特和摩利尔鞋厂共计 15, 776. 51 美元的工资款正在送往工厂的途中。这笔钱装在工资袋里，并被放进了两个钢制箱子里。

下午 3 点，发薪出纳员和工厂保安一起把钱箱子从街上抬回工厂。这时他们看到两个男人靠在围栏上。突然，其中一个人走上前，掏出一支枪并射杀了保安。保安中弹后蹒跚向前跌倒了，又再次中枪。出纳试图跑开，但背部也被击中两枪。

就在此时，一辆坐着数名男子的黑色轿车开了过来。凶手将钱箱丢到车里，跳进车，随后驾车扬长而去。车子离开的时候，车内的人又再次开枪射击保安。保安当场死亡，出纳第二天也死了。

调查

罪案发生时，警察正在调查另一个城镇发生的相似案件。两宗案件中都有驾驶黑色轿车的犯罪团伙，两宗案件的目击证人都说他们认为罪犯是意大利人。

武装抢劫案发生后不久，警察在一个车库里发现了一辆待修理的车，似乎符合证人对逃逸车辆的描述。这辆车属于一个意大利人，名叫迈克·博达。1920 年 5 月 5 日晚上，博达和另外三个男人前来车库取车，事先被警察警告过的车库主人告诉他们，车子还没有修好。

博达和另外一个男人骑着摩托车离开了，目击者看到另外两个男人上了一辆有轨电车。他们离开后，车库主人的妻子报了警。警察逮捕了有轨电车上的两名男子，那原本是为博达设下的圈套，然而博达消失了，再也没有出现过。

警察逮捕的这两个人都没有过任何犯罪记录。当他们被逮捕的时候，两个人都荷枪实弹。他们报出自己的名字是尼古拉·萨科和巴托洛梅奥·万泽蒂。他们都是意大利人，都是外国人。

At the time of the arrest, the police were unaware that the two men were political radicals who were active in anarchist causes. Anarchists generally believe that all forms of political authority are unnecessary and undesirable. When the police chief asked Sacco and Vanzetti questions about their political beliefs, they did not answer honestly. They thought their anarchist associations would get them into trouble.

Although they still had not been told why they had been arrested, the district attorney questioned the suspects. When he asked questions about their political beliefs, they lied once again. When the authorities learned that Sacco and Vanzetti were not being truthful, they assumed that the suspects had more to hide than their political convictions.

 What might be fair procedures when arresting persons who neither speak nor understand English very well?   ☞

　　在电车上逮捕他们的时候，警察并没有告诉萨科和万泽蒂他们为什么被逮捕。这两个人都不太会说英语，也不怎么明白他们所拥有的某种宪法权利。

　　在逮捕两人时，警察没有意识到他们是积极参与无政府主义活动的政治激进主义者。无政府主义者通常认为所有形式的政治权威都是不必要的，也是不受欢迎的。当警长询问萨科和万泽蒂他们的政治信仰时，他们并没有诚实回答。他们认为自己的无政府组织会让他们陷入麻烦当中。

　　尽管仍然没有人告诉萨科和万泽蒂他们为什么被逮捕，地区检察官已经开始审讯这两位嫌疑犯。当他问到他们的政治信仰时，他们又再一次撒谎了。然而当局获悉萨科和万泽蒂没有说实话时，他们推论嫌犯绝不仅仅只是隐瞒了自己的政治信念，还有更多事情他们没说。

逮捕一个既不太会说也不太听得懂英语的人时，公平的程序会是什么？

The Trial

On May 31, 1921, Sacco and Vanzetti were tried for the murders. Their lawyer, Fred Moore, was himself a political radical and made no effort to hide his beliefs. In fact, far from concealing his political views, he let everyone know he thought the case was a clear example of how the capitalist system victimizes downtrodden working people. From the beginning of the trial, there were angry feelings between. Judge Webster Thayer and the defendants' lawyer.

During the seven-week trial, the district attorney who had questioned the two suspects when they were first arrested served as prosecutor. The selection of a jury was a long and difficult process; they examined more than 700 people before choosing the twelve jurors.

As the courtroom proceedings began, the quiet little Massachusetts town of Dedham found itself transformed. Crowds gathered. Law enforcement guarded the courthouse and searched everyone who entered. Armed guards marched the defendants, who were always kept in handcuffs, between the jail and the courthouse. No one could escape the impression that these were desperate and dangerous men.

The first witness for the prosecution, Mary Splaine, identified Sacco as the man who had done the shooting from the car. When questioned by Sacco and Vanzetti's lawyer, however, the witness admitted she had seen the car from a distance of seventy feet for no more than three to five seconds, as it was rapidly speeding away.

Cross-examination also uncovered the fact that a year earlier at the police station, Mary had picked a picture of another man as the gunman. However, after seeing Sacco three times alone in the jail-never in a line-up as was the usual procedure-Mary changed her mind.

Other witnesses had also failed to identify Sacco and Vanzetti until they spent some time alone with the two men. Under these conditions, witnesses who had previously said they had not seen the killers clearly enough to identify them altered their statements to identify Sacco and Vanzetti as the men they had seen.

审判

1921 年 5 月 31 日，萨科和万泽蒂因涉嫌谋杀而当庭受审。他们的律师弗雷德·摩尔，本身就是一位政治激进主义者，并毫不掩饰自己的政治信仰。实际上，他不仅从不隐瞒自己的政治观点，他还让所有人都知道他认为这宗案件是资本主义制度残害底层劳动人民的明显案例。从审判一开始，法官韦伯斯特·塞耶和被告律师之间就互相产生了敌对和愤怒情绪。

在长达 7 个星期的审判过程中，作为第一次被捕时就审问过两个嫌犯的地区检察官担任了本案的控方。对陪审团的挑选也是一个漫长和艰难的过程，他们对超过 700 个人进行了调查，并从中选出了 12 名陪审员。

法庭程序开始后，这个安静的马萨诸塞州戴德姆小镇一下子变得喧闹了。人群都聚集到镇上，执法人员守卫着法院，并对每个进入法院的人进行搜身。荷枪实弹的保安包围着被告穿梭于监狱和法院之间，他们永远都戴着手铐。每个人都免不了有一种印象，那就是这两个男人是绝望而危险的人物。

原告的第一位目击证人叫玛丽·斯普莱恩，她认出萨科就是从车里开枪射击的男人。当萨科和万泽蒂的律师质问她时，证人却承认她是从 70 英尺以外的地方看到车子的，目击的时间总共不超过 5 秒，随后车子就飞快开走了。

交叉质证的环节也披露了很多事实，那就是一年前在警察局，玛丽指认在车内开枪的是另外一个人。然而，在监狱里单独见过萨科三次后（完全没有遵守正常秩序），玛丽改变了自己的想法。

其他证人也无法指认萨科和万泽蒂，直到他们花了一些时间与这两个人单独相处后。在这些前提下，之前声称自己没有很清楚地看到凶手以至于无法辨认他们的证人，现在都改变了他们的证词，指认萨科和万泽蒂就是他们看见的人。

Next, the prosecution showed that Sacco and Vanzetti had lied when questioned at the police station. The district attorney argued that they hid the truth because they were guilty of the murders. The prosecution introduced a cap found at the scene of the crime as evidence. The prosecution claimed it was Sacco's. Sacco, his wife, and his attorney said it was not his and did not even fit him.

The prosecution then produced expert witnesses to show that the gun police. took from Vanzetti actually belonged to the guard who had been shot. The prosecution claimed that Vanzetti had stolen the gun at the time of the murder.

The prosecution also tried to prove that the bullet that had killed the guard had been from Sacco's gun. Sacco and Vanzetti's lawyer failed to challenge this testimony, although later they presented their own ballistics experts who said that the bullet had not come from Sacco's gun. In fact, the police who arrested the two men had failed to mark the guns and ammunition properly.

Guards outside the prison where Sacco and Vanzetti were held. What issues of procedural justice surface during high–profile cases such as the trial of Sacco and Vanzetti?   ☞

　　紧接着，控方说明萨科和万泽蒂在警察局接受讯问的时候撒谎。地区检察官声称他们隐瞒了实情，因为他们为谋杀感到羞愧。控方展示了一顶犯罪现场发现的帽子，控方声称这就是萨科的帽子。萨科、萨科的妻子和他的辩护律师都说这顶帽子不是他的，帽子的大小都不合适。

　　控方接着又提供专业证据，证明警察从万泽蒂身上搜出来的枪实际上属于那位被枪击的警卫。控方认为万泽蒂在谋杀的时候偷了警卫的枪。

　　控方还试图证明杀死警卫的子弹是来自萨科的枪。萨科和万泽蒂的律师没能挑战这个证词，尽管后来他们展示了辩方的弹道学说专家的证据，表明子弹并非来自萨科的枪。实际上，逮捕这两人的警官也没能妥善地标记枪支和弹药。

萨科和万泽蒂被关押的监狱外把手的警卫。像萨科和万泽蒂的审判这样高知名度的案件中，表现出了什么程序正义问题？

Throughout the trial, the prosecutor emphasized the unorthodox political views of the defendants and the fact that they had gone to Mexico during World War I to escape the draft.

After the prosecution presented its case, the defense had its turn. The defense lawyer first called Vanzetti and then Sacco to the witness stand. Both men had trouble proving to the jury's satisfaction where they had been on the day of the murder.

Sacco had not been at work. Vanzetti was self-employed as a fish peddler and could not prove where he had been. When Vanzetti was asked why he carried a gun, he explained that he carried a lot of money when he bought fish for his business and that he needed the gun for self-defense. Vanzetti admitted that he had lied about his political beliefs when questioned by the police, but said it was because he was afraid that he would be sent back to Italy if they knew he was an anarchist.

When Sacco was cross-examined, he admitted that although he had gained many advantages from living in the United States, he had still been quite critical of the government. His defense attorney objected to this line of questioning, saying it had nothing to do with whether Sacco and Vanzetti had committed murder. However, Judge Thayer repeatedly overruled such objections. The defense attorney then produced witnesses that said the defendants had been elsewhere at the time of the murders.

Nicola Sacco   Bartolomeo Vanzetti   ☞

在审判过程中，控方一直强调被告的政治观点的非正统性，以及他们在第一次世界大战期间为逃避兵役跑到墨西哥的事实。

在控方陈述后，轮到被告为自己辩护时，辩方律师首先叫了万泽蒂，然后是萨科到证人席上。有关谋杀案发生当天他们在哪里的问题，两人都很难对陪审团给出令人满意的证明。

萨科没有工作，万泽蒂是卖鱼的个体小贩，无法证明自己当时身处何地。当万泽蒂被问及为什么要随身带着一支枪的时候，他解释道，他带着很多钱要去渔市买鱼，他需要枪来自我防卫。万泽蒂承认当警察讯问他的时候，他对自己的政治信仰撒谎了，但他说这是因为他害怕如果被他们知道自己是一个无政府主义者就会被遣返回意大利。

轮到萨科被交叉讯问的时候，他承认尽管生活在美国让他获得了许多好处，但他还是对政府有不少批评意见。他的辩护律师对这个问题提出了反对，认为这个问题与萨科和万泽蒂是否犯谋杀罪毫无关系。然而，法官塞耶一再宣布律师反对无效。辩方律师接着提供了可以证明谋杀案发生时被告在其他地方的证人。

尼古拉·萨科   巴托洛梅奥·万泽蒂

The Verdict

Both sides gave final arguments on July 14, 1921. When the judge gave instructions to the jury, many observers thought his remarks were prejudiced against Sacco and Vanzetti. In his final charge to the jury, Judge Thayer urged jurors to act "as true soldiers... in the spirit of supreme American loyalty."

During the trial, Thayer permitted numerous questions about the defendants' political beliefs. Some people who had attended the trial also claimed that they had overheard the judge outside the courtroom make sneering and hostile remarks about the defendants. However, these claims were never verified.

The jury deliberated for five hours before reaching a verdict. It was the same for both defendants: guilty of murder in the first degree.

The defense attorneys asked for a new trial. Sacco and Vanzetti waited in prison for six years while motions for a new trial moved slowly through the legal system.

The Appeals

The defense presented new evidence to support the request for another trial. A man named Gould said he had been walking behind the guard and pay master when they were shot. He swore that neither Sacco nor Vanzetti had been in the getaway car. However, according to Massachusetts law at that time, requests for a new trial had to be made to the judge who had heard the original trial. Judge Thayer denied the request, ruling that one piece of evidence was not enough to justify a new trial.

Defense attorneys then claimed that the foreman of the jury which had convicted Sacco and Vanzetti had said that radicals should hang whether they were guilty or not. Judge Thayer denied the second request for a new trial as well.

Months passed. They made another appeal. The prosecution's main ballistics expert said if he had been asked directly if the bullet that killed the guard came from Sacco's pistol, he would have said it did not. Judge Thayer again denied the appeal'.

判决

1921 年 7 月 4 日，控辩双方都进行了最后陈述。当法官向陪审团做出指示时，许多观察者认为法官的评论存在针对萨科和万泽蒂的偏见。在他最后一次指示中，法官塞耶要求陪审员们要"以至高无上的对美国的忠诚"，"作为真正的士兵"行动起来。

在审判过程中，塞耶允许了很多针对被告政治信仰的提问。许多参加审判的人都认为，他们听到法官在法庭外对被告发表了嘲讽和敌对的言论。然而，这些说法从未被追究。

陪审团在做出判决前商讨了 5 个小时。两个被告判决结果是相同的：他们都被判一级谋杀罪。辩方律师请求新的审判。请求重新审判的申诉在法律系统里缓慢传递并审议的时候，萨科和万泽蒂在监狱里等待了六年。

上诉

辩方提出了新的证据，以支持进行新一轮审判的要求。一个叫做古尔德的人说，警卫和出纳被枪击的时候，他就走在他们的后面。他发誓无论是萨科还是万泽蒂都不在那辆逃逸的车辆里。然而，根据马萨诸塞州当时的法律，申请新一轮审判的请求必须提交给聆讯过首轮审判的法官。法官塞耶拒绝了这一请求，并裁定单只有这一项证据不足以重新审判。

辩方律师接着声称，判定萨科和万泽蒂有罪的陪审团长曾经说过，不论他们两人是否有罪，这些激进分子都应当被绞死。法官塞耶又再次拒绝了重新审判的请求。

好几个月过去了，他们又提起了新的上诉。控方的主要弹道专家说，如果审判时直接问他，给了警卫致命一枪的子弹是否来自萨科的手枪，他会说不是。法官塞耶又一次拒绝了重新审判的上诉。

Then on November 18, 1925, Celestino Madeiros, a convicted murderer, confessed that he had participated in the shoe factory robbery and murders as part of the notorious Joe .Morelli gang. Armed with this new evidence, attorneys appealed to the Supreme Court of Massachusetts.

However, according to the law at that time, the high court could only review the records of the original trial and could not review any new evidence. Thus, the court's decision was to let the verdict stand.

Finally, on April 9, 1927, Sacco and Vanzetti went to court for final sentencing. The judge asked them if they had anything to say. Vanzetti rose and spoke:

"I am suffering because I am a radical and indeed I am a radical. I have suffered because I am an Italian and indeed I am an Italian. I would not wish to a dog or a snake, to the most low and unfortunate creature of this world-I would not wish to any of them what I have had to suffer of things I am not guilty of."

Sacco and Vanzetti were sentenced to die in the electric chair.

A Final Appeal

By this time, public opinion had begun to change and many people, conservatives and liberals alike, began to call for a new trial. Protests grew against the executions. A newspaper editorial summarized people's feelings:

"No man, we submit, should be put to death where so much doubt exists."

Although defense attorneys continued to request a new trial and even tried to appeal the case to the United States Supreme Court, they were unsuccessful. They asked the governor of Massachusetts for a stay of execution.

Judge Webster Thayer ☞

　　紧接着，1925 年 11 月 18 日，一名被判有罪的杀人犯——塞莱斯蒂诺·马德罗斯，坦承自己作为臭名昭著的乔·莫雷利团伙的一员参与了鞋厂的抢劫和谋杀案。在这一全新证据的支持下，辩方律师再次提请马萨诸塞州最高法院重新审议此案。

　　然而根据当时的法律，最高法院只能审阅原始审判的记录，无法审查任何新的证据。因此，法院的裁决是维持原判。

　　最终，在 1927 年 4 月 9 日，萨科和万泽蒂在法院接受最后审判，法官问他们还有什么话想说，万泽蒂站起来说：

　　"因为我是一个激进分子，所以我遭受了这些痛苦，而我的确也是一个激进份子。因为我是一个意大利人，所以我遭受了这些痛苦，而我的确也是一个意大利人。我不会向一只狗或一条蛇许愿，我不会向这世界上最低等最不幸的生物许愿，我不会向任何那些让我无辜遭受这些痛苦的人许愿。"

　　萨科和万泽蒂最终被判电椅死刑。

最后呼吁

　　到了这个时候，公众舆论开始发生了改变。许多人，不论是保守派还是自由派都开始呼吁对案件进行重新审判，越来越多的人反对对他们处以死刑。某家报社的社论总结了人们的感受：

　　"我们认为，在还有如此多的地方存在疑点的情况下，没有人应当被处死。"

　　尽管辩方律师持续请求进行新的审判，甚至试图将案件上诉到美国最高法院，但他们没有成功。因此他们请求马萨诸塞州州长批准延期执行死刑。

法官韦伯斯特·塞耶

Critical Thinking Exercise

TAKING, AND DEFENDING A POSITION IN A CLEMENCY BOARD HEARING

Now you will role-play a clemency board hearing. To conduct the exercise, a class member should play the role of the governor of Massachusetts. The governor should appoint an advisory board of five to seven class members to advise him on Sacco and Vanzetti' s request for a stay of execution. The rest of the class should form two groups. One group should prepare arguments in favor of granting a stay of execution and the other group should prepare arguments against granting a stay.

Each group should select two or three spokespersons to present the arguments to the governor's clemency board. Each group's presentation should be limited to five minutes, followed by a question and answer period of five minutes. While each group is preparing its arguments, the members of the governor's clemency board should prepare questions to ask the spokespersons for each side. After the presentations and question and answer periods are completed, the clemency board should discuss what recommendation to make to the governor, and why. Each member of the board should be able to express his or her views to the governor. After hearing the board's recommendations, the governor should decide whether or not to grant a stay of execution, and should explain the reasons for his or her decision to the class.

How does public observation of legal proceedings help achieve the goals of procedural justice? ☞

重点思考练习

在一个赦免委员会听证会上选择和论证一个观点

现在你们要模拟一个赦免委员会的听证会。为了完成此次练习，一名同学应当扮演马萨诸塞州州长的角色。州长应当任命一个 5 到 7 个人组成的顾问委员会，并负责针对萨科和万泽蒂提出的缓期执行死刑的要求，向州长提交委员会的建议。班上剩下的同学应当分成两组，其中一组准备支持准予缓期执行死刑的论据，另一组则准备反对缓刑的论据。

每一组应当选出 2 个或 3 个发言人，向州长赦免委员会陈述自己小组的论据。每一组的陈述应当限制在 5 分钟之内，接着是 5 分钟的提问和回答时间。在每一组准备自己的论据时，代表州长赦免委员会的小组应当准备要问每一方发言人的问题。在陈述发言和问答时间结束后，赦免委员会应当讨论要提交给州长什么建议，以及这一建议的原因。委员会的每一名成员都应当能够向州长表达自己的观点。在听取了委员会的建议后，州长应当决定是否同意实施缓刑，并向全班解释自己做这个决定的原因。

对法律程序的公众观察怎样有助于程序正义的实现？

What do you think?

1. Were the goals of procedural justice met in the Sacco and Vanzetti case? Why or why not?

2. Information made public more than fifty years after the trial ended has been interpreted by some to suggest that Sacco was guilty of murder. He belonged to a Sicilian radical group sworn to secrecy. Recently opened FBI files indicate that the state probably did not have enough evidence to convict Vanzettiof murder, although hit suggest she may have been involved with the armed robbery in some way. Other information, however, seems to point to the Morelli gang. Does this information in any way alter your opinion as to whether or not the procedures used in the case were fair?

3. The Governor of Massachusetts denied the request for a stay of execution. Protests grew all over the world. In some countries, crowds marched on American embassies. In France, Italy, and the United States, workers went on strike. Bombs went off in Philadelphia and New York. Meanwhile, Sacco and Vanzetti continued to maintain their innocence. As the hour for the execution approached, several thousand people gathered outside the jail. Hundreds of armed police held back the crowd. At last, on August 23, 1927, after more than seven years in jail, Sacco and Vanzetti were executed in the electric chair.

After the executions, protest continued. Then in April, 1959, a member of the Massachusetts state legislature proposed that the governor declare a retroactive pardon based on the contention that Sacco and Vanzetti had been denied a fair trial in violation of the due process clause of the Fourteenth Amendment of the U.S. Constitution and protections in the Bill of Rights of the Massachusetts Constitution. If you had been in the legislature, would you have voted for this bill? Why or why not?

4. What, if any, issues of corrective and distributive justice were raised in the Sacco and Vanzetti case?

你怎么看？

1. 程序正义的目标是否在萨科和万泽蒂一案中实现了？为什么？为什么没有？

2. 该案审判结束 50 多年后，案件信息才得以向公众开放，有些人认为这些信息显示出萨科犯有谋杀罪。他从属于并宣誓效忠于意大利西西里的一个秘密激进团体。最近公布的联邦调查局档案表明，州政府可能没有足够的证据来判定万泽蒂谋杀罪名成立，虽然也有证据显示他可能以某种方式参与了武装抢劫。但是，其他信息看上去却是指向莫雷利团伙的。以上信息是否在某种意义上，改变了你对本案中所使用的程序是否公正这一问题的看法？

3. 马萨诸塞州州长最终否决了缓期执行死刑的请求。世界各地都激起了反对的声浪，在某些国家，游行的队伍聚集在美国大使馆门前。在法国、意大利和美国，工人们举行了罢工。费城和纽约发生了爆炸案。与此同时，萨科和万泽蒂继续坚持认为自己是清白的。随着死刑期限的临近，数千人聚集在监狱外，有数百名武警与示威人群对峙。最终，1927 年 8 月 23 日，在监狱服刑长达七年之后，萨科和万泽蒂被处死在电椅上。

在二人被处决后，抗议仍在继续。1959 年 4 月，马萨诸塞州州议会的一名议员提出了一项议案，州长可以宣布一种有追溯力的赦免，这项提案的论据是拒绝对萨科和万泽蒂进行公平审判的行为，违反了《联邦宪法第十四条修正案》的"正当程序"条款，以及触犯了马萨诸塞州宪法中《权利法案》的保护。如果你也是那时的议员，你会投票支持这一法案吗？为什么？为什么不？

4. 如果有的话，萨科和万泽蒂案件中提出了哪些有关矫正正义和分配正义的问题？

Using the Lesson

1. "Due process is that procedure which hears before it condemns, which proceeds upon inquiry, and renders judgment only after trial," wrote American statesman Daniel Webster (1782-1852). According to Webster's definition, how does due process promote the goals of procedural justice?

2. "'The fact of the whole matter is that very-many persons look upon the whole procedure [raids, arrests, and deportations] as all wrong and a travesty of justice. If there was the least evidence against these men of being plotters and agitators against law and order, the burden and duty of the authorities was to see that these charges were either proven or disproven in the law courts." Claremont Eagle Times, September 1920

Unlike Sacco and Vanzetti, many arrested in the Red Raids of the 1920s were never even given the benefit of a trial. Imagine you are an editorial writer in 1927. Write an editorial about the Sacco and Vanzetti case in terms of the three categories of justice you have studied in this program.

4. Arrange to visit and observe an agency of local government at work gathering information or making a decision. List the procedures used and be prepared to discuss their fairness with your class. For example, you might observe a court trial, a board of education hearing, a zoning commission hearing, or a city council hearing.

5. Write an editorial or draw a political cartoon about the procedural justice issues raised in the Sacco and Vanzetti case you have studied in this lesson, or choose other procedural justice issues as your subject. Your editorial or cartoon should emphasize the problems that might occur if there is no procedural justice.

知识运用

1. 美国政治家丹尼尔·韦伯斯特（1782年—1852年）曾写道："正当程序就是在定罪之前必须听取意见，根据调查询问进行审理，并且只有在审讯之后才能做出判决的程序。"根据韦伯斯特的定义，正当程序如何能促成程序正义的目标？

2. 1920年9月的《克莱尔蒙特老鹰时报》评论称："整件事的事实是，许多人都将整个程序（搜查、逮捕和驱逐出境）视为彻底的错误和对正义的嘲弄。如果哪怕有一点点证据可以指控这些违反法律秩序的策划者和煽动者，权威者的责任和职责就是要检查这些指控在法庭上是否可以被证明。"

与萨科和万泽蒂案不同的是，许多在20世纪20年代的"红色突袭"事件中被逮捕的人，甚至从未有机会接受法庭审讯。假设你是1927年的一位报纸评论员，根据在本课中所学到的三类正义，写一篇关于萨科和万泽蒂案件的评论。

3. 安排一次访问，观察一家专职收集信息或制定决策的本地政府机构的工作，列出他们所使用的程序，并准备讨论与班里同学讨论这些程序的正义性。例如，你可以旁听一次法院审理、一次教育委员会的听证会、一次分区委员会的听证会或一次市政厅的听证会。

4. 针对你在本课中学到的萨科和万泽蒂案中的程序正义问题，写一篇评论文章或画一幅政治漫画，或选择其他程序正义问题作为你的主题。在你的评论或漫画中，应当突出强调如果没有程序正义将可能产生的问题。

附录1：
词汇表

assistance of counsel JL2/JL10. Amendment VI of the Bill of Rights-in all criminal prosecutions, the accused is guaranteed the right to have the help of an attorney for his or her defense.

辩护人有效援助（《正义》第二课、第十课）：美国联邦宪法第六修正案（1791年权利法案）规定：在一切刑事诉讼中，保障被告有权取得律师帮助为其进行辩护。

benefits JL1. Things that promote well-being; advantages.

利益（《正义》第一课）：使…得益；优势。

bill of attainder JL2. Legislative act that gives notice of termination of a person's civil rights. Bills of attainder are prohibited by the Constitution in Article I, Section 9.

公民权利剥夺法案（褫夺公权法）（《正义》第二课）：法院颁布的终止一个人的公民权利的法令。美国联邦宪法第一条第九款中禁止实行这一法案。

Bill of Rights JL2/JL10. The first ten amendments to the U.S. Constitution, a summary of fundamental rights and privileges guaranteed to a people against violation by the state.

《权利法案》（《正义》第二课、第十课）：美国联邦宪法的前十项修正案，是对保障人民反抗政府干预的基本权利和特权的总结。

burden JL1. Something oppressive or worrisome.

负担（《正义》第一课）：某些有压制性的或带来烦恼的事情。

capacity JL3. Ability to hold, receive, or contain.

能力（《正义》第三课）：承担、接受或容纳的才能。

caucus JL5. A closed meeting of persons belonging to the same political party.

党团会议（《正义》第五课）：同属于一个政党的人们召开的秘密会议。

common-law JL2. Relating to the body of law developed in England primarily from judicial decisions based on custom and precedent, unwritten in statute or code. The basis of the English legal system and of the system in all of the U.S. except Louisiana.

习惯法（《正义》第二课）：源自英国发展起来的法律体系，司法判定主要基于并未写入成文法令或条例的传统和判例。这是英国和美国联邦各州（除路易斯安那州外）法律体系的基础。

compensate JL8. To make an appropriate payment.

赔偿（《正义》第八课）：对...支付适当的款项。

comprehensiveness JL11. Complete or broad coverage of a topic.

完整性（《正义》第十一课）：对某一主题全面或广泛涉及。

compulsory process JL2. Amendment VI of the Bill of Rights - in all criminal prosecutions, the accused is guaranteed the right to a speedy and fair trial and the right to have the state follow established procedures for obtaining witnesses in his or her favor.

强制程序（《正义》第二课）：美国联邦宪法第六修正案中规定：在一切刑事诉讼中，被告有权利获得迅速和公开的审判；有权利以法定程序获得对被告有利的证人。

correction JL6. An action or instance of bringing into conformity with a standard; an improvement.

矫正（《正义》第六课）：使...符合某种规范或标准的行动或范例；某种改善措施。

corrective justice JL1. Fairness of a response to a wrong or injury to a person or group is an issue of corrective justice; to punish with a view to reforming or improving; to make or set right.

矫正正义（《正义》第一课）：对受到错误对待或伤害的个人或群体的回应的公平性就是有关矫正正义的问题；以重整或改善为目的进行惩罚；调整以使...正确。

corruption of blood JL2. Barring a person from inheriting, retaining, or transmitting any estate, rank, or title due to the commission of a crime (usually treason) that terminates the person's civil rights.

血统玷污（《正义》第二课）：终止犯有某种罪行（通常是叛国罪）的罪犯的公民权，禁止其享有继承、保有或遗赠任何财产、爵位或称号的权利。

desert JL3. Something deserved or merited.

值得（《正义》第三课）：应得的或理所当然的（事）。

detection of error JL11. Discovery of something incorrect or wrong.

发现错误（《正义》第十一课）：发现某些不正确或错误的事情。

deter (deterrence) JL6. To discourage or hinder.

制止（《正义》第六课）：阻碍或拖延。

distributive justice JL1. Fairness of dividing something among several people or groups is an issue of distributive justice. That which is distributed or divided can be a benefit, such as pay for work, the right to speak or vote, or it can be a burden, such as taxes, household chores, or homework.

分配正义（《正义》第一课）：在若干人或群体中分配物品的公平性就是有关分配正义的问题。被分发或分配的可以是某种福利，例如工作的报酬、言论或投票的权利；也可能是某种负担，例如缴税、家务活、或者做功课。

due process of law JL10. Amendment XIV, Section I - ...nor shall any State deprive any person of life, liberty, or property, without due process of law. A course of formal proceedings carried out regularly and in accordance with established rules and principles.

正当法律程序（《正义》第十课）：美国联邦宪法第十四修正案第一款规定：不经正当法律程序，任何一州不得剥夺任何人的生命、自由或财产。一种遵照既定的规则和原则、定期进行的正式诉讼程序。

duration JL7. Period of time.

持续时间（《正义》第七课）：一段时间。

equal protection of the laws JL2. Amendment XIV, Section I - ...nor deny to any persori within its jurisdiction the equal protection of the laws. All citizens no matter their religion, race, gender, age, or status in society are entitled to the same treatment under the law.

平等法律保护（《正义》第二课）：美国联邦宪法第十四修正案第一款规定：任何一州对于在其管辖下的任何人，亦不得拒绝给予平等法律保护。所有公民不论其宗教、种族、性别、年龄或社会地位都有权受到法律的同等对待。

establishment of religion JL2. Recognition by law and support by civil authority of a particular religion as the official church of a nation.

确立国教（《正义》第二课）：某种特定宗教依法确认并得到公民权威支持而成为一个国家的官方教会。

ex post facto law JL2. A law passed retroactively.

追溯既往的法律（《正义》第二课）：可追溯的过去的法律。

extent JL7. The size of a particular area; breadth, degree, or magnitude of something.

程度（《正义》第七课）：某一特定领域的规模；某事（物）的广度、等级或大小。

flexibility JL11. Capability of adapting to new, different, or changing requirements.

灵活性（《正义》第十一课）：能够适应新的、不同的或不断变化的要求。

free exercise of religion JL2. The clause in the First Amendment that states that the government shall make no law forbidding the free practice of religious beliefs.

宗教活动自由（《正义》第二课）：美国联邦宪法第一修正案中的条款规定：政府不得制定关于禁止宗教信仰活动自由的法律。

grand jury JL2. A jury that examines accusations against persons charged with a crime. If the evidence warrants it, the grand jury makes formal charges on which the accused persons are later tried.

大陪审团（《正义》第二课）：针对被控犯罪的被告的指控和罪名进行审查的陪审团。如果（控方的）证据证实了指控，大陪审团会对被告提起正式指控，被告随后将被法院审判。

habeas corpus JL2. See writ of habeas corpus. (writ of habeas corpus. A writ issued to bring a person before a court or judge to obtain protection against illegal imprisonment.

人身保护权（《正义》第二课）：参见"人身保护令（权威第十二课）"：由法院签发的命令，要求羁押者将被羁押者提交法院或法官（以审查羁押的合法性），以保护个人不受非法拘禁。

immunity (immunities) JL2. Freedom from punishment or restrictions.

豁免（《正义》第二课）：免受惩罚或限制的自由。

impact JL7. The effect of something on the feelings or mind of another.

影响（《正义》第七课）：某件事对他人的情感和精神所产生的效果。

impartial (impartiality) JL11. Treating or affecting all equally.

不偏不倚（《正义》第十一课）：对一切都同样对待或产生相同的影响。

inalienable rights JL2. Fundamental rights of people that may not be taken away.

不可剥夺的权利（《正义》第二课）：人民不可被剥夺的基本权利。

indictment JL2. A formal written statement framed by a prosecuting authority and found to have merit by a grand jury charging a person with a crime.

起诉（《正义》第二课）：由检察机关起草的正式的书面声明，针对被告的犯罪指控，提交大陪审团判定指控有效。

injury JL6. Damage, harm, or wound.

伤害（《正义》第六课）：毁坏、危害或创伤。

intent JL7. Aim or purpose.

故意（《正义》第七课）：（有）目的或意图。

interest JL3. A right to or claim on something.

利益（《正义》第三课）：对某事（物）的支配权或有权要求做某事得到某物。

involuntary servitude JL2. The state of being forced to labor for another against one's will.

强迫劳役（《正义》第二课）：违背个人意愿而被迫为他人劳动的状态。

jeopardy JL2/JL10. The danger that an accused person is subjected to when on trial for a criminal offense.

危险（《正义》第二课、第十课）：刑事犯罪被告在审判过程中会遇到的重复审理）的危险。（译者注：这里特指美国宪法第五修正案所禁止的"一罪两罚double jeopardy"）

jurisdiction JL2. The limits or territory within which authority may be exercised.

管辖（《正义》第二课）：可以行使权威的范围或领域。

justify (justification) JL7. To prove or show to be right or reasonable.

辩护（《正义》第七课）：证明或阐述…是正确的或合理的。

just compensation JL10. Amendment V of the Bill of Rights. Payment made to private citizens by the government in cases of government's confiscation of their property.

公平赔偿（《正义》第十课）：美国联邦宪法第五修正案（1791年权利法案）：在政府没收公民私有财产的案例中，政府支付给公民个人的赔偿。

naturalize (naturalized) JL2. To give full citizenship to someone of foreign birth.

归化（《正义》第二课）：给在国外出生的人给予完整的公民权。

need JL3. A condition requiring supply or relief.

需求（《正义》第三课）：需要支援或救助的状况。

negligence JL7. Failure to exercise care.

疏忽（《正义》第七课）：没能注意到，不小心。

notice JL11. A warning or intimation of something.

通知（《正义》第十一课）：有关某事的预警或正式宣告。

oath JL2. A declaration or promise to tell the truth or to act in a certain way made with God or some other sacred object as witness.

宣誓（《正义》第二课）：向上帝或以其他某些神圣对象为见证发出的誓言，承诺要说出事实或以某种方式行动。

offensive (offensiveness) JL7. Causing anger, resentment, or displeasure.

恶劣性（《正义》第七课）：引起愤怒、怨恨或不满。

pardon JL8. To absolve from the consequences of a fault or crime.

宽恕（《正义》第八课）：从某个错误或犯罪行为的后果中免除（责任）。

poll tax JL2. Payment of a fixed amount per person to grant that person the right to vote; forbidden by the Constitution in Amendment XXIV, Section 1.

人头税（《正义》第二课）：每个人缴付一定数额的税款以保证自己投票的权利；美国联邦宪法第二十四修正案第一款中禁止了这一条款。

predictable (predictability) JL11. Capable of being foretold on the basis of observation, experience, or scientific reason.

可预测性（《正义》第十一课）：在观察、经验或科学理性的基础上能够被预言的。

prevention JL6. The act of keeping from happening.

预防（《正义》第六课）：防止某事发生的行为。

principle of similarity JL3. In a particular situation, people who are the same or similar in certain important ways should be treated the same, or equally. In that situation, people who are different in certain important ways should be treated differently, or unequally.

相似原理（《正义》第三课）：在某种特定情况下，对那些在某些重要方面是相同的或相似的人，应当一视同仁或给予同等待遇。在这种情况下，对在某些重要方面有所不同的人则应当区别对待，或给予不同等待遇。

probable cause JL2. A reasonable ground for supposing that a criminal charge is well founded.

合理根据（《正义》第二课）：为假设"某个犯罪指控是有根据的"所给出的合理正当的理由。

probable consequences JL7. Likely results.

可能的结果（《正义》第七课）：可能产生的结果。

procedural justice JL1/10. The fairness of how information is gathered or decisions are made; relating to a series of steps followed in a regular, definite order by a court or other law-administering body.

程序正义（《正义》第一课、第十课）：有关"信息是如何收集的"或"决策是怎样制定的"问题的公平性；与法院或其他法律管理机构所遵循的正规、明确的秩序中的一系列步骤相关。

proportional (proportionality) JL7. Corresponding in size, degree, or intensity.

比例（《正义》第七课）：在规模、程度或强度上保持一致。

reckless (recklessness) JL7. Lacking proper caution; careless of the consequences of one's actions.

鲁莽（《正义》第七课）：缺乏适当的谨慎；不顾个人行为的后果。

redress JL2. To set right; to correct or remedy.

纠正（《正义》第二课）：使...恢复正常；改正或补救。

regret JL7. A sense of distress over a past event or deed.

遗憾（《正义》第七课）：对过去发生的事情或行为感到沮丧 。

relevant JL3. Having significant and demonstrable bearing on the matter at hand

相关的（《正义》第三课）：与正在讨论（考虑）的问题有关键性的、决定性的关联。

reliability JL11. Dependability.

可靠性（《正义》第十一课）：可依赖的。

remorse JL7. Distress or guilt for wrongs committed in the past.

悔恨（《正义》第七课）：为过去所犯的错误而感到痛苦或内疚。

restore JL8. To return something to its original or prior condition.

复原（《正义》第八课）：使某事（物）回复到最初或之前的状况。

value JL3. A principle, standard, or quality considered worthwhile or desirable.

价值观（《正义》第三课）：被认为是有价值的或理想的准则、标准或品质。

wrong JL6. Something that is contrary to conscience, morality, or law.

错误（《正义》第六课）：某些与良知、道德或法律背道而驰的事情。

附录2:

The Constitution of the United States

We the People of the United States, in^{注} Order to form a more perfect Union, establish Justice, insure domestic Tranquility, provide for the common defence, promote the general Welfare, and secure the Blessings of Liberty to ourselves and our Posterity, do ordain and establish this Constitution for the United States of America.

Article. I.

Section. 1   All legislative Powers herein granted shall be vested in a Congress of the United States, which shall consist of a Senate and House of Representatives.

Section. 2   The House of Representatives shall be composed of Members chosen every second Year by the People of the several States, and the Electors in each State shall have the Qualifications requisite for Electors of the most numerous Branch of the State Legislature.

No Person shall be a Representative who shall not have attained to the Age of twenty five Years, and been seven Years a Citizen of the United States, and who shall not, when elected, be an Inhabitant of that State in which he shall be chosen.

Representatives and direct Taxes shall be apportioned among the several States which may be included within this Union, according to their respective Numbers, which shall be determined by adding to the whole Number of free Persons, including those bound to Service for a Term of Years, and excluding Indians not taxed, three fifths of all other Persons. The actual Enumeration shall be made within three Years after the first Meeting of the Congress of the United States, and within every subsequent Term of ten Years, in such Manner as they shall by Law direct. The Number of Representatives shall not exceed one for every thirty Thousand, but each State shall have at Least one Representative; and until

---

注:原文:美国国家档案馆

　　http://www.archives.gov/exhibits/charters/constitution_transcript.html

美利坚合众国宪法

我们合众国人民，为建立更完善的联邦，树立正义，保障国内安宁，提供共同防务，促进公共福利，并使我们自己和后代得享自由的幸福，特为美利坚合众国制定本宪法。

第一条

第一款　本宪法授予的全部立法权，属于由参议院和众议院组成的合众国国会。

第二款　众议院由各州人民每两年选举产生的众议员组成。每个州的选举人须具备该州州议会人数最多一院选举人所必需的资格。

凡年龄不满二十五岁，成为合众国公民不满七年，在一州当选时不是该州居民者，不得担任众议员。

〔众议员名额和直接税税额，在本联邦可包括的各州中，按照各自人口比例进行分配。各州人口数，按自由人总数加上所有其他人口的五分之三予以确定。自由人总数包括必须服一定年限劳役的人，但不包括未被征税的印第安人。〕 ①人口的实际统计在合众国国会第一次会议后三年内和此后每十年内，依法律规定的方式进行。每三万人选出的众议员人数不得超过一名，但每州至少须有一名众议员；在进行上述人口统计以前，新罕布什尔州有权选出三名，马萨诸塞州八名，罗得岛州和普罗维登斯种植地一名，康涅狄格州五名，纽约州六名，新泽西州四名，宾夕法尼亚州八名，特拉华州一名，马里兰州六名，弗吉尼亚州十名，北卡罗来纳州五名，南卡罗来纳州五名，佐治亚州三名。

such enumeration shall be made, the State of New Hampshire shall be entitled to chuse three, Massachusetts eight, Rhode-Island and Providence Plantations one, Connecticut five, New-York six, New Jersey four, Pennsylvania eight, Delaware one, Maryland six, Virginia ten, North Carolina five, South Carolina five, and Georgia three.

When vacancies happen in the Representation from any State, the Executive Authority thereof shall issue Writs of Election to fill such Vacancies.

The House of Representatives shall chuse their Speaker and other Officers; and shall have the sole Power of Impeachment.

Section. 3 The Senate of the United States shall be composed of two Senators from each State, chosen by the Legislature thereof for six Years; and each Senator shall have one Vote.

Immediately after they shall be assembled in Consequence of the first Election, they shall be divided as equally as may be into three Classes. The Seats of the Senators of the first Class shall be vacated at the Expiration of the second Year, of the second Class at the Expiration of the fourth Year, and of the third Class at the Expiration of the sixth Year, so that one third may be chosen every second Year; and if Vacancies happen by Resignation, or otherwise, during the Recess of the Legislature of any State, the Executive thereof may make temporary Appointments until the next Meeting of the Legislature, which shall then fill such Vacancies.

No Person shall be a Senator who shall not have attained to the Age of thirty Years, and been nine Years a Citizen of the United States, and who shall not, when elected, be an Inhabitant of that State for which he shall be chosen.

The Vice President of the United States shall be President of the Senate, but shall have no Vote, unless they be equally divided.

The Senate shall chuse their other Officers, and also a President pro tempore, in the Absence of the Vice President, or when he shall exercise the Office of President of the United States.

The Senate shall have the sole Power to try all Impeachments. When sitting for that Purpose, they shall be on Oath or Affirmation. When the President of the United States is tried, the Chief Justice shall preside: And no Person shall be convicted without the Concurrence of two thirds of the Members present.

任何一州代表出现缺额时，该州行政当局应发布选举令，以填补此项缺额。

众议院选举本院议长和其他官员，并独自拥有弹劾权。

第三款　合众国参议院由［每州州议会选举的］②两名参议员组成，任期六年；每名参议员有一票表决权。

参议员在第一次选举后集会时，立即分为人数尽可能相等的三个组。第一组参议员席位在第二年年终空出，第二组参议员席位在第四年年终空出，第三组参议员席位在第六年年终空出，以便三分之一的参议员得每二年改选一次。［在任何一州州议会休会期间，如因辞职或其他原因而出现缺额时，该州行政长官在州议会下次集会填补此项缺额前，得任命临时参议员。］③

凡年龄不满三十岁，成为合众国公民不满九年，在一州当选时不是该州居民者，不得担任参议员。

合众国副总统任参议院议长，但除非参议员投票时赞成票和反对票相等，无表决权。

参议院选举本院其他官员，并在副总统缺席或行使合众国总统职权时，选举一名临时议长。

参议院独自拥有审判一切弹劾案的权力。为此目的而开庭时，全体参议员须宣誓或作代誓宣言。合众国总统受审时，最高法院首席大法官主持审判。无论何人，非经出席参议员三分之二的同意，不得被定罪。

Judgment in Cases of Impeachment shall not extend further than to removal from Office, and disqualification to hold and enjoy any Office of honor, Trust or Profit under the United States: but the Party convicted shall nevertheless be liable and subject to Indictment, Trial, Judgment and Punishment, according to Law.

Section. 4   The Times, Places and Manner of holding Elections for Senators and Representatives, shall be prescribed in each State by the Legislature thereof; but the Congress may at any time by Law make or alter such Regulations, except as to the Places of chusing Senators.

The Congress shall assemble at least once in every Year, and such Meeting shall be on the first Monday in December, unless they shall by Law appoint a different Day.

Section. 5   Each House shall be the Judge of the Elections, Returns and Qualifications of its own Members, and a Majority of each shall constitute a Quorum to do Business; but a smaller Number may adjourn from day to day, and may be authorized to compel the Attendance of absent Members, in such Manner, and under such Penalties as each House may provide.

Each House may determine the Rules of its Proceedings, punish its Members for disorderly Behaviour, and, with the Concurrence of two thirds, expel a Member.

Each House shall keep a Journal of its Proceedings, and from time to time publish the same, excepting such Parts as may in their Judgment require Secrecy; and the Yeas and Nays of the Members of either House on any question shall, at the Desire of one fifth of those Present, be entered on the Journal.

Neither House, during the Session of Congress, shall, without the Consent of the other, adjourn for more than three days, nor to any other Place than that in which the two Houses shall be sitting.

Section. 6   The Senators and Representatives shall receive a Compensation for their Services, to be ascertained by Law, and paid out of the Treasury of the United States. They shall in all Cases, except Treason, Felony and Breach of the Peace, be privileged from Arrest during their Attendance at the Session of their respective Houses, and in going to and returning from the same; and for any Speech or Debate in either House, they shall not be questioned in any other Place.

弹劾案的判决，不得超出免职和剥夺担任和享有合众国属下有荣誉、有责任或有薪金的任何职务的资格。但被定罪的人，仍可依法起诉、审判、判决和惩罚。

第四款　举行参议员和众议员选举的时间、地点和方式，在每个州由该州议会规定。但除选举参议员的地点外，国会得随时以法律制定或改变这类规定。

国会每年至少开会一次，除非国会以法律另订日期外，此会议在［十二月第一个星期一］④举行。

第五款　每院是本院议员的选举、选举结果报告和资格的裁判者。每院议员过半数，即构成议事的法定人数；但不足法定人数时，得逐日休会，并有权按每院规定的方式和罚则，强迫缺席议员出席会议。

每院得规定本院议事规则，惩罚本院议员扰乱秩序的行为，并经三之二议员的同意开除议员。

每院应有本院会议记录，并不时予以公布，但它认为需要保密的部分除外。每院议员对于任何问题的赞成票和反对票，在出席议员五分之一的请求下，应载入会议记录。

在国会开会期间，任何一院，未经另一院同意，不得休会三日以上，也不得到非两院开会的任何地方休会。

第六款　参议员和众议员应得到服务的报酬，此项报酬由法律确定并由合众国国库支付。他们除犯叛国罪、重罪和妨害治安罪外，在一切情况下都享有在出席各自议院会议期间和往返于各自议院途中不受逮捕的特权。他们不得因在各自议院发表的演说或辩论而在任何其他地方受到质问。

No Senator or Representative shall, during the Time for which he was elected, be appointed to any civil Office under the Authority of the United States, which shall have been created, or the Emoluments whereof shall have been encreased during such time; and no Person holding any Office under the United States, shall be a Member of either House during his Continuance in Office.

Section. 7   All Bills for raising Revenue shall originate in the House of Representatives; but the Senate may propose or concur with Amendments as on other Bills.

Every Bill which shall have passed the House of Representatives and the Senate, shall, before it become a Law, be presented to the President of the United States: If he approve he shall sign it, but if not he shall return it, with his Objections to that House in which it shall have originated, who shall enter the Objections at large on their Journal, and proceed to reconsider it. If after such Reconsideration two thirds of that House shall agree to pass the Bill, it shall be sent, together with the Objections, to the other House, by which it shall likewise be reconsidered, and if approved by two thirds of that House, it shall become a Law. But in all such Cases the Votes of both Houses shall be determined by yeas and Nays, and the Names of the Persons voting for and against the Bill shall be entered on the Journal of each House respectively. If any Bill shall not be returned by the President within ten Days (Sundays excepted) after it shall have been presented to him, the Same shall be a Law, in like Manner as if he had signed it, unless the Congress by their Adjournment prevent its Return, in which Case it shall not be a Law.

Every Order, Resolution, or Vote to which the Concurrence of the Senate and House of Representatives may be necessary (except on a question of Adjournment) shall be presented to the President of the United States; and before the Same shall take Effect, shall be approved by him, or being disapproved by him, shall be repassed by two thirds of the Senate and House of Representatives, according to the Rules and Limitations prescribed in the Case of a Bill.

Section. 8   The Congress shall have Power To lay and collect Taxes, Duties, Imposts and Excises, to pay the Debts and provide for the common Defence and general Welfare of the United States; but all Duties, Imposts and Excises shall be uniform throughout the United States;

参议员或众议员在当选任期内，不得被任命担任在此期间设置或增薪的合众国管辖下的任何文官职务。凡在合众国属下任职者，在继续任职期间不得担任任何一院议员。

第七款　所有征税议案应首先在众议院提出，但参议院得像对其他议案一样，提出或同意修正案。

众议院和参议院通过的每一议案，在成为法律前须送交合众国总统。总统如批准该议案，即应签署；如不批准，则应将该议案同其反对意见退回最初提出该议案的议院。该院应特此项反对见详细载入本院会议记录并进行复议。如经复议后，该院三分之二议员同意通过该议案，该议案连同反对意见应一起送交另一议院，并同样由该院进行复议，如经该院三分之二议员赞同，该议案即成为法律。但在所有这类情况下，两院表决都由赞成票和反对票决定；对该议案投赞成票和反对票的议员姓名应分别载入每一议院会议记录。如任何议案在送交总统后十天内（星期日除外）未经总统退回，该议案如同总统已签署一样，即成为法律，除非因国会休会而使该议案不能退回，在此种情况下，该议案不能成为法律。

凡须由参议院和众议院一致同意的每项命令、决议或表决（关于休会问题除外），须送交合众国总统，该项命令、决议或表决在生效前，须由总统批准，如总统不批准，则按照关于议案所规定的规则和限制，由参议院和众议院三分之二议员重新通过。

第八款　国会有权：

规定和征收直接税、进口税、捐税和其他税，以偿付国债、提供合众国共同防务和公共福利，但一切进口税、捐税和其他税应全国统一；

To borrow Money on the credit of the United States;

To regulate Commerce with foreign Nations, and among the several States, and with the Indian Tribes;

To establish an uniform Rule of Naturalization, and uniform Laws on the subject of Bankruptcies throughout the United States;

To coin Money, regulate the Value thereof, and of foreign Coin, and fix the Standard of Weights and Measures;

To provide for the Punishment of counterfeiting the Securities and current Coin of the United States;

To establish Post Offices and post Roads;

To promote the Progress of Science and useful Arts, by securing for limited Times to Authors and Inventors the exclusive Right to their respective Writings and Discoveries;

To constitute Tribunals inferior to the supreme Court;

To define and punish Piracies and Felonies committed on the high Seas, and Offences against the Law of Nations;

To declare War, grant Letters of Marque and Reprisal, and make Rules concerning Captures on Land and Water;

To raise and support Armies, but no Appropriation of Money to that Use shall be for a longer Term than two Years;

To provide and maintain a Navy;

To make Rules for the Government and Regulation of the land and naval Forces;

To provide for calling forth the Militia to execute the Laws of the Union, suppress Insurrections and repel Invasions;

To provide for organizing, arming, and disciplining, the Militia, and for governing such Part of them as may be employed in the Service of the United States, reserving to the States respectively, the Appointment of the Officers, and the Authority of training the Militia according to the discipline prescribed by Congress;

以合众国的信用借款；

管制同外国的、各州之间的和同印第安部落的商业；

制定合众国全国统一的归化条例和破产法；

铸造货币，厘定本国货币和外国货币的价值，并确定度量衡的标准；

规定有关伪造合众国证券和通用货币的罚则；

设立邮政局和修建邮政道路；

保障著作家和发明家对各自著作和发明在限定期限内的专有权利，以促进科学和工艺的进步；

设立低于最高法院的法院；

界定和惩罚在公海上所犯的海盗罪和重罪以及违反国际法的犯罪行为；

宣战，颁发掳获敌船许可状，制定关于陆上和水上捕获的条例；

招募陆军和供给军需，但此项用途的拨款期限不得超过两年；

建立和维持一支海军；

制定治理和管理陆海军的条例；

规定征召民兵，以执行联邦法律、镇压叛乱和击退入侵；

规定民兵的组织、装备和训练，规定用来为合众国服役的那些民兵的管理，但民兵军官的任命和按国会规定的条例训练民兵的权力，由各州保留。

To exercise exclusive Legislation in all Cases whatsoever, over such District (not exceeding ten Miles square) as may, by Cession of particular States, and the Acceptance of Congress, become the Seat of the Government of the United States, and to exercise like Authority over all Places purchased by the Consent of the Legislature of the State in which the Same shall be, for the Erection of Forts, Magazines, Arsenals, dock-Yards, and other needful Buildings;--And To make all Laws which shall be necessary and proper for carrying into Execution the foregoing Powers, and all other Powers vested by this Constitution in the Government of the United States, or in any Department or Officer thereof.

Section. 9   The Migration or Importation of such Persons as any of the States now existing shall think proper to admit, shall not be prohibited by the Congress prior to the Year one thousand eight hundred and eight, but a Tax or duty may be imposed on such Importation, not exceeding ten dollars for each Person.

The Privilege of the Writ of Habeas Corpus shall not be suspended, unless when in Cases of Rebellion or Invasion the public Safety may require it.

No Bill of Attainder or ex post facto Law shall be passed.

No Capitation, or other direct, Tax shall be laid, unless in Proportion to the Census or enumeration herein before directed to be taken.

No Tax or Duty shall be laid on Articles exported from any State.

No Preference shall be given by any Regulation of Commerce or Revenue to the Ports of one State over those of another; nor shall Vessels bound to, or from, one State, be obliged to enter, clear, or pay Duties in another.

No Money shall be drawn from the Treasury, but in Consequence of Appropriations made by Law; and a regular Statement and Account of the Receipts and Expenditures of all public Money shall be published from time to time.

No Title of Nobility shall be granted by the United States: And no Person holding any Office of Profit or Trust under them, shall, without the Consent of the Congress, accept of any present, Emolument, Office, or Title, of any kind whatever, from any King, Prince, or foreign State.

对于由某些州让与合众国、经国会接受而成为合众国政府所在地的地区（不得超过十平方英里），在任何情况下都行使独有的立法权；对于经州议会同意、由合众国在该州购买的用于建造要塞、弹药库、兵工厂、船坞和其他必要建筑物的一切地方，行使同样的权力；以及制定为行使上述各项权力和由本宪法授予合众国政府或其任何部门或官员的一切其他权力所必要和适当的所有法律。

第九款　现有任何一州认为得准予入境之人的迁移或入境，在一千八百零八年以前，国会不得加以禁止，但对此种人的入境，每人可征不超过十美元的税。不得中止人身保护状的特权，除非发生叛乱或入侵时公共安全要求中止这项特权。

不得通过公民权利剥夺法案或追溯既往的法律。

［除依本宪法上文规定的人口普查或统计的比例，不得征收人头税或其他直接税。］⑤

对于从任何一州输出的货物，不得征税。

任何商业或税收条例，都不得给予一州港口以优惠于他州港口的待遇；开往或开出一州的船舶，不得被强迫在他州入港、出港或纳税。

除根据法律规定的拨款外，不得从国库提取款项。一切公款收支的定期报告书和账目，应不时予以公布。

合众国不得授予贵族爵位。凡在合众国属下担任任何有薪金或有责任的职务的人，未经国会同意，不得从任何国王、君主或外国接受任何礼物、俸禄、官职或任何一种爵位。

Section. 10   No State shall enter into any Treaty, Alliance, or Confederation; grant Letters of Marque and Reprisal; coin Money; emit Bills of Credit; make any Thing but gold and silver Coin a Tender in Payment of Debts; pass any Bill of Attainder, ex post facto Law, or Law impairing the Obligation of Contracts, or grant any Title of Nobility.

No State shall, without the Consent of the Congress, lay any Imposts or Duties on Imports or Exports, except what may be absolutely necessary for executing it's inspection Laws: and the net Produce of all Duties and Imposts, laid by any State on Imports or Exports, shall be for the Use of the Treasury of the United States; and all such Laws shall be subject to the Revision and Controul of the Congress.

No State shall, without the Consent of Congress, lay any Duty of Tonnage, keep Troops, or Ships of War in time of Peace, enter into any Agreement or Compact with another State, or with a foreign Power, or engage in War, unless actually invaded, or in such imminent Danger as will not admit of delay.

Article. II.

Section. 1   The executive Power shall be vested in a President of the United States of America. He shall hold his Office during the Term of four Years, and, together with the Vice President, chosen for the same Term, be elected, as follows:

Each State shall appoint, in such Manner as the Legislature thereof may direct, a Number of Electors, equal to the whole Number of Senators and Representatives to which the State may be entitled in the Congress: but no Senator or Representative, or Person holding an Office of Trust or Profit under the United States, shall be appointed an Elector.

The Electors shall meet in their respective States, and vote by Ballot for two Persons, of whom one at least shall not be an Inhabitant of the same State with themselves. And they shall make a List of all the Persons voted for, and of the Number of Votes for each; which List they shall sign and certify, and transmit sealed to the Seat of the Government of the United States, directed to the President of the Senate. The President of the Senate shall, in the Presence of the Senate and House of Representatives, open all the Certificates, and the Votes shall then be counted. The Person

第十款　任何一州都不得：缔结任何条约，参加任何同盟或邦联；颁发捕获敌船许可状；铸造货币；发行纸币；使用金银币以外的任何物品作为偿还债务的货币；通过任何公民权利剥夺法案、追溯既往的法律或损害契约义务的法律；或授予任何贵族爵位。

任何一州，未经国会同意，不得对进口货或出口货征收任何税款，但为执行本州检查法所绝对必需者除外。任何一州对进口货或出口货所征全部税款的纯收益供合众国国库使用；所有这类法律得由国会加以修正和控制。

任何一州，未经国会同意，不得征收任何船舶吨位税，不得在和平时期保持军队或战舰，不得与他州或外国缔结协定或盟约，除非实际遭到入侵或遇刻不容缓的紧迫危险时不得进行战争。

第二条

第一款　行政权属于美利坚合众国总统。总统任期四年，副总统的任期相同。总统和副总统按以下方法选举：每个州依照该州议会所定方式选派选举人若干人，其数目同该州在国会应有的参议员和众议员总人数相等。但参议员或众议员，或在合众国属下担任有责任或有薪金职务的人，不得被选派为选举人。

［选举人在各自州内集会，投票选举两人，其中至少有一人不是选举人本州的居民。选举人须开列名单，写明所有被选人和每人所得票数；在该名单上签名作证，将封印后的名单送合众国政府所在地，交参议院议长收。参议院议长在参议院和众议院全体议员面前开拆所有证明书，然后计算票数。得票最多的人，如所得票数超过所选派选举人总数的半数，即为总统。如获得此种过半数票的人不止一人，且得票相等，众议院应立即投票选举其中一人为总统。如无人获得过半数票；该院应以同样方式从名单上得票最多的五人中选举一人为总统。但选举总统时，以州为单位计票，每州代表有一票表决权；三分之二的州各有一名或多名众议员出席，即构成选举总统的法定人数，选出总统需要所有州的过半数票。

having the greatest Number of Votes shall be the President, if such Number be a Majority of the whole Number of Electors appointed; and if there be more than one who have such Majority, and have an equal Number of Votes, then the House of Representatives shall immediately chuse by Ballot one of them for President; and if no Person have a Majority, then from the five highest on the List the said House shall in like Manner chuse the President. But in chusing the President, the Votes shall be taken by States, the Representation from each State having one Vote; A quorum for this purpose shall consist of a Member or Members from two thirds of the States, and a Majority of all the States shall be necessary to a Choice. In every Case, after the Choice of the President, the Person having the greatest Number of Votes of the Electors shall be the Vice President. But if there should remain two or more who have equal Votes, the Senate shall chuse from them by Ballot the Vice President.

The Congress may determine the Time of chusing the Electors, and the Day on which they shall give their Votes; which Day shall be the same throughout the United States.

No Person except a natural born Citizen, or a Citizen of the United States, at the time of the Adoption of this Constitution, shall be eligible to the Office of President; neither shall any Person be eligible to that Office who shall not have attained to the Age of thirty five Years, and been fourteen Years a Resident within the United States.

In Case of the Removal of the President from Office, or of his Death, Resignation, or Inability to discharge the Powers and Duties of the said Office, the Same shall devolve on the Vice President, and the Congress may by Law provide for the Case of Removal, Death, Resignation or Inability, both of the President and Vice President, declaring what Officer shall then act as President, and such Officer shall act accordingly, until the Disability be removed, or a President shall be elected.

The President shall, at stated Times, receive for his Services, a Compensation, which shall neither be increased nor diminished during the Period for which he shall have been elected, and he shall not receive within that Period any other Emolument from the United States, or any of them.

在每种情况下，总统选出后，得选举人票最多的人，即为副总统。但如果有两人或两人以上得票相等，参议院应投票选举其中一人为副总统。]⑥

国会得确定选出选举人的时间和选举人投票日期，该日期在全合众国应为同一天。

无论何人，除生为合众国公民或在本宪法采用时已是合众国公民者外，不得当选为总统；凡年龄不满三十五岁、在合众国境内居住不满十四年者，也不得当选为总统。

[如遇总统被免职、死亡、辞职或丧失履行总统权力和责任的能力时，总统职务应移交副总统。国会得以法律规定在总统和副总统两人被免职、死亡、辞职或丧失任职能力时，宣布应代理总统的官员。该官员应代理总统直到总统恢复任职能力或新总统选出为止。]⑦

总统在规定的时间，应得到服务报酬，此项报酬在其当选担任总统任期内不得增加或减少。总统在任期内不得接受合众国或任何一州的任何其他俸禄。

Before he enter on the Execution of his Office, he shall take the following Oath or Affirmation:--"I do solemnly swear (or affirm) that I will faithfully execute the Office of President of the United States, and will to the best of my Ability, preserve, protect and defend the Constitution of the United States."

Section. 2   The President shall be Commander in Chief of the Army and Navy of the United States, and of the Militia of the several States, when called into the actual Service of the United States; he may require the Opinion, in writing, of the principal Officer in each of the executive Departments, upon any Subject relating to the Duties of their respective Offices, and he shall have Power to grant Reprieves and Pardons for Offences against the United States, except in Cases of Impeachment.

He shall have Power, by and with the Advice and Consent of the Senate, to make Treaties, provided two thirds of the Senators present concur; and he shall nominate, and by and with the Advice and Consent of the Senate, shall appoint Ambassadors, other public Ministers and Consuls, Judges of the supreme Court, and all other Officers of the United States, whose Appointments are not herein otherwise provided for, and which shall be established by Law: but the Congress may by Law vest the Appointment of such inferior Officers, as they think proper, in the President alone, in the Courts of Law, or in the Heads of Departments.

The President shall have Power to fill up all Vacancies that may happen during the Recess of the Senate, by granting Commissions which shall expire at the End of their next Session.

Section. 3   He shall from time to time give to the Congress Information of the State of the Union, and recommend to their Consideration such Measures as he shall judge necessary and expedient; he may, on extraordinary Occasions, convene both Houses, or either of them, and in Case of Disagreement between them, with Respect to the Time of Adjournment, he may adjourn them to such Time as he shall think proper; he shall receive Ambassadors and other public Ministers; he shall take Care that the Laws be faithfully executed, and shall Commission all the Officers of the United States.

Section. 4   The President, Vice President and all civil Officers of the United States, shall be removed from Office on Impeachment for, and Conviction of, Treason, Bribery, or other high Crimes and Misdemeanors.

　　总统在开始执行职务前，应作如下宣誓或代誓宣言："我庄严宣誓（或宣言）我一定忠实执行合众国总统职务，竭尽全力维护、保护和捍卫合众国宪法"。

　　第二款　总统是合众国陆军、海军和征调为合众国服役的各州民兵的总司令。他得要求每个行政部门长官就他们各自职责有关的任何事项提出书面意见。他有权对危害合众国的犯罪行为发布缓刑令和赦免令，但弹劾案除外。

　　总统经咨询参议院和取得其同意有权缔结条约，但须经出席参议员三分之二的批准。他提名，并经咨询参议院和取得其同意，任命大使、公使和领事、最高法院法官和任命手续未由本宪法另行规定而应由法律规定的合众国所有其他官员。但国会认为适当时，得以法律将这类低级官员的任命权授予总统一人、法院或各部部长。

　　总统有权委任人员填补在参议院休会期间可能出现的官员缺额，此项委任在参议院下期会议结束时满期。

　　第三款　总统应不时向国会报告联邦情况，并向国会提出他认为必要和妥善的措施供国会审议。在非常情况下，他得召集两院或任何一院开会。如遇两院对休会时间有意见分歧时，他可使两院休会到他认为适当的时间。他应接见大使和公使。他应负责使法律切实执行，并委任合众国的所有官员。

　　第四款　总统、副总统和合众国的所有文职官员，因叛国、贿赂或其他重罪和轻罪而受弹劾并被定罪时，应予免职。

Article III.

Section. 1   The judicial Power of the United States shall be vested in one supreme Court, and in such inferior Courts as the Congress may from time to time ordain and establish. The Judges, both of the supreme and inferior Courts, shall hold their Offices during good Behaviour, and shall, at stated Times, receive for their Services a Compensation, which shall not be diminished during their Continuance in Office.

Section. 2   The judicial Power shall extend to all Cases, in Law and Equity, arising under this Constitution, the Laws of the United States, and Treaties made, or which shall be made, under their Authority;--to all Cases affecting Ambassadors, other public Ministers and Consuls;--to all Cases of admiralty and maritime Jurisdiction;--to Controversies to which the United States shall be a Party;--to Controversies between two or more States;-- between a State and Citizens of another State,--between Citizens of different States,--between Citizens of the same State claiming Lands under Grants of different States, and between a State, or the Citizens thereof, and foreign States, Citizens or Subjects.

In all Cases affecting Ambassadors, other public Ministers and Consuls, and those in which a State shall be Party, the supreme Court shall have original Jurisdiction. In all the other Cases before mentioned, the supreme Court shall have appellate Jurisdiction, both as to Law and Fact, with such Exceptions, and under such Regulations as the Congress shall make.

The Trial of all Crimes, except in Cases of Impeachment, shall be by Jury; and such Trial shall be held in the State where the said Crimes shall have been committed; but when not committed within any State, the Trial shall be at such Place or Places as the Congress may by Law have directed.

Section. 3   Treason against the United States, shall consist only in levying War against them, or in adhering to their Enemies, giving them Aid and Comfort. No Person shall be convicted of Treason unless on the Testimony of two Witnesses to the same overt Act, or on Confession in open Court.

The Congress shall have Power to declare the Punishment of Treason, but no Attainder of Treason shall work Corruption of Blood, or Forfeiture except during the Life of the Person attainted.

第三条

第一款　合众国的司法权，属于最高法院和国会不时规定和设立的下级法院。最高法院和下级法院的法官如行为端正，得继续任职，并应在规定的时间得到服务报酬，此项报酬在他们继续任职期间不得减少。

第二款　司法权的适用范围包括：由于本宪法、合众国法律和根据合众国权力已缔结或将缔结的条约而产生的一切普通法的和衡平法的案件；涉及大使、公使和领事的一切案件；关于海事法和海事管辖权的一切案件；合众国为一方当事人的诉讼；两个或两个以上州之间的诉讼；〔一州和他州公民之间的诉讼；〕⑧不同州公民之间的诉讼；同州公民之间对不同州让与土地的所有权的诉讼；一州或其公民同外国或外国公民或国民之间的诉讼。

涉及大使、公使和领事以及一州为一方当事人的一切案件，最高法院具有第一审管辖权。对上述所有其他案件，不论法律方面还是事实方面，最高法院具有上诉审管辖权，但须依照国会所规定的例外和规章。

除弹劾案外，一切犯罪由陪审团审判；此种审判应在犯罪发生的州内举行；但如犯罪不发生在任何一州之内，审判应在国会以法律规定的一个或几个地点举行。

第三款　对合众国的叛国罪只限于同合众国作战，或依附其敌人，给予其敌人以帮助和鼓励。无论何人，除根据两个证人对同一明显行为的作证或本人在公开法庭上的供认，不得被定为叛国罪。

国会有权宣告对叛国罪的惩罚，但因叛国罪而剥夺公民权，不得造成血统玷污，除非在被剥夺者在世期间，也不得没收其财产。

Article. IV.

Section. 1   Full Faith and Credit shall be given in each State to the public Acts, Records, and judicial Proceedings of every other State. And the Congress may by general Laws prescribe the Manner in which such Acts, Records and Proceedings shall be proved, and the Effect thereof.

Section. 2   The Citizens of each State shall be entitled to all Privileges and Immunities of Citizens in the several States.

A Person charged in any State with Treason, Felony, or other Crime, who shall flee from Justice, and be found in another State, shall on Demand of the executive Authority of the State from which he fled, be delivered up, to be removed to the State having Jurisdiction of the Crime.

No Person held to Service or Labour in one State, under the Laws thereof, escaping into another, shall, in Consequence of any Law or Regulation therein, be discharged from such Service or Labour, but shall be delivered up on Claim of the Party to whom such Service or Labour may be due.

Section. 3   New States may be admitted by the Congress into this Union; but no new State shall be formed or erected within the Jurisdiction of any other State; nor any State be formed by the Junction of two or more States, or Parts of States, without the Consent of the Legislatures of the States concerned as well as of the Congress.

The Congress shall have Power to dispose of and make all needful Rules and Regulations respecting the Territory or other Property belonging to the United States; and nothing in this Constitution shall be so construed as to Prejudice any Claims of the United States, or of any particular State.

Section. 4   The United States shall guarantee to every State in this Union a Republican Form of Government, and shall protect each of them against Invasion; and on Application of the Legislature, or of the Executive (when the Legislature cannot be convened), against domestic Violence.

第四条

第一款　每个州对于他州的公共法律、案卷和司法程序，应给予充分信任和尊重。国会得以一般法律规定这类法律、案卷和司法程序如何证明和具有的效力。

第二款　每个州的公民享有各州公民的一切特权和豁免权。

在任何一州被控告犯有叛国罪、重罪或其他罪行的人，逃脱法网而在他州被寻获时，应根据他所逃出之州行政当局的要求将他交出，以便解送到对犯罪行为有管辖权的州。

[根据一州法律须在该州服劳役或劳动的人，如逃往他州，不得因他州的法律或规章而免除此种劳役或劳动，而应根据有权得到此劳役或劳动之当事人的要求将他交出。]⑨

第三款　新州得由国会接纳加入本联邦；但不得在任何其他州的管辖范围内组成或建立新州；未经有关州议会和国会的同意，也不得合并两个或两个以上的州或几个州的一部分组成新州。

国会对于属于合众国的领土或其他财产，有权处置和制定一切必要的条例和规章。对本宪法条文不得作有损于合众国或任何一州的任何权利的解释。

第四款　合众国保证本联邦各州实行共和政体，保护每州免遭入侵，并应州议会或州行政长官（在州议会不能召开时）的请求平定内乱。

Article. V.

The Congress, whenever two thirds of both Houses shall deem it necessary, shall propose Amendments to this Constitution, or, on the Application of the Legislatures of two thirds of the several States, shall call a Convention for proposing Amendments, which, in either Case, shall be valid to all Intents and Purposes, as Part of this Constitution, when ratified by the Legislatures of three fourths of the several States, or by Conventions in three fourths thereof, as the one or the other Mode of Ratification may be proposed by the Congress; Provided that no Amendment which may be made prior to the Year One thousand eight hundred and eight shall in any Manner affect the first and fourth Clauses in the Ninth Section of the first Article; and that no State, without its Consent, shall be deprived of its equal Suffrage in the Senate.

Article. VI.

All Debts contracted and Engagements entered into, before the Adoption of this Constitution, shall be as valid against the United States under this Constitution, as under the Confederation.

This Constitution, and the Laws of the United States which shall be made in Pursuance thereof; and all Treaties made, or which shall be made, under the Authority of the United States, shall be the supreme Law of the Land; and the Judges in every State shall be bound thereby, any Thing in the Constitution or Laws of any State to the Contrary notwithstanding.

The Senators and Representatives before mentioned, and the Members of the several State Legislatures, and all executive and judicial Officers, both of the United States and of the several States, shall be bound by Oath or Affirmation, to support this Constitution; but no religious Test shall ever be required as a Qualification to any Office or public Trust under the United States.

Article. VII.

The Ratification of the Conventions of nine States, shall be sufficient for the Establishment of this Constitution between the States so ratifying the Same.

第五条

国会在两院三分之二议员认为必要时，应提出本宪法的修正案，或根据各州三分之二州议会的请求，召开制宪会议提出修正案。不论哪种方式提出的修正案，经各州四分之三州议会或四分之三州制宪会议的批准，即实际成为本宪法的一部分而发生效力；采用哪种批准方式，得由国会提出建议。但［在一千八百零八年以前制定的修正案，不得以任何形式影响本宪法第一条第九款第一项和第四项］；⑩任何一州，不经其同意，不得被剥夺它在参议院的平等投票权。

第六条

本宪法采用前订立的一切债务和承担的一切义务，对于实行本宪法的合众国同邦联时期一样有效。

本宪法和依本宪法所制定的合众国法律，以及根据合众国的权力已缔结或将缔结的一切条约，都是全国的最高法律；每个州的法官都应受其约束，即使州的宪法和法律中有与之相抵触的内容。

上述参议员和众议员，各州州议会议员，以及合众国和各州所有行政和司法官员，应宣誓或作代誓宣言拥护本宪法；但决不得以宗教信仰作为担任合众国属下任何官职或公职的必要资格。

第七条

经九个州制宪会议的批准，即足以使本宪法在各批准州成立。

Done in Convention by the Unanimous Consent of the States present the Seventeenth Day of September in the Year of our Lord one thousand seven hundred and Eighty seven and of the Independance of the United States of America the Twelfth In witness whereof We have hereunto subscribed our Names.

G°. Washington

Presidt and deputy from Virginia

Delaware

Geo: Read

John Dickinson

Jaco: Broom

Gunning Bedford jun

Richard Bassett

Maryland

James McHenry

Danl. Carroll

Dan of St Thos. Jenifer

Virginia

John Blair

James Madison Jr.

North Carolina

Wm. Blount

Hu Williamson

Richd. Dobbs Spaight

South Carolina

J. Rutledge

Charles Pinckney

Charles Cotesworth Pinckney

Pierce Butler

Georgia

William Few

Abr Baldwin

New Hampshire

John Langdon

Nicholas Gilman

本宪法于耶酥纪元一千七百八十七年，即美利坚合众国独立后第十二年的九月十七日，经出席各州在制宪会议上一致同意后制定。我们谨在此签名作证。

乔治·华盛顿
主席、弗吉尼亚州代表
特拉华州

乔治·里德　　　　　　　　　　小冈宁·贝德福德

约翰·迪金森　　　　　　　　　理查德·巴西特

雅各布·布鲁姆

马里兰州

詹姆斯·麦克亨利　　　　　　　圣托马斯·詹尼弗的丹尼尔

丹尼尔·卡罗尔

弗吉尼亚州

约翰·布莱尔　　　　　　　　　小詹姆斯·麦迪逊

北卡罗来纳州

威廉·布朗特　　　　　　　　　理查德·多布斯·斯佩特

休·威廉森

南卡罗来纳州

约翰·拉特利奇　　　　　　　　查尔斯·科茨沃斯·平克尼

查尔斯·平克尼　　　　　　　　皮尔斯·巴特勒

佐治亚州

威廉·费尤　　　　　　　　　　亚伯拉罕·鲍德温

新罕布什尔州

约翰·兰登　　　　　　　　　　尼古拉斯·吉尔曼

Massachusetts

Nathaniel Gorham   Rufus King

Connecticut

Wm. Saml. Johnson   Roger Sherman

New York

Alexander Hamilton

New Jersey

Wil: Livingston   David Brearley

Wm. Paterson   Jona: Dayton

Pennsylvania

B Franklin   Thomas Mifflin

Robt. Morris   Geo. Clymer

Thos. FitzSimons   Jared Ingersoll

James Wilson   Gouv Morris

Attest William Jackson Secretary

The Bill of Rights:

Amendment I

Congress shall make no law respecting an establishment of religion, or prohibiting the free exercise thereof; or abridging the freedom of speech, or of the press; or the right of the people peaceably to assemble, and to petition the Government for a redress of grievances.

马萨诸塞州

纳撒尼尔·戈勒姆　　　　　鲁弗斯·金

康涅狄格州

威廉·塞缪尔·约翰逊　　　罗杰·谢尔曼

纽约州

亚历山大·汉密尔顿

新泽西州

威廉·利文斯顿　　　　　　戴维·布里尔利

威廉·帕特森　　　　　　　乔纳森·戴顿

宾夕法尼亚州

本杰明·富兰克林　　　　　托马斯·米夫林

罗伯特·莫里斯　　　　　　乔治·克莱默

托马斯·菲茨西蒙斯　　　　贾雷德·英格索尔

詹姆斯·威尔逊　　　　　　古·莫里斯

证人：威廉·杰克逊，秘书

《权利法案》：

（依照原宪法第五条、由国会提出并经各州批准、增添和修改美利坚合众国宪法的条款。译者注）

第一条修正案

［前十条修正案于 1789 年 9 月 25 日提出，1791 年 12 月 15 日批准，被称为"权利法案"。］

国会不得制定关于下列事项的法律：确立国教或禁止信教自由；剥夺言论自由或出版自由；或剥夺人民和平集会和向政府请愿伸冤的权利。

Amendment II

A well regulated Militia, being necessary to the security of a free State, the right of the people to keep and bear Arms, shall not be infringed.

Amendment III

No Soldier shall, in time of peace be quartered in any house, without the consent of the Owner, nor in time of war, but in a manner to be prescribed by law.

Amendment IV

The right of the people to be secure in their persons, houses, papers, and effects, against unreasonable searches and seizures, shall not be violated, and no Warrants shall issue, but upon probable cause, supported by Oath or affirmation, and particularly describing the place to be searched, and the persons or things to be seized.

Amendment V

No person shall be held to answer for a capital, or otherwise infamous crime, unless on a presentment or indictment of a Grand Jury, except in cases arising in the land or naval forces, or in the Militia, when in actual service in time of War or public danger; nor shall any person be subject for the same offence to be twice put in jeopardy of life or limb; nor shall be compelled in any criminal case to be a witness against himself, nor be deprived of life, liberty, or property, without due process of law; nor shall private property be taken for public use, without just compensation.

Amendment VI

In all criminal prosecutions, the accused shall enjoy the right to a speedy and public trial, by an impartial jury of the State and district wherein the crime shall have been committed, which district shall have been previously ascertained by law, and to be informed of the nature and cause of the accusation; to be confronted with the witnesses against him; to have compulsory process for obtaining witnesses in his favor, and to have the Assistance of Counsel for his defence.

第二条修正案

管理良好的民兵是保障自由州的安全所必需的，因此人民持有和携带武器的权利不得侵犯。

第三条修正案

未经房主同意，士兵平时不得驻扎在任何住宅；除依法律规定的方式，战时也不得驻扎。

第四条修正案

人民的人身、住宅、文件和财产不受无理搜查和扣押的权利，不得侵犯。除依据可能成立的理由，以宣誓或代誓宣言保证，并详细说明搜查地点和扣押的人或物，不得发出搜查和扣押状。

第五条修正案

无论何人，除非根据大陪审团的报告或起诉书，不受死罪或其他重罪的审判，但发生在陆、海军中或发生在战时或出现公共危险时服役的民兵中的案件除外。任何人不得因同一犯罪行为而两次遭受生命或身体的危害；不得在任何刑事案件中被迫自证其罪；不经正当法律程序，不得被剥夺生命、自由或财产。不给予公平赔偿，私有财产不得充作公用。

第六条修正案

在一切刑事诉讼中，被告有权由犯罪行为发生地的州和地区的公正陪审团予以迅速和公开的审判，该地区应事先已由法律确定；得知控告的性质和理由；同原告证人对质；以强制程序取得对其有利的证人；取得律师帮助为其辩护。

Amendment VII

In Suits at common law, where the value in controversy shall exceed twenty dollars, the right of trial by jury shall be preserved, and no fact tried by a jury, shall be otherwise re-examined in any Court of the United States, than according to the rules of the common law.

Amendment VIII

Excessive bail shall not be required, nor excessive fines imposed, nor cruel and unusual punishments inflicted.

Amendment IX

The enumeration in the Constitution, of certain rights, shall not be construed to deny or disparage others retained by the people.

Amendment X

The powers not delegated to the United States by the Constitution, nor prohibited by it to the States, are reserved to the States respectively, or to the people.

The Constitution: Amendments 11-27

AMENDMENT XI

Passed by Congress March 4, 1794. Ratified February 7, 1795.

Note: Article III, section 2, of the Constitution was modified by amendment 11.

The Judicial power of the United States shall not be construed to extend to any suit in law or equity, commenced or prosecuted against one of the United States by Citizens of another State, or by Citizens or Subjects of any Foreign State.

第七条修正案

在习惯法的诉讼中，其争执价额超过二十美元，由陪审团审判的权利应受到保护。由陪审团裁决的事实，合众国的任何法院除非按照习惯法规则，不得重新审查。

第八条修正案

不得要求过多的保释金，不得处以过重的罚金，不得施加残酷和非常的惩罚。

第九条修正案

本宪法对某些权利的列举，不得被解释为否定或轻视由人民保留的其他权利。

第十条修正案·

宪法未授予合众国、也未禁止各州行使的权力，由各州各自保留，或由人民保留。

第十一条修正案

［1794 年 3 月 4 日提出，1795 年 2 月 7 日批准 ］

合众国的司法权，不得被解释为适用于由他州公民或任何外国公民或国民对合众国一州提出的或起诉的任何普通法或衡平法的诉讼。

AMENDMENT XII

Passed by Congress December 9, 1803. Ratified June 15, 1804.

Note: A portion of Article II, section 1 of the Constitution wa superseded by the 12th amendment.

The Electors shall meet in their respective states and vote by ballot for President and Vice-President, one of whom, at least, shall not be an inhabitant of the same state with themselves; they shall name in their ballots the person voted for as President, and in distinct ballots the person voted for as Vice-President, and they shall make distinct lists of all persons voted for as President, and of all persons voted for as Vice-President, and of the number of votes for each, which lists they shall sign and certify, and transmit sealed to the seat of the government of the United States, directed to the President of the Senate; -- the President of the Senate shall, in the presence of the Senate and House of Representatives, open all the certificates and the votes shall then be counted; -- The person having the greatest number of votes for President, shall be the President, if such number be a majority of the whole number of Electors appointed; and if no person have such majority, then from the persons having the highest numbers not exceeding three on the list of those voted for as President, the House of Representatives shall choose immediately, by ballot, the President. But in choosing the President, the votes shall be taken by states, the representation from each state having one vote; a quorum for this purpose shall consist of a member or members from two-thirds of the states, and a majority of all the states shall be necessary to a choice. [And if the House of Representatives shall not choose a President whenever the right of choice shall devolve upon them, before the fourth day of March next following, then the Vice-President shall act as President, as in case of the death or other constitutional disability of the President. --]* The person having the greatest number of votes as Vice-President, shall be the Vice-President, if such number be a majority of the whole number of Electors appointed, and if no person have a majority, then from the two highest numbers on the list, the Senate shall choose the Vice-President; a quorum for the purpose shall consist of two-thirds of the whole number of Senators, and a majority of the whole number shall be necessary to a choice. But no person constitutionally ineligible to the office of President shall be eligible to that of Vice-President of the United States.

第十二条修正案

[1803 年 12 月 9 日提出，1804 年 7 月 27 日批准]

选举人在各自州内集会，投票选举总统和副总统，其中至少有一人不是选举人本州的居民。选举人须在选票上写明被选为总统之人的姓名，并在另一选票上写明校选为副总统之人的姓名。选举人须将所有被选为总统之人和所有被选为副总统之人分别开列名单，写明每人所得票数；在该名单上签名作证，将封印后的名单送合众国政府所在地，交参议院议长收。参议院议长在参议院和众议院全体议员面前开拆所有证明书，然后计算票数。获得总统选票最多的人，如所得票数超过所选派选举人总数的半数，即为总统。如无人获得这种过半数票，众议院应立即从被选为总统之人名单中得票最多的但不超过三人中间，投票选举总统。但选举总统时，以州为单位计票，每州代表有一票表决权。三分之二的州各有一名或多名众议员出席，即构成选举总统的法定人数，选出总统需要所有州的过半数票。[当选举总统的权力转移到众议院时，如该院在次年三月四日前尚未选出总统，则由副总统代理总统，如同总统死亡或宪法规定的其他丧失任职能力的情况一样。] (11)得副总统选票最多的人，如所得票数超过所选派选举人总数的半数，即为副总统。如无人得过半数票，参议院应从名单上得票最多的两人中选举副总统。选举副总统的法定人数由参议员总数的三分之二构成，选出副总统需要参议员总数的过半数票。但依宪法无资格担任总统的人，也无资格担任合众国副总统。

*Superseded by section 3 of the 20th amendment.

AMENDMENT XIII

Passed by Congress January 31, 1865. Ratified December 6, 1865.

Note: A portion of Article IV, section 2, of the Constitution was superseded by the 13th amendment.

Section 1　Neither slavery nor involuntary servitude, except as a punishment for crime whereof the party shall have been duly convicted, shall exist within the United States, or any place subject to their jurisdiction.

Section 2　Congress shall have power to enforce this article by appropriate legislation.

AMENDMENT XIV

Passed by Congress June 13, 1866. Ratified July 9, 1868.

Note: Article I, section 2, of the Constitution was modified by section 2 of the 14th amendment.

Section 1　All persons born or naturalized in the United States, and subject to the jurisdiction thereof, are citizens of the United States and of the State wherein they reside. No State shall make or enforce any law which shall abridge the privileges or immunities of citizens of the United States; nor shall any State deprive any person of life, liberty, or property, without due process of law; nor deny to any person within its jurisdiction the equal protection of the laws.

Section 2　Representatives shall be apportioned among the several States according to their respective numbers, counting the whole number of persons in each State, excluding Indians not taxed. But when the right to vote at any election for the choice of electors for President and Vice-President of the United States, Representatives in Congress, the Executive and Judicial officers of a State, or the members of the Legislature thereof, is denied to any of the male inhabitants of such State, being twenty-one years of age,* and citizens of the United States, or in any way abridged, except for participation in rebellion, or other crime, the basis of representation therein shall be reduced in the proportion which the number of such male citizens shall bear to the whole number of male citizens twenty-one years of age in such State.

第十三条修正案

[1865 年 1 月 31 日提出，1865 年 12 月 6 日批准]

第一款　在合众国境内受合众国管辖的任何地方，奴隶制和强制劳役都不得存在，但作为对于依法判罪的人的犯罪的惩罚除

第二款　国会有权以适当立法实施本条。

第十四条修正案

[1866 年 6 月 13 日提出，1868 年 7 月 9 日批准]

第一款　所有在合众国出生或归化合众国并受其管辖的人，都是合众国的和他们居住州的公民。任何一州，都不得制定或实施限制合众国公民的特权或豁免权的任何法律；不经正当法律程序，不得剥夺任何人的生命、自由或财产；在州管辖范围内，也不得拒绝给予任何人以平等法律保护。

第二款　众议员名额，应按各州人口比例进行分配，此人口数包括一州的全部人口数，但不包括未被征税的印第安人。但在选举合众国总统和副总统选举人、国会众议员、州行政和司法官员或州议会议员的任何选举中，一州的 [年满二十一岁]^② 并且是合众国公民的任何男性居民，除因参加叛乱或其他犯罪外，如其选举权道到拒绝或受到任何方式的限制，则该州代表权的基础，应按以上男性公民的人数同该州年满二十一岁男性公民总人数的比例予以削减。

Section 3 No person shall be a Senator or Representative in Congress, or elector of President and Vice-President, or hold any office, civil or military, under the United States, or under any State, who, having previously taken an oath, as a member of Congress, or as an officer of the United States, or as a member of any State legislature, or as an executive or judicial officer of any State, to support the Constitution of the United States, shall have engaged in insurrection or rebellion against the same, or given aid or comfort to the enemies thereof. But Congress may by a vote of two-thirds of each House, remove such disability.

Section 4 The validity of the public debt of the United States, authorized by law, including debts incurred for payment of pensions and bounties for services in suppressing insurrection or rebellion, shall not be questioned. But neither the United States nor any State shall assume or pay any debt or obligation incurred in aid of insurrection or rebellion against the United States, or any claim for the loss or emancipation of any slave; but all such debts, obligations and claims shall be held illegal and void.

Section 5 The Congress shall have the power to enforce, by appropriate legislation, the provisions of this article.

*Changed by section 1 of the 26th amendment.

AMENDMENT XV

Passed by Congress February 26, 1869. Ratified February 3, 1870.

Section 1 The right of citizens of the United States to vote shall not be denied or abridged by the United States or by any State on account of race, color, or previous condition of servitude--

Section 2 The Congress shall have the power to enforce this article by appropriate legislation.

AMENDMENT XVI

Passed by Congress July 2, 1909. Ratified February 3, 1913.

Note: Article I, section 9, of the Constitution was modified by amendment 16.

第三款　无论何人，凡先前曾以国会议员、或合众国官员、或任何州议会议员、或任何州行政或司法官员的身份宣誓维护合众国宪法，以后又对合众国作乱或反叛，或给予合众国敌人帮助或鼓励，都不得担任国会参议员或众议员、或总统和副总统选举人，或担任合众国或任何州属下的任何文职或军职官员。但国会得以两院各三分之二的票数取消此种限制。

第四款　对于法律批准的合众国公共债务，包括因支付平定作乱或反叛有功人员的年金和奖金而产生的债务，其效力不得有所怀疑。但无论合众国或任何一州，都不得承担或偿付因援助对合众国的作乱或反叛而产生的任何债务或义务，或因丧失或解放任何奴隶而提出的任何赔偿要求；所有这类债务、义务和要求，都应被认为是非法和无效的。

第五款　国会有权以适当立法实施本条规定。

第十五条修正案
［1869 年 2 月 26 日提出，1870 年 2 月 3 日批准］

第一款　合众国公民的选举权，不得因种族、肤色或以前是奴隶而被合众国或任何一州加以拒绝或限制。

第二款　国会有权以适当立法实施本条。

第十六条修正案
［1909 年 7 月 12 日提出，1913 年 2 月 3 日批准］

The Congress shall have power to lay and collect taxes on incomes, from whatever source derived, without apportionment among the several States, and without regard to any census or enumeration.

AMENDMENT XVII

Passed by Congress May 13, 1912. Ratified April 8, 1913.

Note: Article I, section 3, of the Constitution was modified by the 17th amendment.

The Senate of the United States shall be composed of two Senators from each State, elected by the people thereof, for six years; and each Senator shall have one vote. The electors in each State shall have the qualifications requisite for electors of the most numerous branch of the State legislatures.

When vacancies happen in the representation of any State in the Senate, the executive authority of such State shall issue writs of election to fill such vacancies: Provided, That the legislature of any State may empower the executive thereof to make temporary appointments until the people fill the vacancies by election as the legislature may direct.

This amendment shall not be so construed as to affect the election or term of any Senator chosen before it becomes valid as part of the Constitution.

AMENDMENT XVIII

Passed by Congress December 18, 1917. Ratified January 16, 1919. Repealed by amendment 21.

Section 1   After one year from the ratification of this article the manufacture, sale, or transportation of intoxicating liquors within, the importation thereof into, or the exportation thereof from the United States and all territory subject to the jurisdiction thereof for beverage purposes is hereby prohibited.

Section 2   The Congress and the several States shall have concurrent power to enforce this article by appropriate legislation.

Section 3   This article shall be inoperative unless it shall have been ratified as an amendment to the Constitution by the legislatures of the several States, as provided in the Constitution, within seven years from the date of the submission hereof to the States by the Congress.

国会有权对任何来源的收入规定和征收所得税，无须在各州按比例进行分配，也无须考虑任何人口普查或人口统计。

第十七条修正案

[1912 年 5 月 13 日提出，1913 年 4 月 8 日批准]

合众国参议院由每州人民选举的两名参议员组成，任期六年；每名参议员有一票表决权。每个州的选举人应具备该州州议会人数最多一院选举人所必需的资格。

任何一州在参议院的代表出现缺额时，该州行政当局应发布选举令，以填补此项缺额。但任何一州的议会，在人民依该议会指示举行选举填补缺额以前，得授权本州行政长官任命临时参议员。

本条修正案不得作如此解释，以致影响在本条修正案作为宪法的一部分生效以前当选的任何参议员的选举或任期。

第十八条修正案

[1917 年 12 月 18 日提出，1919 年 1 月 16 日批准]

[第一款　本条批准一年后，禁止在合众国及其管辖下的一切领土内酿造、出售和运送作为饮料的致醉酒类；禁止此类酒类输入或输出合众国及其管辖下的一切领土。

第二款　国会和各州都有权以适当立法实施本条。

第三款　本条除非在国会将其提交各州之日起七年以内，由各州议会按本宪法规定批准为宪法修正案，不得发生效力。][13]

AMENDMENT XIX

Passed by Congress June 4, 1919. Ratified August 18, 1920.

The right of citizens of the United States to vote shall not be denied or abridged by the United States or by any State on account of sex.

Congress shall have power to enforce this article by appropriate legislation.

AMENDMENT XX

Passed by Congress March 2, 1932. Ratified January 23, 1933.

Note: Article I, section 4, of the Constitution was modified by section 2 of this amendment. In addition, a portion of the 12th amendment was superseded by section 3.

Section 1   The terms of the President and the Vice President shall end at noon on the 20th day of January, and the terms of Senators and Representatives at noon on the 3d day of January, of the years in which such terms would have ended if this article had not been ratified; and the terms of their successors shall then begin.

Section 2   The Congress shall assemble at least once in every year, and such meeting shall begin at noon on the 3d day of January, unless they shall by law appoint a different day.

Section 3   If, at the time fixed for the beginning of the term of the President, the President elect shall have died, the Vice President elect shall become President. If a President shall not have been chosen before the time fixed for the beginning of his term, or if the President elect shall have failed to qualify, then the Vice President elect shall act as President until a President shall have qualified; and the Congress may by law provide for the case wherein neither a President elect nor a Vice President shall have qualified, declaring who shall then act as President, or the manner in which one who is to act shall be selected, and such person shall act accordingly until a President or Vice President shall have qualified.

第十九条修正案

［1919 年 6 月 4 日提出，1920 年 8 月 18 日批准 ］

合众国公民的选举权，不得因性别而被合众国或任何一州加以拒绝或限制。

国会有权以适当立法实施本条。

第二十条修正案

［1933 年 3 月 2 日提出，1933 年 1 月 23 日批准 ］

第一款　总统和副总统的任期应在本条未获批准前原定任期届满之年的一月二十日正午结束，参议员和众议员的任期在本条未获批准前原定任期届满之年的一月三日正午结束，他们继任人的任期在同时开始。

第二款　国会每年至少应开会一次，除国会以法律另订日期外，此会议在一月三日正午开始。

第三款　如当选总统在规定总统任期开始的时间已经死亡，当选副总统应成为总统。如在规定总统任期开始的时间以前，总统尚未选出，或当选总统不合乎资格，则当选副总统应代理总统直到一名总统已合乎资格时为止。在当选总统和当选副总统都不合乎资格时，国会得以法律规定代理总统之人，或宣布选出代理总统的办法。此人应代理总统直到一名总统或副总统合乎资格时为止。

Section 4   The Congress may by law provide for the case of the death of any of the persons from whom the House of Representatives may choose a President whenever the right of choice shall have devolved upon them, and for the case of the death of any of the persons from whom the Senate may choose a Vice President whenever the right of choice shall have devolved upon them.

Section 5   Sections 1 and 2 shall take effect on the 15th day of October following the ratification of this article.

Section 6   This article shall be inoperative unless it shall have been ratified as an amendment to the Constitution by the legislatures of three-fourths of the several States within seven years from the date of its submission.

AMENDMENT XXI

Passed by Congress February 20, 1933. Ratified December 5, 1933.

Section 1   The eighteenth article of amendment to the Constitution of the United States is hereby repealed.

Section 2   The transportation or importation into any State, Territory, or Possession of the United States for delivery or use therein of intoxicating liquors, in violation of the laws thereof, is hereby prohibited.

Section 3   This article shall be inoperative unless it shall have been ratified as an amendment to the Constitution by conventions in the several States, as provided in the Constitution, within seven years from the date of the submission hereof to the States by the Congress.

AMENDMENT XXII

Passed by Congress March 21, 1947. Ratified February 27, 1951.

Section 1   No person shall be elected to the office of the President more than twice, and no person who has held the office of President, or acted as President, for more than two years of a term to which some other person was elected President shall be elected to the office of President more than once. But this Article shall not apply to any person holding the office of President when this Article was proposed by Congress, and shall not prevent any person who may be holding the office of President, or acting as President, during the term within which this Article becomes operative from holding the office of President or acting as President during the remainder of such term.

第四款　国会得以法律对以下情况作出规定：在选举总统的权利转移到众议院时，而可被该院选为总统的人中有人死亡；在选举副总统的权利转移到参议院时，而可被该院选为副总统的人中有人死亡。

第五款　第一款和第二款应在本条批准以后的十月十五日生效。

第六款　本条除非在其提交各州之日起七年以内，自四分之三州议会批准为宪法修正案，不得发生效力。

第二十一条修正案
［1933 年 2 月 20 日提出，1933 年 12 月 5 日批准］

第一款　美利坚合众国宪法修正案第十八条现予废除。

第二款　在合众国任何州、领地或属地内，凡违反当地法律为在当地发货或使用而运送或输入致醉酒类，均予以禁止。

第三款　本条除非在国会将其提交各州之日起七年以内，由各州制宪会议依本宪法规定批准为宪法修正案，不得发生效力。

第二十二条修正案
［1947 年 3 月 24 日提出，1951 年 2 月 27 日批准］

第一款　无论何人，当选担任总统职务不得超过两次；无论何人，在他人当选总统任期内担任总统职务或代理总统两年以上，不得当选担任总统职务一次以上。但本条不适用于在国会提出本条时正在担任总统职务的任何人；也不妨碍本条在一届总统任期内生效时正在担任总统职务或代理总统的任何人，在此届任期结束前继续担任总统职务或代理总统。

Section 2   This article shall be inoperative unless it shall have been ratified as an amendment to the Constitution by the legislatures of three-fourths of the several States within seven years from the date of its submission to the States by the Congress.

AMENDMENT XXIII

Passed by Congress June 16, 1960. Ratified March 29, 1961.

Section 1   The District constituting the seat of Government of the United States shall appoint in such manner as Congress may direct:

A number of electors of President and Vice President equal to the whole number of Senators and Representatives in Congress to which the District would be entitled if it were a State, but in no event more than the least populous State; they shall be in addition to those appointed by the States, but they shall be considered, for the purposes of the election of President and Vice President, to be electors appointed by a State; and they shall meet in the District and perform such duties as provided by the twelfth article of amendment.

Section 2   The Congress shall have power to enforce this article by appropriate legislation.

AMENDMENT XXIV

Passed by Congress August 27, 1962. Ratified January 23, 1964.

Section 1   The right of citizens of the United States to vote in any primary or other election for President or Vice President, for electors for President or Vice President, or for Senator or Representative in Congress, shall not be denied or abridged by the United States or any State by reason of failure to pay poll tax or other tax.

Section 2   The Congress shall have power to enforce this article by appropriate legislation.

AMENDMENT XXV

Passed by Congress July 6, 1965. Ratified February 10, 1967.

Note: Article II, section 1, of the Constitution was affected by the 25th amendment.

第二款　本条除非在国会将其提交各州之日起七年以内，由四分之三州议会批准为宪法修正案，不得发生效力。

第二十三条修正案

［1960 年 6 月 16 日提出，1961 年 3 月 29 日批准］

第一款　合众国政府所在的特区，应依国会规定方式选派：一定数目的总统和副总统选举人，其人数如同特区是一个州一样，等于它在国会有权拥有的参议员和众议员人数的总和，但不得超过人口最少之州的选举人人数。他们是在各州所选派的举人以外增添的人，但为了选举总统和副总统的目的，应被视为一个州选派的选举人；他们在特区集会，履行第十二条修正案所规定的职责。

第二款　国会有权以适当立法实施本条。

第二十四条修正案

［1962 年 8 月 27 日提出，1964 年 1 月 23 日批准］

第一款　合众国公民在总统或副总统、总统或副总统选举人、或国会参议员或众议员的任何预选或其他选举中的选举权，不得因未交纳任何人头税或其他税而被合众国或任何一州加以拒绝或限制。

第二款　国会有权以适当立法实施本条。

第二十五条修正案

［1965 年 7 月 6 日提出，1967 年 2 月 10 日批准］

Section 1   In case of the removal of the President from office or of his death or resignation, the Vice President shall become President.

Section 2   Whenever there is a vacancy in the office of the Vice President, the President shall nominate a Vice President who shall take office upon confirmation by a majority vote of both Houses of Congress.

Section 3   Whenever the President transmits to the President pro tempore of the Senate and the Speaker of the House of Representatives his written declaration that he is unable to discharge the powers and duties of his office, and until he transmits to them a written declaration to the contrary, such powers and duties shall be discharged by the Vice President as Acting President.

Section 4   Whenever the Vice President and a majority of either the principal officers of the executive departments or of such other body as Congress may by law provide, transmit to the President pro tempore of the Senate and the Speaker of the House of Representatives their written declaration that the President is unable to discharge the powers and duties of his office, the Vice President shall immediately assume the powers and duties of the office as Acting President.

Thereafter, when the President transmits to the President pro tempore of the Senate and the Speaker of the House of Representatives his written declaration that no inability exists, he shall resume the powers and duties of his office unless the Vice President and a majority of either the principal officers of the executive department or of such other body as Congress may by law provide, transmit within four days to the President pro tempore of the Senate and the Speaker of the House of Representatives their written declaration that the President is unable to discharge the powers and duties of his office. Thereupon Congress shall decide the issue, assembling within forty-eight hours for that purpose if not in session. If the Congress, within twenty-one days after receipt of the latter written declaration, or, if Congress is not in session, within twenty-one days after Congress is required to assemble, determines by two-thirds vote of both Houses that the President is unable to discharge the powers and duties of his office, the Vice President shall continue to discharge the same as Acting President; otherwise, the President shall resume the powers and duties of his office.

第一款　如遇总统被免职、死亡或辞职，副总统应成为总统。

第二款　凡当副总统职位出缺时，总统应提名一名副总统，经国会两院都以过半数票批准后就职。

第三款　凡当总统向参议院临时议长和众议院议长提交书面声明，声称他不能够履行其职务的权力和责任，直至他向他们提交一份相反的声明为止，其权力和责任应由副总统作为代理总统履行。

第四款　凡当副总统和行政各部长官的多数或国会以法律设立的其他机构成员的多数，向参议院临时议长和众议院议长提交书面声明，声称总统不能够履行总统职务的权力和责任时，副总统应立即作为代理总统承担总统职务的权力和责任。

此后，当总统向参议院临时议长和众议院议长提交书面声明，声称丧失能力的情况不存在时，他应恢复总统职务的权力和责任，除非副总统和行政各部长官的多数或国会以法律设立的其它机构成员的多数在四天之内向参议院临时议长和众议院议长提交书面声明，声称总统不能够履行总统职务的权力和责任。在此种情况下，国会应决定这一问题，如在休会期间，应为此目的在四十八小时以内集会。如国会在收到后一书面声明后的二十一天以内，或如适逢休会期间，则在国会按照要求集会以后的二十一天以内，以两院的三分之二的票数决定总统不能够履行总统职务的权力和责任，副总统应继续作为代理总统履行总统职务的权力和责任；否则总统应恢复总统职务的权力和责任。

AMENDMENT XXVI

Passed by Congress March 23, 1971. Ratified July 1, 1971.

Note: Amendment 14, section 2, of the Constitution was modified by section 1 of the 26th amendment.

Section 1   The right of citizens of the United States, who are eighteen years of age or older, to vote shall not be denied or abridged by the United States or by any State on account of age.

Section 2   The Congress shall have power to enforce this article by appropriate legislation.

AMENDMENT XXVII

Originally proposed Sept. 25, 1789. Ratified May 7, 1992.

No law, varying the compensation for the services of the Senators and Representatives, shall take effect, until an election of representatives shall have intervened.

第二十六条修正案

［1971 年 3 月 23 日提出，1971 年 7 月 1 日批准］

第一款　年满十八岁和十八岁以上的合众国公民的选举权，不得因为年龄而被合众国或任何一州加以拒绝或限制。

第二款　国会有权以适当立法实施本条。

第二十七条修正案

［1989 年 9 月 25 日提出，1992 年 5 月 7 日批准］

改变参议员和众议员服务报酬的法律，在众议员选举举行之前不得生效。

（本译本引用自李道揆《美国政府和美国政治》，商务印书馆，1999-03 版）